JOHN HORGAN

JOHN HORGAN

IN HIS OWN WORDS

JOHN HORGAN *with* ROD MICKLEBURGH

HARBOUR PUBLISHING

For Ellie, Nate and Evan

---

1 2 3 4 5 — 29 28 27 26 25

HARBOUR PUBLISHING CO. LTD.
P.O. Box 219, Madeira Park, BC, V0N 2H0
www.harbourpublishing.com

EDITED by Noel Hudson
COVER DESIGN by John Montgomery
TEXT DESIGN by Libris Simas Ferraz / Onça Publishing
TEXT IS PRINTED on 100% recycled paper
PRINTED AND BOUND in Canada

HARBOUR PUBLISHING acknowledges the support of the Canada Council for the Arts, the Government of Canada, and the Province of British Columbia through the BC Arts Council.

LIBRARY AND ARCHIVES CANADA CATALOGUING IN PUBLICATION
Title: John Horgan : in his own words / John Horgan with Rod Mickleburgh.
Names: Horgan, John, 1959-2024, author | Mickleburgh, Rod, author.
Identifiers: Canadiana (print) 20250239132 | Canadiana (ebook) 20250239159 | ISBN 9781998526260 (hardcover) | ISBN 9781998526277 (EPUB)
Subjects: LCSH: Horgan, John, 1959-2024. | LCSH: Premiers (Canada)—British Columbia—Biography. | LCSH: Legislators—British Columbia—Biography. | LCSH: British Columbia—Biography. | LCGFT: Autobiographies.
Classification: LCC FC3831.1.H67 A3 2025 | DDC 971.1/05092—dc23

CONTENTS

INTRODUCTION

ROD MICKLEBURGH

IN THE DAYS AND WEEKS AFTER HE RESIGNED AS PREMIER OF BRITISH Columbia, John Horgan experienced the dramatic deceleration of life familiar to most former politicians suddenly out of the public eye. Emails end. Phone calls stop. An uncertain future stretches ahead. He volunteered at his local food bank, working as a swamper on the delivery truck. He went fishing and doubled down on his favourite hobby, rock polishing. But it was not enough for someone who had been active all his life. There were no job offers that seemed right, and hints of diplomatic postings did not initially materialize. Inevitably, perhaps, his mind turned to recording his legacy, a project first suggested to him by literary agent John Pearce not long after his resignation.

These tentative early thoughts eventually led to a series of interviews he did for Royal Roads University in mid-August of 2023. They would be preserved in the university archives, under his control, until he decided how to proceed. Horgan chose me to do the interviews. He was appreciative of my BC labour history book, *On the Line*, and knew of my long career in journalism. The interviews stretched out over two days. They covered the key issues he and his government encountered during his five years as premier, the major hurdles they confronted and overcame, and their many progressive measures and achievements. A third, shorter session took place in November with Horgan and his closest political ally and former finance minister, Carole James, steered by his ex-press secretary Sheena McConnell.

With Horgan's candour and straightforwardness on full display, the Royal Roads interviews were so productive that discussions about a book-length memoir began in earnest. When an equally rewarding podcast interview was added to the mix, it became even more evident there was far and away sufficient material for a book, and the deal was sealed. This would be John Horgan's story, an oral history told to me—with exceptions noted—in his own uniquely Horganesque words.

The heart of the book is a fulsome account of his time as leader of the NDP government that squeaked into power in 2017, then romped to a lopsided victory in 2020, the first time in BC political history that an NDP premier had been re-elected. Added to that is a narrative of Horgan's rollicking personal life and the ups and downs of his career in politics before becoming premier. We began interviews for this section of the book in the spring of 2024. They were conducted via Zoom, since Horgan was then in Berlin, where he had taken up his post as Canada's ambassador to Germany. They came to a halt in June, after he was diagnosed with thyroid cancer—his third cancer diagnosis. As he explained in a brief email: "I had to have a tracheotomy, so our gab sessions will have to stop, at least temporarily." He remained in hospital in critical condition for weeks.

Despite his health challenges, he was determined to press on. In late August, he notified me that he felt able to resume our interviews: "My health has improved, and I now have a talking device for my tracheotomy. My voice does not sound like Stephen Hawking. It is pretty much the same as ever." And indeed it was. Though there was a noticeable trace of frailty, his spirit and clarity were undiminished. With Horgan sitting up comfortably in his hospital bed, we had four more sessions before his cancer took a final turn for the worse.

By then, remarkably, his memoir was pretty well complete. There were maybe a few issues we might have canvassed with a bit more time, but little of significance.

This is anything but a dry political memoir. It is unvarnished Horgan, a tale recounted with gusto, replete with zingers, blunt assessments, comical anecdotes and candid admissions of his own shortcomings—plus, of course, his thorough detailing of decisions and events during those momentous five years in office. Yet the book is more than that. As the memoir proceeded, it took on elements of a personal statement from someone who has thought deeply about politics and has strong beliefs about how it should be practised. As a staunch social democrat, he also offered his views on the path the NDP needs to follow for future electoral success, particularly at the federal level.

Sadly, he did not get a chance to review the finished product. We will never know what changes and additions he might have made, and some of his observations may seem a bit dated, given the pace of change in the past year. But the book is anything but incomplete. He saw to that, insisting that we continue even while he was confined to his hospital bed in Berlin. And as I worked to whittle the wealth of material into form, having to make editing decisions without being able to consult the author, my number one goal was to ensure that every word, every paragraph, every chapter was full-on John Horgan. I hope he would be happy with the result.

CHAPTER ONE

EARLY DAYS

MY MOTHER WAS ALICE MAY CLUTTERBUCK. THAT'S RIGHT, Clutterbuck. She was born in Toronto in 1922 to Daisy and Joe Clutterbuck. They came to Canada from England sometime after the First World War, in which Joe had been severely gassed. He was a painter. My mother grew up in Toronto, the middle child of three kids. I only saw my grandparents a few times, but from what I can gather, Daisy was a tyrant, and that had an impact on my mother. Her childhood memories were not pleasant, except when she talked about my grandfather, whom she loved dearly. When I asked her about growing up, she would visibly stiffen. Marge, the older daughter, could do no wrong, and her brother, Bill, was the son they always wanted. Alice was in the middle, quite tall and ungainly. I have photographs of her that show a beautiful woman, but she was five foot ten, and there weren't a lot of tall women in those days. Her sister, Marge, was a perfect size two or whatever, and five foot three. My mom always felt like the thorn in the garden. That's how she characterized herself, which is very sad. When the war started, she joined the Women's Army Corps as a communications person. She trained in Montreal and was then sent to the Patricia Bay airbase in Victoria as part of the air force communications group.

My father, Patrick John Horgan, was born in County Cork, Ireland, in 1916 to Anne Doherty and John Coveney Horgan. He had a younger brother, Jack, and an older sister named Pauline, who was known as Pansie. My paternal grandfather died of the Spanish flu in 1918. Nana brought the family to Canada in the early 1930s. They landed in Halifax and took the train across Canada to Vancouver. She had some connection with the family that owned the big Spencer's department store downtown and worked as a nanny for the Spencer children. Pansie died in 1934, leaving Jack and Pat, two rough-hewn Cork boys, living in Vancouver. When World War II came along, both of them signed up. Jack was wounded in Italy, and Pat, my dad, was assigned to help protect the airbase at Patricia Bay. That's where he met and courted my mom.

She got pregnant with my older brother, Pat, who was born in 1946. That's why they got married. Of course, that was scandalous for an Irish Catholic, and my grandmother would sometimes refer to my mom, who was not Catholic, as "that bitch from the Church of England." Despite that, my mother always spoke well of my Irish grandmother. I liked her because she had cookies. My other brother, Brian, was born in 1947. My sister, Kathy, was born in 1953. My dad died from a brain hemorrhage in 1962, at the age of forty-six. I was just a toddler at the time, so I have no real memories of him, but I have heard lots of stories from my brothers. They were just teens when he died, so he had a big impact on their lives.

He was a drunk, but by all accounts, he was a happy drunk. A fast-talking Irishman, not unlike me, he could talk angels out of their underwear. And he would do these absolutely outrageous things. Everyone loved him at the pub. When the pub closed, he would say: "Alice will cook us some dinner. Let's go back to the house." We didn't have a pot to piss in, but everyone had space to piss in our pot. He didn't really have a craft or trade. He was more or less a salesman. These were difficult times. It was a struggle to make ends meet. My mom had to raise four kids in a time when there was no social safety net. But she managed that—got us married off, and we had kids, which was important to her. She did everything pretty much by herself. My dad really wasn't part of me, so I wouldn't do this often, but every now and then I would ask my mom about him. I'd say, "Give me a Dad story." And she would just brighten, you know. A smile would come over her face. It was like it took her back to a certain period in her life, even though it had been hard.

My dad was a bit of a boxer, basically what you would call an Irish scrapper. He also got into sports on the managing side. He managed Victoria's senior basketball team for a number of years. They were known as the Victoria Individuals. He was the money guy. Norm Baker was part of the team for a while. He's in the Canadian Sports Hall of Fame and was named Canada's most outstanding basketball player of the century in 1950, decades before Victoria's Steve Nash came along! His son, Norm Baker Jr., was a great lacrosse player, built like a fire hydrant, and a key part of the fine Victoria Shamrocks teams of the seventies and eighties. My dad often worked the penalty box at lacrosse games. The Victoria newspaper carried a cartoon that showed him with his arms crossed, keeping players apart in the sin bin, pointing out that he was an ex-boxer. Media outlets would characterize him that way. I don't think he'd been in any Golden Gloves or anything. I think what it really meant was that he was an Irish guy who got into a lot of fights. He knew how to take care of himself. That probably came from being a scrapper from Cork and having to work his way through a lot of drunken incidents—because when the sun went down, most of the time he was drunk.

He was a promoter as well. He handled things whenever the famous Harlem Globetrotters came to town. I used to have a stack of letters their owner, Abe Saperstein, had written to my dad. Everything was cash. You went around, you collected the cash, and my dad would stuff it into a paper bag. You gave the players their share. You gave the travelling management some, and then Abe Saperstein got his take. That's the way he did business. My brother Brian tells a great story about having to share a bed with one of the Globetrotters, because in the early days, they wouldn't let them check into the hotels in Victoria: "You can't stay here, you're Black." So they would stay at our house, which was not a palatial manor by any means. My mother remembered how they would all be sitting at the kitchen table, passing me around like a basketball—these huge hands and this little baby. She was terrified they were going to drop me, but there was zero chance of that. I was in more trouble if I was passed to a nanny walking down the street. A Globetrotter was never going to drop me.

One more story about my dad. At one time, I drove a truck delivering food to restaurants and convenience stores, which were all Chinese in those days. That was a connection back to my dad, because he got along with all the Chinese in Chinatown. It was a busy place in those days. At one point, he worked at Swift Meats. One of his jobs was to pick up the meat that couldn't be sold by Friday and take it to the dump, which was basically a barge. The barge would go out into the Strait of Georgia and dump the meat into the ocean. That's how we managed waste in those days. Henry Eng had started Oakcrest Food Store, but he was only allowed to sell vegetables. There was some law that prevented him from selling meat. So my dad would take him the meat that was going to be thrown out anyway—there was nothing wrong with it, except it was the end of the week. Dad would give it to the folks in Chinatown. It was barter. He would barter this for something else. That was how the system worked in Chinatown. He became the supplier of meat from Swift Meats to Chinese restaurants and the grocery stores. My mom used to say that Pat liked the Chinese because they were treated the same way the Irish were, as second-class citizens. He felt a kinship with them.

I used that anecdote several times when speaking in Victoria. The city's Chinatown is one of the oldest in North America. There's now a block of granite there commemorating the challenges of the Chinese community, apologizing for the way they were treated and all that. It also says "Premier John Horgan," which is a bit ironic, and here's why. One night, as I was being driven home by the security people, I looked down, and there was a little bronze plaque on a piece of cement commemorating the Capital Regional District and the Union of BC Municipalities and someone else for the Craigflower Corridor Phase Three or something like that, and I said, "What's the deal with plaques?" I started ranting about Christy Clark and [Transport Minister] Todd Stone spending something like $70,000 on a plaque to commemorate the thirtieth anniversary of the Coquihalla Highway just so they could have their names on it. They had nothing to do with the Coquihalla except putting the plaque there. So I was ranting away to the two cops who drove me around about how stupid it was to have plaques. Andrew, the driver, who had a very dry wit, got a smile on his face and said to me, "Are we not going to Chinatown on Sunday, sir?" And I said, "What do you mean?" He said, "Apparently we're unveiling a plaque with your name on it." And I said, "Well, I'll make an exception in this case, but otherwise I hate plaques!"

But that stone in Chinatown really meant something to me. My dad's little company was in Bastion Square. I've still got business cards from it that basically promote him as a jack-of-all-trades: "Whatever you need to do, I can do it." He was always in and around Chinatown, and now there's a plaque with his kid's name on it where he used to do business. Despite what I think about plaques, I'm very happy about that.

Our family lived in what was called the Hillside area of Victoria. After I was born, August 7, 1959, they moved to Saanich. There were now four kids, so we needed a bigger house. Pat and Brian shared a room. Kathy had her own room, and I was the baby, so I got my own room, too. We ended up selling that house, where my dad died, for another house about two kilometres away. It was on the other side of a mall called Town and Country, which was the dividing line between what was considered the city of Victoria and Saanich and Central Saanich and North Saanich and South Saanich and all of the other Saaniches. There's a million of them. Saanich is where I grew up.

I went to Lake Hill Elementary School. In grade 1, I was elected King of Hearts on Valentine's Day. It was my first elected office. I had to go into the cloakroom, ballots were cast, and there I was, King of Hearts. My queen was Lori Hallier. We were in the same class from grade 1 to grade 12. She went on to be an actor and managed to make a living out of standing in front of a camera. She was in a *Star Trek* episode. She played a Borg in *Star Trek: Voyager*. I am a total *Star Trek* geek, so that was awesome. Anyway, I remember coming home from being King of Hearts, with my crepe paper crown and some kind of robe. Of course it was raining, and the crepe paper turned to mush, but I sat there until my mom came home so she could see it. I don't know what I must have looked like when she opened the door, but I was just so proud.

Things were difficult after my father died. My mom didn't have a driver's licence. She didn't have any job skills. But she got her driver's licence, went to Sprott Shaw College, and managed to make her way into the tax department at Saanich City Hall. Saanich was a growing community in those days, and that became job security. It's what saved us. And it was a union job. She was a member of CUPE. The union was important to her because one time her boss made an inappropriate comment. She told him to go to hell and marched out of the municipal hall. But the union rep said, "Don't be so hasty, Alice. We've got a case here." She ended up salvaging her job, and from then on never looked unkindly on the union. She was able to accumulate a pension and retire at sixty.

As a kid, I'd go over to friends' who had fathers, since I didn't have one. Some of their dads would take me fishing or get me into Cubs. I started playing lacrosse because one of my buddies was playing. His dad would pick me up and maybe pay for my equipment and registration. I was kind of taken in by people, even though my mom was fierce: "I'm fine. I can take care of this." My brothers were gone by then. They married young. I remember when my niece was born. I was nine and so disappointed it was a girl because I thought that made me an aunt, not an uncle. We still laugh about that. So my brothers were out of the house, and my sister, God bless her, who was six years younger than they were, had to be the rock. At sixteen, she got pregnant, and she had three kids by the time she was nineteen, including twins.

We weren't a religious family at all, but the basic decency of Christianity permeated our existence. I can't remember a time when we weren't talking about doing unto others. My mother instilled that in me almost from the get-go. Those elements of faith that used to be foundational in most families were in our house too. After she was on her own, people would constantly show up at the door: "What do you need? How can I help?" Eventually that stopped, but it was never far from her mind that there, but for the Grace of God, go we. If anyone needed help, she was always there. She volunteered for stuff all the time, doing a lot for Silver Threads after she retired. And that became part of who I was.

Another lesson she taught me was "Don't burn your bridges. You've got your father's mercurial personality. Try and curb that, because you never know when someone may be in a position to help you." I don't know how relevant this is, but I say "bless you" every time somebody sneezes. That's from my mom offering up help to everyone, even someone who's had their head shaken up in a sneeze. You want to make sure that their soul stays with them and doesn't get taken by the fairies, which was part of the Irish lore hanging around when I was little.

Despite the hardships, all four of us kids—the result of an Irish immigrant and an uptight woman from Toronto coming together—did pretty well. We all had children of our own, and nobody was living rough on the streets. Everyone found their way. But I think I was special to my mother. She loved us all, but I was the apple of her eye, the kid she had after my dad agreed to stop drinking. She knew how important I was to my dad. The fact I was into sports when my brothers really weren't, the fact that I seemed to have an aptitude for academics when my brothers didn't, and then my going off to university and getting a master's degree, these were things that would have been unimaginable to her when I was in her arms and they were putting my dad into the ground. I became what kept her going. I don't know how many times she said that. I'm getting a bit choked up thinking about it.

In those days, if someone was widowed, the community was aware of it. Our neighbours babysat me. There was no universal child care. I would come home to *Gilligan's Island* and *Bewitched* and *I Dream of Jeannie*. I was also blessed that the principal at Lake Hill Elementary kept an eye on me, and I got a bit of a break. He had seen my brothers come through, not quite Irish twins but only thirteen months apart, and they scrapped with each other all the time. He'd managed them, and then my sister, so when I rolled in, he knew all about our family and that it was tough for my mother.

My mom remarried a guy she didn't love. Thankfully, he died, so she was rid of him. It's terrible to say that, but he wasn't my dad, so he didn't have a chance—not with my brothers, not with my mom, and not with me. It was like, I have a good thing going here, who's this jerk? He wasn't abusive in any way, but he was gormless, you know, and that was such a contrast to all the stories of the devil-may-care guy who was my father, full of vigour and madness. It was during this time that I descended into rebellion, doing all the things that twelve- and thirteen-year-old kids are not supposed to do.

I was an above-average student in grade 7. By the time I got to grade 8, I was heading into the ditch. I had started to seriously smoke cigarettes, then weed, and drink beer. There was a guy who broke into the local winery at the end of the tracks, so we had an endless supply of plonk, as well. The next year, in grade 9, I failed four classes. I was skipping school, getting high every day. Then, in grade 10, I started to turn myself around. I began dating a girl named Karen who played basketball. I was six foot one. I could jump. I had ability. Jack Lusk, the basketball coach, kind of took me under his wing. And that's what really brought me around. It was actually twofold. One, I really liked Karen. She was a great student and basketball player. And two, the basketball coach saw more in me than I saw myself. So did the principal. So did the counsellor. All of these people, for reasons that are really hard to fathom, decided that I was a salvageable product. By grade 12, I was captain of the basketball team. I was president of the student council. I was on a completely different trajectory from where I was in grades 8 and 9.

The principal and Jack Lusk felt they could work on this kid. I'm sure the fact that I had a troubled background, a single mom and all that stuff, played into it. I'm so grateful because, had they not made a choice to help me, I would never have had the opportunities I ended up with. I was so far away from what I'm doing right now. For anyone who knew me when I was fourteen, it would have been incomprehensible that this kid was going to grow up and be the premier of British Columbia and go off to be a diplomat in Europe. Like, are you kidding? He failed French in grade 9. He didn't really speak English. We owe so much to teachers.

I wasn't the best player on our basketball team. I was a better lacrosse player. But Jack Lusk instilled in me that I didn't have to be the best. It's a team game. You just have to be the guy everyone wants to play with. That's far more important than being the superstar. Everyone has a role to play, and quite honestly that philosophy shaped how I looked at cabinet-making later on. I needed a whole bunch of utility fielders who would rise to the occasion when needed. You look at the potential in people and hope they'll realize it. That's what Jack saw in me: There's potential there, and if he realizes it, the sky's the limit.

He also gave me humility. My dad was not humble. He was brash. He was loud. He was out there. But my mom was humble—hard-working, earnest, shoulders to the wheel, do your level best, never stop trying. Jack Lusk was the male equivalent to that. He directed me through my adolescence because my mom couldn't do that. She was a woman, and she was working. She was keeping the balls in the air. She'd already got through two rambunctious boys who were always in trouble, and I don't know if she had a third one in her. That's why the time I came upon Jack was so critically important. It was the shaping of my character. You have this raw material. You have your DNA. You have your predispositions. But all of that can go sideways unless you have a navigator for all those avenues of life. Jack also made me go into high-school theatre, which he had a real passion for. All the basketball players helped make the sets and had bit roles on stage. Jack wanted well-rounded people. Don't just be a gym rat. There's more to life than that. You need to explore other things. And if you're a dick, no one's going to want you around. That's what took me away from the dope smokers. I could hang around with them, or I could hang around with the jocks. I chose the jocks, only because Jack let me. I wasn't a starter when he pulled me in, but I was by the end.

Besides Jack Lusk, there was the principal, Bill Garner, who helped set me on the right path. I have a letter that he wrote to my mom at graduation. It was something like: "Dear Alice, I just want to let you know what a fine young man your son has turned out to be." Even though I did a whole lot of things after that, my mom kept that letter. For her, it was that feeling of "Thank goodness, mission accomplished." Of the four of us kids, I'm the only one who graduated from high school.

Years later, I learned just how much that mattered to her. Towards the end of the summer after grade 11, my brother Pat, who was already working for Safeway, got me a job as a warehouseman. The union, Retail Wholesale, was a real juggernaut in those days, and my wages for the first week were, like, are you kidding me? Before that, I'd been selling newspapers. But after that first week, my brother told me that I wasn't allowed to work there anymore because we were related. And I thought, "Oh, that's a shame. Too bad." Much, much later, my brother told me the real story. My mother had pinned him against the wall and said, "If that boy's not back at school in September, you're never allowed back in this house." She literally threatened my brother to get me fired or she would never forgive him. And that's why I didn't become a warehouseman. My mother said I needed to be in school.

Another early influence I had was Bruce Hutchison. I became friends with him, which was remarkable for me as a young teenager. He was a legend. Although not very well known today, he wrote popular books about BC and Canada and was a famous political columnist. His views were taken seriously by the country's political leaders for decades. You could say he invented the term "political reporting" in Canada. I grew up with his grandkids, and we used to party. At that age, we were just out of our heads. Meanwhile, Bruce Hutchison would be meeting with the lieutenant governor or someone like that on the other side of the huge house they lived in. I remember he gave me a job cutting wood at his camp at Shawnigan Lake. It involved driving up the Malahat Highway, getting to the camp, and splitting maybe two or three pieces of wood. Then he would invite me inside, with the wood stove going, and we would spend the rest of the day talking about politics, past and present. It was unbelievable. What a great opportunity.

It was an unlikely friendship. I was young and rambunctious, and he was this serious-looking guy almost sixty years older than me. But he took a shine to me. Years later, when I was a staffer in Ottawa and he was in his eighties, he would still make an annual trek to Ottawa and Washington to talk to the mandarins there. That was his trapline. He was aging and no longer as relevant as he used to be, but nonetheless he would make the trip. I remember one time in particular, he phoned me up and said, "Horgan, have you got time for a coffee?" And I said, "Absolutely. You name the time." He said, "Well, I'm seeing Simon Reisman at two o'clock, and Michael Wilson at four. Can we squeeze something in there?" And I thought, this guy is squeezing me in between the minister of finance and our trade representative during the great free trade debate of 1988.

I kept kind of pinching myself. How did I fall into the lap of living history? He would tell me all of these stories. They weren't things that I could use effectively to tear down an opponent, but they helped me gain more experience and more understanding of the human condition from the perspective of someone who had spent sixty years writing about politics. They were all about things that he had observed, through one war, one massive depression, and a whole host of events and changing political personalities. He interviewed every prime minister from William Lyon Mackenzie King all the way through to Brian Mulroney. He was an icon in the media business and wrote a glowing letter of recommendation for me to get into the one-year program of journalism at Carleton University in Ottawa. They rejected me, thank goodness, because otherwise I would have ended up being a journalist. I had a passion for media because of my relationship with Bruce and watching how he had spent a lifetime chronicling the events of our time. That really appealed to me. Instead of chronicling them, however, I became an actor in them.

CHAPTER TWO

SPORTS

I STARTED PLAYING LACROSSE AROUND EIGHT YEARS OLD. MY FRIENDS were already playing, but I couldn't get in the first year because we didn't have the money, and we weren't in the sports stream. I didn't have a dad trying to get his boy on the team. Later on, I became a hockey dad, so I know all about the role of politics in minor sport. I don't need to get into that, suffice to say my mom wasn't in that circle. I was a bit of a chubby kid at the start, but I started to lean out as I grew up. I became quite a good lacrosse player. I played defence. I could knock people over, I could score, and I was quick. I became the guy everyone wanted to have on their team.

In my midget or intermediate year, we had a very good team. We beat Burnaby in the provincial finals. Their team included the well-known sportscaster Don Taylor, and I always bugged him about it. When they came over to Victoria to play, he stayed at my house, and I sometimes stayed at his house when we played over there. Those were the days when you would put your kids on a ferry without much adult supervision, let them stay at a stranger's house, and expect them to come back in the same shape two or three days later. I can't imagine that today. We bunked with other families so that trips were affordable. No hotels or anything like that. I played lacrosse up to Junior B. I got cut from the Junior A team in my first year of eligibility, and then I moved to Peterborough, in Ontario, to go to university. Peterborough was a hotbed of lacrosse, and that was one of the reasons I ended up going there. In the summer, I went to their junior tryouts. There's a clipping in the local paper with a picture of me doing a sit-up, saying I'm one of the potential new players for the team. But they couldn't get me a job. It was 1980. Times were tough, so I came back to BC, where I knew I could get work. I worked in the Cowichan Valley at a small value-added joinery operation that was union. Even though I was still a junior, I ended up playing Senior B lacrosse. That was kind of cool because these were people I used to go and watch, and now I was playing with them. That was as close as I got to realizing my childhood dream of playing in BC's top lacrosse league.

My passion for lacrosse meant going to Victoria Shamrocks games. My mom wouldn't take me: "Oh my god, I can't possibly do that. And you can't go on the bus by yourself!" So I would have to go with someone's parent. I fell in love with Memorial Arena. We would go around the concourse and bark "Green ball!" at the refs every time the ball went out. It was like a festival. I used to say that the hot dogs at Memorial Arena were so good because they kept the water in big vats in the basement. They just kept using it over and over again. I fell in love with the Shamrocks. Plus, there was the fact that my dad had been associated with them, and it was a chance to talk about him. When people would say "My dad did this" or "My dad did that," I could say, "My dad used to work the penalty box at the Shamrocks games."

I didn't only play lacrosse. As a kid, I played soccer because it was cheap. You just needed boots, and you could use someone else's old ones. With basketball, you already had your running shoes. They were the ones you walked around in. You would be out in the mud with them, throw them in the washing machine, play a game at night, and they'd be just fine. I always wanted to play hockey, but skates were expensive and registration was off the charts, so I never played hockey. I played sports that were cheap and were team based. At Trent, the university in Ontario where I ended up going, I was good enough to play on the school's basketball team. Every year that went by, I became a better basketball player because I was playing more and more against better players.

For me, team sports were where you realized that everyone's role was important. If you were the best on the team, that was great, but if the team lost, what was the point? The values of mateship—helping each other out, supporting people, and making sure there was room for everyone to participate—were higher values as far as I was concerned. For me, sports are a microcosm of society. You have a task ahead of you. What's the plan to take on that task? How do we use the talents available to achieve the outcome we all want? We love to watch the highlights of the great goal, the great save or the outstanding catch, but the beauty of the game is that all of these snapshots are the result of a bunch of people from different backgrounds and different skills coming together and finding that sweet spot that will lead to success. That's what sports have always meant to me.

When I watch sports now, I don't necessarily look at the Connor McDavids. I look at the guy who plays all two hundred feet of the rink, goes into corners, takes a punch, gives a punch, and who rallies the troops. That's the kind of person I became. I was that guy in my senior year at high school. I made the city all-star basketball team, not because I could hit thirty-footers all day or crash the boards, but because I was working hard. I would get ten to fifteen points a game, some boards, some assists, some steals, and a little bit of everything else. I tried to be the teammate you wanted to have in all circumstances. That's how I like to look at everyone. What's your potential? If you realize it, fantastic, but even if you realize only half your potential, you can still make a contribution.

There's another thing about me that likely came from sports. When I first ran for the leadership of the BC NDP, I got an endorsement from one of my good friends from university. The essence of what he wrote was that when he met John Horgan, I was the life of the party. I was the centre of attention. But what really stuck with him, and why we have remained friends to this day, is that I was always looking to see who was not included. How can we make the circle bigger so that everyone is part of the party? And that, I think, typifies how I've looked at things. I was with the druggies, and I was with the jocks. When I joined the jocks, I didn't turn my back on the druggies, because they were my friends, too. I still smoke weed today, so it's not like I became abstinent and decided not to do any of that. Of course, having said that, I think there's obviously a lot more to be gained by being sober and focusing on what's in front of you. But I was always trying to keep as many people included as possible, always trying to make the table bigger. I don't know where that came from, other than through sports. It was just instinctive. People made room for me, so I should make room, too. I think that humility came from my mom and from Jack Lusk. Don't get too high on yourself, because what happens before the fall? Hubris comes before the fall.

I played on the Sydney University basketball team in Australia, where I went after graduating from Trent, but that was a step down. They didn't play university sports much in Australia. Universities were for eggheads. The rugby players, cricketers, and most everyone else played club sports. Basketball was kind of an afterthought, but I played there until I was twenty-five, at a pretty high level. When I came back to Canada, I would still throw the ball around, and when I was in my thirties, in Victoria, working for the NDP, there was a group of MLAs and staff who played lunch-hour basketball at the United Church basement with people like Emery Barnes, Barry Jones, Mike Harcourt and the legendary Cliff Serwa. They were always saying to me, "You gotta dial it back, kid. We're not at your level." That was basically the last basketball I played, and it wasn't serious at all.

My most vivid sports memory took place in Australia, because it also involved a frightful experience for my wife, Ellie. There was some tournament outside Sydney, and I remember I hit nine three-pointers in a single game. I was the best guy on the floor that night. I couldn't miss. And the three-pointers were from further and further out, like Caitlin Clark, who's so incredible doing that in women's basketball. Everything I threw up in the air went in. Ellie and I were newlyweds, and we were tenting with the team at a caravan park in a place called Wollongong. That night, Ellie developed a very bad migraine. She's resilient, and her pain threshold is beyond my imagination. This was the first time I'd ever seen her incapacitated by pain. Even though I was the best guy on the basketball floor, that was a secondary memory to this night of Ellie's extraordinary pain, getting her to the hospital, getting her hydrated and all these other things. She never had a headache like that again. But we'd just been married. There was no support network, only the two of us.

Just to finish up, I have some interests that have nothing to do with sports. I love polishing rocks. And science fiction is something I really get into.

There's not usually a big crossover between sports people, druggie people and geeks, but I was comfortable with all of them. I was also comfortable with smokers. I smoked until 2001. When I was playing basketball in Australia, I would usually have a few smokes at halftime.

I enjoyed music, too. I have no musical ability, but I do love music. At university, there were lots of bars and lots of bands, and we would go out wherever there was music.

And of course there was my career in high-school drama, which Jack Lusk had forced me into—although I enjoyed it. My greatest role was as a dung beetle in one of the productions. Some might say it was typecasting, rolling balls of dung across the stage. Sort of like politics.

CHAPTER THREE

LOVE AND UNIVERSITY

AS I MENTIONED, I WOUND UP AT TRENT UNIVERSITY, IN PETERBOROUGH, in south-central Ontario. How I got there is a pretty fascinating story. Part of it has to do with my passion for the Victoria Shamrocks. After high school, I wanted to work at the bar, because I needed to make some money, and it was also a chance to meet women. But you couldn't work there unless you were a student. So I registered at Camosun College. I didn't really go to many classes and didn't complete the year. Pretty shameless, I know. My dream had been to play for the Shamrocks. I had every expectation that would happen, but it didn't. By then, I felt I needed to get out of Victoria to be a success.

There was no internet then, so what universities had I heard of? University of Toronto, Queen's, McGill, and a friend was going to the University of Prince Edward Island. I thought I would make that my goal. I travelled by Greyhound bus. To go right across Canada, making stops along the way, it was like ninety-nine dollars or something.

I was on my way to Kingston to check out Queen's, but I made a side trip to Peterborough because the Shamrocks were playing there for the Mann Cup. I got a seat in the arena, and every time the Shamrocks scored, this one guy in the stands would stand up and go "Yay!" Everyone else would look at me and ask me what I was doing there. I said I was looking for a university, and they said that I should take a look at Trent. And I said, "What's Trent?" They said it's a small university just outside of town. So I went by the university. It had these relatively modern buildings built in the 1960s. They had colleges like Oxford and Cambridge. And they had rowing teams. That was the big thing. I thought, well, that's nice and carried on my way. McGill was too big, and all the French just freaked me out, so I went to PEI to see my friend. I liked it there, plus the synergy of leaving an island on the West Coast for an island on the East Coast kind of made sense, so I pretty much set my sights on PEI.

Now comes the Ocean Falls part of the story. I knew some guys from Ocean Falls who had come down to Victoria to play high-school basketball. There was really nothing for them in Ocean Falls. You play against Bella Coola, then you play against Bella Coola, and then you play against Bella Coola, and the season's over. They would go back in the summer and work in the pulp mill there. I had got to know them, so I went up to Ocean Falls and stayed there for a year making pulp. I started working in the sawmill, but I wanted to make as much money as possible, so I transferred to the pulp mill, where someone was always sick or didn't show up. I got a lot of double shifts, and I made a bucket of money.

There were about twelve hundred people in Ocean Falls, way down from the five thousand the town used to have, but that was still enough to have basketball teams. I helped coach the girls' high-school basketball team. We played Bella Coola, then we played Bella Coola. Of course, I was still thinking about university, and I looked in the high school's library. They had exactly two university calendars. One was for UBC, which made complete sense, and the other was for—of all universities—Trent. And I started thinking, "What are the chances of that?" If I carried that calendar around, no one in Ocean Falls would know what

Trent University was. But I did, because I'd been there, and I knew where it was, so I thought, why not, and I applied.

This was the summer of 1979. I got a note from Trent that I had been accepted, and they had assigned me to Catharine Parr Traill College. But that was downtown, and I wanted to be on campus, where everything was happening. They offered to put me in some student townhouses that were a straight line to the campus along Water Street, and I thought, "Well, townhouses, that could be good. I'm in." The townhouses were all coed, except mine, which was six guys. Think *Animal House*. It turned out that I was in No. 18, and Ellie Mast was in No. 16.

The first day I was there, there was a pub crawl, and I said, "What the hell, let's go." I got sufficiently lubricated to be sitting on the piano singing songs at the top of my lungs, badly. It turns out this attractive blonde took a shine to me and walked me home. I had no memory of any of it. The next day at campus, I ran into her at the library, where the bus would come. I had sunglasses on, very heavily hungover, and I was desperate to get home. Ellie came up to me and said, "Hi, how are you doing?" I said I was fine, and we chatted away on the bus back into town. I asked if she wanted to go out that night. She said, "Sure, that would be great." We agreed to go to the Jolly Hangman pub. I went back to the townhouse and said to the guys, "Am I the only one going out with a beautiful blonde tonight?" And one of them said, "Is that the same one who brought you home last night?" I hadn't remembered a thing. That was forty-five years ago, and we've been married forty years as of February 2024.

None of that would have happened if I hadn't gone to Ocean Falls and stumbled upon the Trent calendar, which I would not have cared about if I hadn't stopped off in Peterborough to watch the Shamrocks play, and on and on. I'm not a particularly spiritual person or a "things happen for a reason" kind of person, but, boy, there are a lot of coincidences in the world, and that's one of them. The love of my life, the person who finished moulding the rough clay that my mom shaped out in Saanich, was Ellie.

There's actually one more thing about Ocean Falls being a factor in meeting my soulmate. I learned later that my application to Trent had originally been rejected. My grades had been inadequate. But Thomas H.B. Symons, the founding president of the university, had pulled my application out of the reject pile and put it in the accept file. Why? Because he saw I was from British Columbia, from a place called Ocean Falls. No one from there had ever come to Trent, and he thought that was interesting enough to accept me. He told me that in my graduating year. They had been watching me ever since I first arrived, and I had turned out pretty well. I'd gone from being a mediocre student to an A-plus student who would go on to get a master's degree in history. And it was all because this guy pulled my name out of the reject pile and put it into the accept pile because of where I came from. Had he not done that, I might be driving a truck delivering food for Safeway. It was so absolutely random.

This might be a good time to say something more about my working experience at Ocean Falls, which played such a role in my future. It was the end of the road, no way in or out except by boat or seaplane. There were some real hard-life stories in Ocean Falls, and I learned a lot. The NDP government under Dave Barrett had bought the pulp mill in 1973 from Crown Zellerbach, which was going to shut it down, so there had been a bit of a renaissance. The operation was an integrated sawmill, pulp mill, paper mill, all in one place, with cheap energy. They had a dam up at the lake and fourteen feet of rain a year. They used to say: "Dirty days have September, April, June and November. All the rest have thirty-one, with little chance of any sun. If all the months had two and thirty, they'd be twice as wet and twice as dirty." It rained a lot in Ocean Falls. Residents called themselves "the Rain People."

There were two bars. One was in the Martin Inn, a six-storey hotel that for a time, I think, was the largest building in BC outside Vancouver. You could either go to that bar or the Legion. If you were barred from the bar, you weren't necessarily barred from the Legion, since they were a little distance apart. And every Saturday night, the ferry would come into town. Now, living on Vancouver Island my entire life, the idea of "let's go down to watch the ferry come in" was never ever something I thought about. By the time I left Ocean Falls, however, I had a better appreciation of why people did that. Sometimes people just walked on, and you never saw them again. They said, "I'm done. I'm not staying here a minute longer." They'd buy their ticket, head off to Prince Rupert, and go back to wherever they'd come from. Ocean Falls was also filled with people who'd been there a lifetime. Kids who had then raised their own kids there. There was that stream, and there were the hard-lifers who had maybe rolled in with the salmon fleet, which showed up every year. There were a lot of drugs, hard drugs. Fortunately, at that point, I was no longer in that stream. But I had some good friends who were. It was jarring for me to see the deterioration, when they had that first fix and knew they had to have the next one. My introduction to the destructive force of addiction was in Ocean Falls.

My anti-gambling views came from Ocean Falls, as well. I would watch people sign the back of their paycheques and throw them into a poker pot when that was the last thing they should be doing. I was only there to make money, I wasn't going to give it to those asshats, so I wasn't playing poker—and I loved poker. We used to play in high school all the time. Go on basketball trips, you play poker. Lacrosse trips, you play poker. Sometimes it was serious money, but I wasn't going to do that again. Another lesson from my mom: Don't waste your money.

I often went to my friend Dale's place. His dad was foreman in the pulp mill. His mom, Kitty, worked at the bar. They'd raised their family, four boys and a daughter, in Ocean Falls. They had invested their entire life in the community. I was exposed to those kind of people, and there were lots of them. There were also a lot of good athletes from Ocean Falls. In the summer, for those weeks it didn't rain, there was track and field, basketball, baseball, and swimming at the lake, rather than the pool, because the pool was only fifteen metres or something. It was like stroke stroke turn, stroke stroke turn. That's why some of their swimmers were so good: They never missed a second on the turns. Ralph Hutton from Ocean Falls won a silver medal at the Olympics in 1968. Ian MacKenzie swam against Mark Spitz at the Olympics in 1972. Another Olympic swimmer from Ocean Falls was Dick Pound, who became well known as a member of the International Olympic Committee for many years. Those idyllic elements were very much part of Ocean Falls, but throughout its history, there were also a lot people, like me, who would just roll in and then roll out again. By the time I was there, they were the majority.

As for the work, it was hard. Before switching to the pulp mill, I worked in the sawmill. Some of the logs we ground up into pulp make me weep. But at that time, when you were working on the grinders, the bigger the log you could jam into the end with the grinding stones, the longer it would grind, and the less work you had to do. You've got this kind of keyboard thing, and you've got these jacks that jump up and shoot the logs this way or that way, and you've got four pockets on the conveyor. There were four stations with four pockets each, and if you were up at the front, that was the best place to be. The worst place to be was at the end, because all you got was the small wood. The small wood ground down very quickly, so you were constantly putting small wood into the pockets because all the big wood was in pocket one, pocket two, pocket three. By the time you got to station four, there was no big wood left. It was dangerous work, and you had to be awake.

I only did a couple of shifts in the paper mill. That was considered to be the job that took the most energy because you had to do a lot of moving around. In groundwood, you just leaned back and basically played the keyboard, loading up the pockets. Same thing in the sawmill. The wood came up the conveyor belt, and you just separated it this way, separated it that way, cut it up into four-foot chunks and sent it on its way. But people were always sweating in the paper mill. While we were in jackets, they were in T-shirts because it was so hot. Lots of steam and lots of chemicals, as well, coming out of the groundwood.

Ocean Falls was my introduction to a whole bunch of things. Global economics for one. When the *LA Times* all of a sudden didn't want our newsprint anymore, the pulp mill said that we could make money selling kraft, which is just basically raw pulp cut into stacks to be sent to papermakers somewhere else. I remember being in the premier's office later on as a staffer, talking about trying to find a way to innovate in the pulp sector, changing from newsprint to tissue to magazine paper to various cartons. But the markets just kept disappearing, or we got replaced as suppliers by lower-cost jurisdictions—bamboo instead of Douglas fir, that sort of thing. I learned that you have to have an integrated supply chain. When I was being briefed on supply chains during the pandemic, for example, and how fundamental that issue is to our global economy, I morphed back to what I had heard after the *LA Times* pulled the plug in Ocean Falls. That meant the town's paper component was no longer viable, which meant that the sawmill was redundant. And what can you really do with pulp if you're not making paper with it? That ultimately led to the demise of the town not that long after I left.

I can't remember ever having a fight with Ellie. That's not to say she's without strong opinions, but whenever anything might have risen up between us, it wasn't that important to her. She's been supportive of me from the start. She helped make me a better student by her being a good student. I wanted to be like her. She's had my back the whole time. She's helped me out in every endeavour.

She grew up in a rigid Christian Reform church family in an Ontario Dutch community, where if you're not Dutch, you're not much. Christian Reform is a right-wing sect of Protestantism, so she had a sheltered upbringing. Then she met me at university, this impetuous guy from an exotic island in the North Pacific, not like any of the blond boys she'd gone to church or hockey games with. Maybe they had grasped a hand in a romantic, reckless moment on a Saturday night, but here was this guy singing "I love tequila" on a piano in a bar, and she says she was in love with me from that moment on.

At Trent I started taking philosophy, sociology, psychology, maybe a first-year history course, but my plan was to be a social worker. I was not a political animal in any way, shape or form. But in second year, one of my roommates said that Tommy Douglas was speaking at the university and invited me to go. I was like, "Who the heck is Tommy Douglas?" I was the jock that had been drunk or high much of the time growing up, and I was just chipping away at what the world was all about. I honestly had no idea who Tommy Douglas was. But my friend promised to buy me a beer, so we hopped on the bus to go hear him. And there was this tiny little man, and he had this booming voice, and I was enthralled, simply captivated by this guy. The campus was kind of a lefty place, and I'd scratched the surface of a few organizations, but after Tommy Douglas, that was it. The next year I switched to history. I learned about the League for Social Reconstruction and the creation of the CCF, which became the NDP. The veils came off my eyes. All I wanted to do after that meeting was get an education and help people. Social work might have been the way, but I was learning about political structures and how you lift up communities and societies. This was serious stuff. I loaded up on courses about Canada, and just about everything I wrote was about the Left's response. There were all these little clubs and debates, and it's what you're talking about in the pub. And Marxism, of course. What else do you talk about on a campus in the 1980s? That's how I began my political journey. By accident. All because of this chance meeting that I didn't want to go to.

Once Ellie and I were both finished at Trent, I went back to BC. The plan was that I was going to go to Australia to do graduate work. I was just waiting for acceptance. But the Australian

National University in Canberra rejected me—which turned out to be great, because I was accepted instead by the university in Sydney, and Sydney was so much better than Canberra.

I spent the summer working at the Keg in Victoria: "My name's John. The specials tonight are x, y and z. I'll bring some people up to sing you a birthday song. And please leave me a big tip." What other job would you expect with an undergraduate degree from a liberal arts university in 1983?

Ellie came out to visit me. It was in her mind that it was going to be a long goodbye because she was going back to Ontario. I clearly had a plan, and she wasn't part of it. But in my mind, we just hadn't had that conversation. Job one was to get our university degrees. I was poor as a church mouse by the time we graduated. I didn't have two dimes to rub together, and I had massive student debts. I weighed about 165 pounds, which was less than when I first arrived at Trent. I was emaciated. I lived off Kraft Dinner. We wouldn't use all the sprinkled cheese, because we could make that hot and put it on toast. I was as poor as poor could be.

Ellie was with me in BC when I got the letter from Sydney University saying that I was in. We went out to celebrate at a place called Coffee Max. It was really just a diner with a $1.99 special, toast, soup and a salad. We're sitting at the table. It's lunchtime, and the place is full. I say, "This is fantastic. I can't wait for us to go to Australia." And Ellie says, "I could never do that to my parents, the two of us just up and going like that." I'm scooping up a spoonful of soup, and I say, "Well, we can get married... but I don't have any money." And as I'm bringing the soup to my mouth, Ellie says, "I've got money." And I spit the soup all over the table. We went from the restaurant down to Victoria's Inner Harbour. I got down on one knee in front of a sailing vessel called, appropriately enough, the *Bohemian* and asked her to marry me. She said she would. That was in the fall of 1983, and we got married in her hometown on February 18, 1984. It was a rushed wedding. All the Dutch relatives were convinced that Ellie was pregnant.

They're going off to Australia, right? So she's obviously going to have a baby when they're gone. They kept looking very closely at her dress.

We had a rigid wedding. Ellie's father was dead against dancing. Apparently the Lord doesn't like dancing. We had a marriage in their Christian church. My family was there, and a handful of friends from BC, and all these Dutch people I had never seen before in my life. When we left the wedding, we drove up to Peterborough and went to the bar where we first met. About a hundred people from school were there waiting for us. Every surplus area was covered with beer. They closed the doors at one a.m., as they had to, but we stayed until four in the morning sucking back beers.

On our thirtieth wedding anniversary, I commemorated the day with a small speech in the Legislature. Christy Clark had just moved Question Period to the morning. It was one of her tactics to screw the Opposition because it didn't give us time to prepare and no one in the media cared about anything but drinking coffee at that time of day. Ellie had come down to the Legislature, since it was our anniversary, and we were going to have lunch together. She was sitting in the public gallery. I stood up in the House and said something like: "Thirty years ago today, Canada was playing Sweden for the bronze medal at the Olympics in Sarajevo. Unfortunately, Canada lost. Now I can see some members wondering why I would remember that. Well, I remember that because it was also my wedding night. The Canadian team got shut out, but I did pretty well. So I want to introduce the House to Ellie, my alpha, my omega, my reason for living, because nothing says 'I love you' like an early morning Question Period." You can find it on Google, February 18, 2014.

Ellie was my secret weapon when we moved to Australia because she worked there. She's a biologist by training, a freshwater ecologist. She got a job at the New South Wales Egg Marketing Board just as we arrived. It was a union job, and she was happy with it. We were making money, life was good, the sun was out all the time. She applied for another gig, doing renal research at St. Leonard's, the teaching hospital attached to the University of Sydney, across the bridge on the north shore. She would cut rats open, pull out their kidneys and put little capillaries in, then draw blood and go to the electron microscope at the main campus near our house and submit all the materials so that the techs could do their stuff. She was doing kidney research. What a great thing to be doing. I ended up getting a job at the phone company, Telecom Australia. I had gone there looking for papers and discovered a treasure trove of documents. They hired me as their historical officer.

When I finished my thesis, both of us had good jobs and we assumed we were going to stay in Australia forever. Then the immigration people said, "Get the heck out of here. You're not a student anymore." We said that we wanted to stay because back in Canada I'd been a waiter and Ellie was unemployed. The last summer in Canada, Ellie had actually worked on the assembly line at a glue factory someplace in southern Ontario. We were living large in Australia. Money was coming in. We had office jobs, no heavy lifting. Nothing better. And they kicked us out of the country. They said you can apply from Canada to stay, but you have to wait two years. So we came back to BC.

We drove across the country to see Ellie's family, and while we were in Ontario we figured, well, how about Ottawa? I had a master's degree, and Ottawa has a whole bunch of museums. The public archives are there. "Let's go to Ottawa and see what's what." I ended up going to see Ian Waddell because a job in his office was advertised. He was the NDP's MP for Vancouver–Kingsway. I could tell stories about Ian all day long. I loved him dearly, and his heart was absolutely in the right place, but he was a weird dude. He didn't want to give me the job. He suggested I try Jim Manly, who was the NDP member for Cowichan–Malahat–The Islands. I applied, and Manly said I was way too qualified for the job, which was basically opening mail. I said, "Well, I need to qualify for paying my rent. I'll do whatever you want me to do. I need a job." He hired me, reluctantly, and that's how I started on Parliament Hill. Ellie, meanwhile, was literally cleaning apartments. Here she was, going from doing kidney research with her BSc to being a cleaner. A year later, she became pregnant, and all of a sudden going back to Australia didn't seem that appealing. Nate was born in April of 1988, and she stayed home, tending to the baby. By that time, I'd been working on the Hill for a year.

CHAPTER FOUR

PARLIAMENT HILL

WITH ELLIE AT HOME AND MY LARGE ONGOING STUDENT DEBT, KEEPING my job was very important. But 1988 was an election year. If the election went badly, I might be out of luck. Political staff come and go with the wind. Jim Manly wasn't running again, and his constituency had been redrawn to be part of three new ridings. Dave Stupich got one of the NDP nominations. Dave Barrett got the nomination in Esquimalt–Juan de Fuca, and Lynn Hunter, a little-known campaigner for Oxfam, was running in Saanich–Gulf Islands, which is currently Elizabeth May's seat. I was stoked, thinking I was going to take all of my brilliance and offer it up to Dave Barrett. But Jim said to me, "You know, Barrett doesn't need any help from you, but Lynn Hunter could sure use a hand." That was wise advice from my United Church minister. I would have been just another body in the room for Barrett. It was the end of his illustrious career. He wasn't going to work particularly hard, but NDP leader Ed Broadbent had asked him to run.

I took Jim's advice and worked on Lynn Hunter's campaign. She ended up winning because of the split that resulted from the Reform Party being on the ballot. I became her adviser. I went from opening the mail for a seasoned MP to a guy advising someone who, in terms of politics, had just fallen off the turnip truck. She valued my views and my perspective. The NDP made a big breakthrough in BC, going from eight seats to nineteen. I felt I was actually participating in events rather than observing them. I was becoming more of a political animal. That was a change.

Despite the party's success in BC, the election was a disappointment for the NDP. The party had been on a roll. Liberal leader John Turner wasn't resonating, and we'd been riding high in the polls. We were going to storm the country and leapfrog over the Liberals. They were heady days. Then we got soft on free trade and a lot of our vote collapsed. But I was glad to still have a job. I had to feed three people now instead of just one. Then Evan was born in 1989. Suddenly there were four of us. By that time, I was well regarded, with fairly decent pay. It was better than drywalling, working at the Keg, or all those other things I had done before going to Australia. Gradually, this became something that I could call a career.

I was in Ottawa for five years, from 1986 to 1991. After the election, there were a lot of New Democrats from BC and a lot of staff. I was part of the team that was always preparing for whatever was coming down the pike, making sure everyone was ready for Question Period and seeing that BC MPs got their share of questions. I wasn't exactly in the vanguard, but these were formative years for me, learning about the country. There was a Saskatchewan group, an Ontario group, and there was Stanley Knowles. At that point, he was an honorary clerk of the House of Commons, a position that Prime Minister [Pierre] Trudeau had bequeathed him. He would take his place at the clerk's table during Question Period, beloved by everyone because he was such a wonderful guy. But he was in his eighties, and he had had a stroke. He would meet with young staffers, and you'd go and have tea and biscuits with him. I used to say the biscuits had come with him on the train from Manitoba in 1942 when he was first elected for the CCF, and he was just getting through them. They were very stale, but you were obliged to eat one because it was on your cup and saucer. Those were the kind of personalities I was seeing.

I got to watch Svend J. Robinson, who, in his own way, was very effective, even if it was often for Svend J. Robinson and not so much for anybody else. Ian Waddell was also a good Opposition member. And I had the good fortune of getting to know Pauline Jewett. She was impressive, even if she was a real smoker and didn't spend a lot of time in the House because of the no-smoking rules. Margaret Mitchell was delightful as well. Those two stood out in my mind. They were feminists before Gloria Steinem was a feminist. Nelson Riis, from Kamloops, always impressed me. One incident really stands out in my mind. He was meeting some obscure group of representatives from BC, and they wanted to talk to our BC caucus about something or other. Even though he got there late, he commanded the room and everything went fine. They all left, and I was thinking how well-prepared he was. He kind of slumped in his chair and said, "I had no bloody idea what I was talking about." He was simply reading the room as he sat down. He could see the subject matter on the handout in front of him, and off he went. That really impressed me. To be successful in politics, you have to be quick on your feet, and you have to be able to engage with people and hold your own on a variety of different subjects. I was kind of fashioning my career as a bit of an expert on things around energy, but Nelson Riis showed me that in order to be a decent politician you need to be able to talk about almost everything. Not in a condescending way, but knowing enough about the subject that the people you're talking to believe you care about what they're saying.

As luck would have it, I'm extremely curious. What I liked about working in politics for as long as I did was the opportunity to meet people I wouldn't normally have got to meet and hear their stories and different perspectives. From CEOs to workers, and everybody in between, you had a chance to drop in on them. As premier, they're lining up to talk to you, and it was fantastic. What could be better for someone who just wants to know stuff? It wasn't to be boorish at cocktail parties. It was because it's good to know. I liked retaining information. How many home runs did

Willie McCovey hit in 1969? Who were the four twenty-game winners for the Baltimore Orioles in 1971? This was all before Google.

The person I was most fond of was Jim Fulton, the NDP's MP from Skeena. He was outstanding, a larger-than-life figure, always with a mischievous smile on his face, as if he was up to something. Everyone liked him. I remember a speech he gave when they created Gwaii Haanas, the national park in Haida Gwaii. He was so eloquent and passionate about it, the words were just falling out of his mouth. I marvelled at his ability as a politician. There were stories that he would go away at Christmas, and he would come back with a pretty rich tan, but he would tell people that he'd been home on the island over Christmas. Of course it was Jamaica, not Haida Gwaii. On Fridays, his staff would call the bar of the Crest Hotel in Prince Rupert and ask for Jim to be paged. Now Jim was nowhere near Prince Rupert, but in the bar of the Crest Hotel, they'd ask him to come to the phone. And people would go, "Oh, Jim's in town." That's just one of the things he would do. I suppose that's deceitful, but it's also smart, and funny, too. We would do whatever Jim wanted, follow him over the cliff if need be, because he was just that kind of guy.

I had become pretty good at what I was doing. I had watched and learned. But I was still mindful of the vagaries of elections. The longer I stayed working as a political staffer, the more I started thinking about the need to become more permanent. There were provincial NDP governments in Ontario, BC and Saskatchewan, and Tony Penikett's Yukon government was also NDP. But in Ottawa, we'd become the fourth party after Lucien Bouchard left Brian Mulroney and started his blockheads [Bloc Québécois]. I very much wanted to get out of Ottawa. It was too cold, until it was too hot. And I'm colour-blind, so I didn't notice the leaves changing that everybody got all excited about for the week that it happened in the fall. It didn't do anything for me. I wanted to get out of Ottawa and come back home.

CHAPTER FIVE

WORKING FOR GOVERNMENT

MIKE HARCOURT AND THE NDP HAD BEEN ELECTED IN 1991. I EXPECTED to be lured back to work for them. It didn't happen. I wasn't very happy about that, especially when I saw some of the people who were hired out of Ottawa. I was told no one was going to hire me unless they could look me in the eyes in person. That's when we loaded up and headed back home. For the first few weeks, we lived in my mom's basement. We had some equity from our house in Ottawa, and we began looking for a place we could afford. I wanted to be in the Saanich area, where I grew up, but our equity wasn't enough, and we kept being pushed further and further away from the areas we wanted. Meanwhile, the truck was coming with our stuff, and my mom wasn't going to let us unload it into the basement. At last, we found a house we could afford. It was in Langford. The realtor said we could move in right away. We said we'd take it. It was St. Patrick's Day. For an Irish guy, what could be better than that? We lived in that house for the next thirty years, until we moved to Berlin.

Mike Harcourt was sworn in as premier in December of 1991. I ended up getting a job with Dave Zirnhelt, who was minister of economic development. He kept wanting more and more information. That was the complete opposite of Nelson Riis, who just needed the subject. But Riis was in opposition. Zirnhelt felt the weight of being a cabinet minister. He felt he had to be better prepared than anyone on planet Earth about every single subject. Preparing for Question Period was a nightmare. Then, at some point, one of Harcourt's chief staffers, John Heaney, asked me to come and join the premier's office.

But loyalty was something I valued. Although it was very hard working for Dave, we became good friends, and I think very highly of him. It was tough for everyone as they tried to find their footing. Zirnhelt was from the Cariboo, and he had to go home to a hostile neighbourhood every weekend. He was a right-of-centre New Democrat who really wanted to be the economic guy. So I told Heaney that we were just starting to get things together, and I wanted to stay with Dave. Eventually, however, I did move on to more responsible positions with the Harcourt government, and then with Glen Clark, who succeeded him. It was such a big change from Ottawa, where the NDP was in opposition and every day was dead simple. It was all about throwing rocks. Now I had a taste of what you could actually do by being government. The reason I got inspired by Tommy Douglas in the first place was that he had made me realize all the things we could do to make a difference and help people with public investment. I did some really exciting things working for Harcourt. I was involved with the Columbia River Treaty discussions and the decision to stop Alcan's Kemano Dam Completion Project up north. That was the thing—when you're in government, you're not just working with NDP people who are smart, you're working with many other people who are also smart.

I know Mike Harcourt took a lot of grief, but from my point of view, he ran a very good government. Mike sometimes seemed a bit like a 6/49 machine. There were forty-nine ideas in there, and you didn't know which ones were going to pop out. I don't mean he didn't have a vision. He did. I don't mean he wasn't intelligent. He was. But having been premier, I realize stuff's coming at you all the time. People were always telling him: "Mike, you need to deliver this message." And I don't think he was particularly good at delivering messages. He often sounded like he was repeating something someone else had said to him—and in fact he was. I think it diminished his time as premier. Then, afterwards, when Glen flamed out so spectacularly, everyone within the NDP started talking about Harcourt as the good old days. The problem was that Glen was such a spectacular campaigner and so quick on his feet, Mike looked like a dullard beside him. But I believe history will judge Mike on his accomplishments. He had a lot of very capable people who came to work for him. Many were formerly in government in Manitoba and Saskatchewan. And Tony Penikett showed up after he lost in Yukon. Harcourt got stuff done. Looking back, it was a good period of progressive government. Was he the best premier of all time? No, but he was good. He was competent. He was stable. He was moderate. Moderate light.

As for me, I was doing big things. Unlike in Ottawa, I wasn't observing and criticizing, I was doing stuff. That was the change. It was intoxicating, quite frankly, to be hanging around cabinets and people having confidence in me. I'm a likeable guy. People liked being around me. Admittedly, if you crossed me, I could be frightening. I was big physically, and under Glen Clark I was a fixer. I exposed problems and eliminated them, so there were a lot of people who probably didn't like me at the end of the day, and a lot of public servants who maybe felt, in some circumstances, that I was a bit too harsh. Usually, they were in files that sucked. If things were going smashingly, they wouldn't have seen me at all.

But I finally had enough. Glen had been premier for two years, after succeeding Harcourt and winning a narrow election in 1996, and the troubles were piling up. It seemed like every day there was a new problem to fix. I thought, I can't do this anymore. In 1998, I moved into the Crown Corporation Secretariat and the next year to the Columbia Power Corporation. I want to say something about that. This was a Crown corporation that we created under Harcourt to put the final elements of the Columbia River Treaty in place. I was part of that. I also worked closely with Corky Evans, who was one of our MLAs from the region. We became buddies, although I would say we are estranged now. But I was a disciple of Corky. You'd sit in the room and listen to him, and he was captivating—until you read the words, and often they didn't make a lot of sense. But back then I had a lot of time for Corky. He thought of himself as the great orator of the 1990s.

We wanted to use the downstream benefits of the Columbia River dams and make amends for the flooding of the valleys and the Kootenays. Keenleyside was one of the dams, but it didn't have any turbines on it. It was a drone dam. It just held water for the Americans, to help with flood control. We wanted to repower it by using the money the Americans owed us for the power we'd sold them under the Columbia River Treaty for the past thirty years. We felt that if BC Hydro did it, the cost would be a bajillion dollars, so we created a company, Columbia Power Corporation, to do the job. We used the Allied Hydro Agreement with the unions, which was also a commitment to jobs in the region. Later, we bought the Brilliant and the Waneta dams from Cominco, which is now Teck. We bought them and repowered them as well. It all added up to a $500-million deal, and the benefits that have gone back to the region ever since have been incalculable. Not only did they get the work, they got the revenue from selling energy generated by those three dams. Two of them had been private and the other didn't have any turbines. Now, all three were public. I'm pretty proud of my role in that.

I became director of corporate relations for Columbia Power. It was a small company, and people wondered where I'd disappeared to. I found that being a cog in the wheel is quite different from creating the vehicle. We created Columbia Power. We created the Columbia River Treaty benefits package, and we did the negotiations to get to a place where off it went. That's what I was proud of. Did I need to be around when they were pouring the cement and purchasing the turbines and all of that? No. That was boring.

One day we were having a staff meeting. It was all about some exciting new filing system. I tried to get out of it, but they said everyone had to be there, so we go into this room, and it's dark, no windows, and they were showing transparencies. Remember the good old transparency? You put it on the light, and it would be shot up onto the wall. And this guy is explaining to me why I should care about this, and my head is snapping back: "Okay, okay, I've got it." Then the door opens a crack, and the receptionist is waving frantically and pointing at me. I go out, and she says, "It's the premier on the line for you." It was Dan Miller. Glen Clark had resigned, and Dan was selected by caucus to take over. I had no knowledge of any of this. I was in this new place. I was no longer part of politics. I pick up the phone and I go, "Hey, Dan." And he goes, "Hey, yeah. Johnny, listen, I need you to be my chief of staff." I looked back at the door where that meeting was going on, and I said, "I'll be right there." It was probably a stupid thing to do because it put a big bull's eye on my head for the BC Liberals, who were sure to win the next election. No one would be looking for me if I stayed at Columbia Power. It was relatively successful. I would likely have survived under the Liberals and been able to keep my good-paying job. Dan probably picked me for that reason. I wasn't visible. He surveyed the landscape and asked, "Where's Horgan? What happened to him?" Everyone else was just trying to keep their heads on their shoulders at that point. By then, the NDP ship was sinking. In fact, it had already sunk, so coming back was a challenge.

I had all the time in the world for Dan. He and I were similar guys. We'd both worked in pulp mills. Two pulp mill premiers. Everyone who worked for Dan smoked. Sharon Prescott, who was deputy chief of staff, smoked enough for two people. If there was anyone who didn't think they were a smoker, Sharon said, "Don't worry, I got you covered. I'm smoking two at a time." I spent six months as chief of staff.

As to exactly why Dan picked me, you'd have to ask him. But caucus was fractured at the time. The Kyoto Protocol had come about. People were starting to talk about climate change in a meaningful way, really for the first time. Thanks to Joan Sawicki, our environment minister, we had a climate action plan. I think it was the first one in North America. People looked at me as both green and brown. I could talk to John Cashore, I could talk to Joan Sawicki—both ministers of the environment at various times—I could also talk to the leaders of the woodworkers' union, the IWA. I could cross over into all these different components, while Dan was very much the brown guy.

Meanwhile, the summer drilling and tax credits for oil and gas were opening up the industry. We don't get nearly enough credit for that. It made billions of dollars to be used later by Carole Taylor when she was the Liberals' finance minister. I like Carole Taylor, but she was never able to give credit to anyone else. We were dirty, tawdry New Democrats. It's true that only a right-wing government could have brought in a carbon tax when they did, but only a left-wing government would not get credit for bringing in a royalty regime. In the same vein, Glen Clark never got credit for the film tax credits, which have created a massive industry in BC. When I was premier, I don't know how many times my deputy, Don Wright, said we had to get rid of them. They were killing us. I said, "That's great, Don, but no chance. No chance." The benefits were established. We had a well-trained workforce. Producers wanted to come here not just for the credits but because we had people who could make movies. If we took away the credits, they would all go to other jurisdictions that had the credits, and our skilled workers would go with them. There's no chance we would ever do away with them.

The NDP did a lot of things with the private sector. One of them was mining. When we were in opposition, I was our energy and mines critic virtually uninterrupted for ten years. I always went to the annual meeting of the BC Association for Mineral Exploration. Every year there was a new Liberal cabinet minister for mining—Bill Bennett, Kevin Krueger, Blair Lekstrom, and on and on. One year it was Gordie Hogg. God love him, but he didn't know a rock from a mineral. At the chairman's dinner on the Sunday night, I would roll in and say, "Yeah, it's me, Horgan, again, the NDP guy who supports mining. Who's the Liberal minister this year? I can't keep track." And they'd laugh. But as soon as their minister walked into the room, they all swooned toward him. They'd tell me: "We like you, Horgan, but, you know, what can you do for us? Bugger all." I got a lot of my interest in mining by hanging out with Dan Miller and with Glen Clark when he was doing economic development, before he became premier. Yep, social democrats, my NDP, doing those things for the private sector.

I liked being chief of staff. I was able to use all the experience I had gathered working in Ottawa, in different ministers' offices, behind the scenes in two premiers' offices and working on economic files. Now I was in the office of a guy who really didn't want the job. But when people saw the field of candidates to replace him, they wanted him to stay. They were Ujjal Dosanjh, Corky Evans, Gordon Wilson and Joy MacPhail, who later dropped out. By then, Glen had made Gordon Wilson the finance minister. Dan told me to tell him that he couldn't remain in the cabinet if he was running for the leadership, which I did. We replaced him as finance minister with Paul Ramsey, a really good guy, an English prof who was really good at math. He balanced the budget.

We managed to do that because of Powerex [BC Hydro's marketing subsidiary] selling power to the Americans. That was my thing. Deregulation of the energy sector was happening in California. Enron wasn't yet a scandal, but they were driving up prices. Enron never created an electron. They just moved them around. They didn't even move them on their own lines. They bought energy in one place and sold it somewhere else. But we actually generated electricity. We sold it to California and made billions. That allowed us to balance the budget. Ken Peterson was CEO of Powerex at the time. He made up two red T-shirts. On the top was the Powerex logo. Underneath it said: "Keeping socialism solvent." He gave one to me and one to Paul Ramsey. It was fun.

During that time, there was a by-election in Delta South. We got 2.5 per cent of the vote. I remember Eddie Goldenberg, who was working for Jean Chrétien at the time, phoned me up and said, "It doesn't look too good." And I said, "Eddie, we've got them right where we want them." Admittedly it was not an incumbent NDP seat, but you might as well not run a candidate at all for 2.5 per cent. We were in a dark place, and then Ujjal Dosanjh took over. Dan and I had met with the four primary leadership candidates. We wanted to know what issues they wanted to bury and what did they want us to get started so they could hit the ground running, because we were really just caretakers. Joy MacPhail was the only one with any ideas. She had a million of them. Gordon Wilson had no ideas, Corky was in his sort of country bumpkin mode, and Ujjal Dosanjh was like, "What do you think, Dan?" And I remember Dan saying, "If I had something to say, I would be running against you." Dan didn't have much time for Dosanjh. But he won. Hundreds and hundreds of South Asians rolled in, and they all voted for Ujjal. He wasn't the best choice, but he had the best organization. It was racial politics. I get that. I think that's both an asset and a liability in any political movement. You want to engage with ethnic communities, you want them to be full participants, and then you complain when they do engage as full participants. I don't mean that in a negative way. It's just something to acknowledge. We said, come join us, be part of our movement. And they said, okay, and we're going to bring a lot of friends, and we're going to make sure we elect people.

The diversity of the NDP caucus today is something I'm very proud of. And that's a direct result of us opening up the doors, particularly in Surrey, but not only in Surrey. We had an equity mandate that we got kicked in the face about for years, but it worked, and we're better for it. It's not just better for the NDP, everybody's better for it. There's now an expectation that our Legislature will be as diverse as the communities they represent.

After becoming leader and premier, Ujjal replaced me with Chris Chilton, who'd been my boss under Harcourt. That was fine. I joined Paul Ramsey as associate deputy finance minister. I worked on energy and related issues, mostly on electricity sales and scrutinizing oil and gas subsidies. They were the things that I had been doing in the past, and I just kept doing them, only under the ministry of finance rather than in energy.

Ujjal really didn't have anything he wanted to do other than go to India, and he did. "I grew up in a dusty village in India," he would say. I remember those dusty village stories all the time. Looking back on it now, it was a great accomplishment to have a South Asian as premier of British Columbia, but it was not unlike Adrian Dix winning the leadership in 2011. He wasn't the best choice. He was the best organizer. We kept waiting for the election to be called, let's stop with the dusty village in India. Traditionally, after a leadership change, you go to the people quickly, when you've still got what bump there is from the leadership race. But there really wasn't a bump for Dosanjh. He waited for over a year. I think it was just because he liked being in the corner office. Chris Chilton had a heart issue and had been replaced by Elizabeth Cull as chief of staff. I talked to Elizabeth almost every day, and I kept saying, "Call the bloody election. Every day, it's getting worse, not better. Let's go."

And the government was precarious. We had only a one-seat majority. Ed Conroy, a bull of a guy, had a couple of transplants. Penny Priddy had cancer. Thanks to Gordon Wilson becoming a New Democrat after leaving his own party, we had just barely enough seats to hang on. The right thing to do would have been to say: "I've been selected leader. I have a new vision. I'm not the past. I'm the future." But you can't do that fifteen months later. You're just the guy who doesn't want to leave.

That really stuck with me. Time was up. Not for me, but for the NDP and the government. The public wanted a change. It may have been unfair, but the NDP was done. We had no credibility on any issue. Every day was another gong show. John Heaney was a director of communications for Ujjal, and I remember someone in the press gallery said to me, "Every time we see John Heaney coming, we know he's going to lie to us." And John Heaney wasn't lying. He was spinning. He was trying to put the best face on the circumstances. He wasn't a liar by any stretch. Nobody is, left or right. They're just trying to reinterpret. This isn't Kellyanne Conway stuff. It's trying to say, "Well, you know, if you look at it this way, it's not as bad." Or if you're on the other side, "If you look at it this way, it's worse." But I was thinking that if we can't have a fair hearing with the media, let's go. Let's ask the people and see what happens.

When Dosanjh finally did call the election, John Heaney and I anchored the campaign in Victoria. That's where all the staffers come, and you make sure you've got your daily events prepared, and you're shooting the information out to everyone. Our events were basically Ujjal driving in the bus from Jenny Kwan's riding in Mount Pleasant to Joy MacPhail's riding in East Vancouver, then having a nap, and then doing something in and around the Lower Mainland in the afternoon. He literally had daily naps built into the schedule. He was a terrible campaigner, and it was a disastrous campaign. In his defence, we didn't have anything to say. We were over. The public was so done with us that Gordon Campbell, who's a pretty wooden guy—though he did get better—slaughtered us. We ended up with two seats, the most lopsided result in BC history. Total carnage.

CHAPTER SIX

A POLITICIAN AT LAST

I KEPT WAITING FOR THE PHONE CALL FROM THE LIEUTENANT GOVernor to advise me that my services were no longer required. I could have fought to get my old job back with Columbia Power, or could have taken severance, which is traditional when new people come in. Because I was a deputy minister, the call came from the cabinet secretary. She was someone I'd known and respected for a long time. She said, "It's with great regret that I advise you..." And she went through the whole thing. And I said, "Well, if the lieutenant governor doesn't want me, it's an arrow through my heart." In truth, I danced a bit of a jig. I was happy to be out of government. There had been some challenging times, and I was very ready not to do that anymore. It had been exciting. I loved the adrenaline. I loved not knowing what was going to happen every day. That was usually a good thing, but by the end, it was not a good thing.

What happened after that is that Ian Reid, John Heaney, one or two others and myself formed a consulting company we called IdeaWorks. We had worked together as youngsters in the early 1990s. By 2001, I was the last one standing. IdeaWorks did polling and interpreted it. We did strategies for private sector companies to deal with government, including quite a lot of work at city hall in Vancouver. Larry Campbell was mayor, and they had some issues they wanted to push. Ian Reid was their main guy. He was the pollster. He had the secret sauce on interpreting focus groups and stuff that were just numbers to me. Numbers always seemed dire to me. At least that was my memory until I became premier, and then, holy crap—those numbers for me are really high. Geoff Meggs, who'd been my chief of staff, sent me something the other day from the good old days. It was a CBC story that said I was at 68 per cent popularity, which was virtually unheard of in polling history. Sorry for the aside.

The file that got the most media attention was slot machines. I don't support gambling. I think it's a tax on stupidity, and we shouldn't do that to people. But it's everywhere, and government should get its take. And with that take, they should put programs in place to deal with people who have gambling addictions. I guess that's the best of all the bad circumstances that come from gambling.

Then there was my mom. She was always saying, don't waste your money, but she ended up going to casinos. It was something to do. She felt it was her right. One night she called me up and said, "Are you still opposed to gambling, dear?" And I said, "Yeah, Mom. Why? What's up?" And she said, "Well, I just won $25,000 at the casino, and they want someone to come and pick me up." I was shocked. She was always so frugal, a coupon-clipper when we were growing up. But she started listening to the horse races at Sandown Park on the radio. And then she's going there, and next thing she's on a seniors' bus trip to Reno. And now this was happening.

It was some card game—I can't remember the name—so I go in and say, "I'm looking for Alice." They tell me she's in the back. I go into the back room and she's sitting there with her purse on her lap. She was like the queen, always holding onto her purse. We start walking our way through the casino, and all these people are saying the same thing, "Way to go, Alice," and telling me to take good care of her. What struck me was that these were her new friends. Most of her other friends were dead. This was her new social network. And if she lost a bit that she'd been able to accumulate, who cared at that point? It was another lesson she taught me. Because of her, I softened my views on gambling.

At the time, there were five casinos in Vancouver. None were licensed for slot machines. The previous mayor, Philip Owen, and Gordon Campbell, the mayor before him, were dead set against casinos and slot machines: "Not on our watch. They're the devil's work." There was all this jargon. Advocates called them Video Lottery Terminals so they didn't sound like slot machines, and they spoke about "gaming" instead of "gambling." I was a reluctant participant. But it wasn't as if people in Vancouver couldn't find slot machines if they wanted them. They were just a transit ride away, in the suburbs. Vancouver had a COPE city council at the time. They had some real fruit loops in that group. But one of our points was that as soon as the paint dries in the premier's office, Gordon Campbell is going to do whatever he wants anyway. He only hated slot machines when he didn't need the revenue. Now he needed the revenue, so at some point, slot machines were going to come in. We argued they should come in on the city's terms.

We ended up consolidating the casinos into the Edgewater Casino at the Plaza of Nations. Meanwhile, there were eighty-eight charities that got a lot of their revenue from the popular charitable enterprise on Main Street, Planet Bingo. Slot machines would have killed Planet Bingo by taking away a big chunk of its business. My job was to build an alliance between the casino operators and the not-for-profits. We worked out a deal so that a stream of revenue from the slot machines would be funnelled to Planet Bingo and then be distributed to the eighty-eight charities. We made the best out of a tough situation.

Charlie Smith wrote in the *Georgia Straight* that we were Glen Clark's gambling buddies, using inside information to jam slot machines down people's throats. It was nothing like that. It was a clean slate. The city still had to vote on it. We made sure labour people were at the public meetings and hearings because there was going to be a benefit to the Hastings Park racecourse, as well. These were vulnerable people who had union jobs. Many of them actually lived out there on a bale of hay with the horses. We worked out a bunch of benefits for Hastings Park, including a daycare. Despite the negative consequences from an expansion of gambling, there were going to be some good things.

That was one of the lessons from all the casino work we did. Businesses can be persuaded not to stomp on people if you make it worth their while. We told the casino operators that if they wanted slot machines, they needed to demonstrate to a council that mostly hated their guts that they were going to be helping people city councillors cared a great deal about—and also make sure they were still profitable. Casinos don't always make money. Just ask Donald Trump. But a majority of people perceived them as dens run by the Monopoly guy that suck money out of people's pockets, so for me to insert myself into what I would characterize as an unseemly underbelly was eye-opening. With the right nudge, you can get a positive outcome. Not just the government can do good deeds, so can the private sector.

I worked on another project, for the Huu-ay-aht First Nation in Bamfield. They wanted some cultural tourism, and I wrote a report for them. I enjoyed writing again. It was nice to get back to creating something rather than just giving input on someone else's creation. As luck would have it, my master's history thesis had been focused on the Pacific Cable, which went all the way to Australia, and its terminus was right there in Bamfield. The Pacific Cable station was the largest building on the west coast of Vancouver Island. It's now the Marine Biology Station, connected to the University of Victoria. They had found the remnants of a four-hundred-year-old longhouse nearby, and they were trying to get the UN to designate it as a biosphere reserve. They hoped to stamp it as something people should go and see. You could get there on the famous *Lady Rose* or other coastal vessels. The road, however, was appalling.

Nothing really came of our proposal, but tragically, in 2019, a bus full of students who were going to the Marine Station went off the road. A couple of them died. I was premier then, and I went up to see Chief Robert Dennis, who I knew because he was Chief of the Huu-ay-aht when I gave them our ecotourism proposal. I vowed to fix the road. It was complicated because it was not a provincial highway, it was a logging road. But we figured out a way to do it, and their village held a big celebration. Chief Dennis told them, "You know, I've learned a very valuable lesson. You should always treat your contractors well because one day they may grow up to be premier of British Columbia."

I had been profoundly affected by the way the NDP ended its time of office in 2001. I had no intention whatsoever of running for office, but every time I went to Vancouver on business, I would get together with Adrian Dix. I'd first met Adrian when we were both working for the NDP on Parliament Hill. We also worked for the NDP government in Victoria, and we'd become good friends. He would always ask me how my campaign was going. I'd say, "Oh, fuck off. I have no campaign." It was the last thing on my mind. Then there was this cathartic moment. Gordon Campbell announced that the government would be building new ferries in Germany. I started yelling at my TV set: "That's the stupidest goddamn thing I've ever heard of in my life. What's he doing!?"

It happened that my son had a high-school garage band, and they were taking a break, and the drummer, a kid named John C. Russell, was grazing in our refrigerator. He came out into the front room and asked me, "Why are you yelling at the TV?" I said, "Look at those stupid idiots. They're doing this really dumb thing." And he said, "Well, what are you going to do about it?" And all of a sudden, at that moment, I said, "Well, I'm going to run for the

Legislature, and you're going to help me." And he did. He came and did stuff like handing out leaflets with me. The next time I got together with Adrian, he asked me how my campaign was going, expecting the same old answer. Instead, I said that I had signed up all the people at my United Church, and I thought most of the parents I knew were going to be with me. He perked right up: "You're going to do it?" I said, "Yeah, I think I will." And that's how it happened. If the drummer with my son's garage band hadn't been there, I would likely have just carried on yelling at the TV, and the history of BC would have been entirely different.

The great irony is that the ferries were being built in Germany, and I would later become Canada's ambassador there. I don't know how my German friends would take it if I told them that the reason I got directly involved in politics was because Canada was spending BC money in Germany. I'd try to say it in a way that wouldn't cost me my job.

I had worked on campaigns, I had created words for people to say, I had pushed them out the door, I had stood behind them as they door-knocked—and criticized them afterwards—but I had never been the front guy. It was a bit daunting, quite frankly. Julie Thomas ran against me for the nomination. She was a school trustee. She had been elected to something. I had not. The constituency [Malahat–Juan de Fuca] was everything from the Cowichan River down to Langford. The northern part had all these tiny little places: Glenora, Cowichan Bay, Cobble Hill, Shawnigan Lake, Mill Bay, Malahat, Cowichan Station, which is just a dot in the Cowichan Valley. They were fiercely proud communities with a long history of voting NDP. The southern part of the riding was Sooke, Langford and out to Port Renfrew. I lived in Langford, which was literally right on the edge of the riding. I knew more people in Esquimalt and Metchosin than I knew in this constituency. There was a guy from the Cowichan Valley, Richard Hughes, who wanted to run. He had run in 2001 and lost.

He felt he deserved another chance, and he probably did. He was likely thinking: "This hack from Victoria wants to come and tell us in the Republic of Cobble Hill what to do. Not a chance." But he got into some political trouble on the Cowichan Valley Regional District over a zoning thing, and he ended up not running. We subsequently became good friends. So I ran against Julie Thomas. I got about 70 per cent of the votes. She was convinced she could have won if there hadn't been snow on the Malahat Highway that night, because her support was from the north part of the riding, where she lived, and the vote was in Langford.

It was all good except for one thing. Carole James was now the leader, and all these dudes were being nominated and not many women. Here was another contest where the guy beats the woman. Carole was asked questions about that, not really knowing who the hell I was, since I'd been a behind-the-scenes worker. But at the same time, the comment by my son's drummer, John C. Russell, that got me going was perfect. That's the beauty of fixed elections, says the guy who called a snap election. You can plan your life around them. I can keep working until a set date, then I have to go and campaign. That's good for paying the mortgage. I simply told some clients that I was going to take a few weeks off, and if I didn't win, I'd be back and life would go on. But I ended up winning.

Election night was great. There was a big party at the Empress Hotel. We'd done very well. We'd gone from three to thirty-three seats. We came close to sweeping Vancouver Island and almost cleared the table in Victoria. It was exciting, and I was looking forward to being an MLA. I'd become one of the go-to people for the media. That was interesting, because the media terrified me. Speaking to people was a challenge. Joy MacPhail was very helpful. She said, "Fuck, Horgan, just talk. You're good at that." She said the media will use some of it, and they won't use some of it. That's it. But it took me a while to get to a place where I understood that. In fact, some might argue it took me twelve years in opposition before I finally acknowledged that people weren't out to get me.

The media just needed to fill space. Their story was already written. You want to be in it? Say something. You don't want to be in it? I could care less, I'm done. I'm going to send the story now. If you keep talking, you're going to slow me up and you're not going to be in it, so why don't you just give me these words? A lot of times it was pretty well like that.

My election was pretty much the end of IdeaWorks. The others were also starting to go off and do something else. It had worked really well. I enjoyed it. We all brought something different. They were people I liked working with. I respected their skills. I also made more money by a long shot than I ever did as an MLA, but that's never been a motivator for me. What I'd been doing was also less interesting than what I did in government, and the adrenaline wasn't the same.

Just on money, when the MLAs voted to give ourselves a big raise halfway through the term, some of my colleagues and I convinced the NDP caucus to give back any compensation above what the salary had been when we agreed to run. We gave the money to charity. That's what started my relationship with the Goldstream Food Bank, which remains active to this day. They said, "You're giving us how much money?" And I said, "Well, I didn't earn it. You need it more than I do." The media would ask whether we were going to continue to take less money. I said, "No. I'm worth every penny that [Liberal] Rich Coleman is." That wasn't the point. The point was that I knew what the salary was when I ran. If the salary goes up and you run and win again, that's fine. That's what you should get paid. Some of our people argued that we didn't get paid enough, and they were right. But that's the salary. If you don't like it, quit. You don't like being here—indoor work, no heavy lifting—get the hell out. Let someone else do it.

Carole James asked all of us to write down what ministries we wanted to focus on. I was light years ahead of everyone on energy. I assumed that's what I was going to do. It was kind of a no-brainer. But Carole said, "You're going to be education critic." I started shuffling through my papers and going, "I know it starts with an 'e'..." Her rationale was that I been around legislation for a number of years, and the Liberals had brought in back-to-work legislation to end the teachers' strike. She felt I would be able to dive right in and dissect it while everyone else in the caucus was getting up to speed. That was an overreach on her part. I had worked on legislation surrounding the Columbia River Basin, but by and large the drafters do all the work. I had no notes on legislation. It was a misunderstanding of the role of an Opposition critic. We were all so green.

But going to education exposed me to a social side that I hadn't experienced. When I worked for Harcourt, it was all hard-dirt stuff. Same with Glen Clark, same with Dan Miller. That was what I knew. I knew the people in government. I knew where the bodies were buried. I knew where opportunities rested. It just seemed the best use of my skills. But education allowed me to be front and centre very early as a spokesperson on something that was top of mind in the province. Before that, nobody knew who John Horgan was. All of a sudden, I was showing up a lot. I was asking questions. I gave good sound bites. I was on Rafe Mair's radio show on CKNW to talk about it. Near the end, I said, "Gotta go, Rafe, I have to give a two-hour speech on the back-to-work legislation." Rafe reminded me that Edward Everett spoke for two hours at Gettysburg and no one remembers his name. Abraham Lincoln spoke for two minutes, and they're still reciting what he said. "Don't waste your energy," said Rafe. It was wise advice.

However, it was my first speech in the Legislature, and I did get up and talk for two hours. I went from grade 1 to grade 12, talking about all my teachers, about the challenges they faced and how important educators are. It was an opportunity to tell some of the stories I've already mentioned, and more. I even remembered the red cardigan I wore in those days. That became a thing: "Hey, Horgan, where's your red cardigan?" I would say it doesn't fit anymore. It's a little snug in the shoulders. I talked about being elected class president in grade 12 by campaigning for more dances. It was a slam dunk. I seemed to have a nose for politics even then. I drew from my personal experiences without making it about me.

Although I was not always a fan of the leadership of the BC Teachers' Federation, it was good to walk the picket line with the teachers and hear their stories. It was also a great opportunity to have parent-teacher interviews because they were telling me about my kids, and I didn't have to sit in a tiny little desk with my knees scrunched up. And it gave me a chance to tell every teacher I met how grateful I was for the work they were doing to shape the lives of the people who will get us through the challenges ahead. "You don't get enough credit," I said. "You may not ever get enough money, but I want you to know that you're respected and beloved by a whole bunch of parents and a whole bunch of people in the Legislature as well."

That was the start of me in the House. Education was a good training ground for a newly elected representative. I'm glad I did it. Carole is convinced it made me a better human being. She had been head of the BC School Trustees Association and a trustee on the Victoria School Board. I thought she would be looking over my shoulder. She didn't. She left me alone. So did David Chudnovsky, who was in the caucus. He had been president of the BC Teachers' Federation, but he was given transportation rather than education. And you know what? He was great. I wasn't convinced that would be the case, but he was always supportive, always helpful. Jinny Sims was leading the teachers' strike, and she could be a handful. But I didn't mess it up, so neither Carole nor David had anything to be unhappy about.

I was also the new MLA for Malahat–Juan de Fuca. I tried different things, including town hall meetings, which were then in vogue. But it became clear to me pretty quickly that those were opportunities for blowhards to come and bitch about things they thought were important, and no one else had a chance to say anything. You're always trying to manage the crowd so the nutters don't dominate the microphones. Fewer and fewer normal people were showing up. It was the same old grievances. How come you haven't fixed this thing I've been complaining about since the 1950s? Well, because it's not bloody fixable, that's why! I sit on the other side of the House all day. I can't fix anything.

I also started going to every single event in the riding because something was always going on. I remember one nice sunny day at the Mother's Day paint-in at Royal Roads University. There were lots of young families with their kids. I was walking around looking at the kids' art, and this woman comes around the corner and says, "Horgan sighting!" She puts her hand over her mouth and runs away. It startled me. Then she comes back with another woman and says she wants to apologize: "We're big fans of yours, and we see you everywhere we go, so we have this little game of who sees you first. I'm really sorry I said that out loud." By this point I'm blushing. I tell them not to worry. It's fine. But that had become their thing because they couldn't go anywhere without seeing John Horgan. He's at the sporting events. He's at the ballet. He's at the music hall. He's lugging speakers up the stairs for his kid's band, packing a hockey bag for his kid's hockey game. He goes to church. He's loud in the Legislature. I was also on the radio every week with Joe Easingwood on CFAX. He was an old-timer who was the Victoria equivalent of Rafe Mair on the talk-show circuit.

Then I started getting on the bus at the Legislature, taking it all the way out to Sooke and talking to people who were sitting down: "How you doing? I'm your local MLA." If they didn't want to talk to me, fine. But many did. It became a thing. I would advertise in the paper that I would be on the 414 from Belleville Street. It was a chance for people to bring things up and talk to me without having to rush home, cook dinner for the kids, or get in the car and go to another of those town-hall meetings and hear some jerk go on and on about whatever he'd been complaining about at the last one. It was an opportunity to have a candid conversation, and I could say, "Well, look, I'll give you a call about this and we can talk about it in privacy."

There was one guy I spent the whole trip to Sooke talking to. He was like nineteen years old and was on his way to Afghanistan. He'd been in the military only twelve months. Eighteen months later, a guard at the Legislature told me, "My boy's home from Afghanistan. There are no holes in him." I said that's fantastic and invited them to lunch at the Legislature. His son was the kid I'd talked to on the bus, so that was great.

At some point, everyone knew Horgan was on the bus, because I'd advertised it. Then they'd be disappointed when I wasn't on the bus that they took. After a while I started taking Gravol because the trip out to Sooke was quite windy, and when you're spinning around talking to different people, it can wear on you. Barfing on people is a good way to lose votes really quickly. I started to do the bus ride less and less. I think I only did it once as premier. There were diminishing returns. After nearly two terms, my polling numbers were good, and by then I was very much a household name: John from Langford.

CHAPTER SEVEN

OPPOSITION

I AGREE WITH THE SAYING THAT ALL POLITICS IS LOCAL. I WANTED TO be a good constituency person. I took it seriously. When you're in opposition, that's all you've got. I tried very hard to work with the BC Liberals, to get them to spend money in my community, which hadn't voted Liberal. I had a good relationship with Shirley Bond, their education minister, because I wanted her to build a school. But it took a long time. It was another education minister, George Abbott, who finally got the school built. I like George Abbott. He's funny and he's smart. As premier, I appointed him to help me out with a report on wildfire management.

There were other good people on the opposite side, like their attorney general during my first term, Wally Oppal. Wally's really a New Democrat in the BC context of being a pragmatic centrist and a little bit left of centre. Blair Lekstrom, who had several different jobs in the Liberal cabinet, is a pack of contradictions. He's more conservative than he is social democrat, but he's an IBEW union guy. I like him. We got along well because he's a decent person. He's not a left-wing guy who happens to be in a right-wing party. He's a right-wing guy who happens to have a conscience. There were a few others I worked hard to be friends with, not because I wanted to have beers with them, but because I wanted to try and get stuff done in my constituency.

One time, there was a logjam on the San Juan River up in Port Renfrew. The broadcast media were telling everyone there was going to be a disaster. The logjam could break, come rushing down the river, take out the bridge, strand people and blah blah blah. None of that was likely to occur, but it became an issue. John Les, not my favourite person, was the cabinet minister responsible for emergency preparedness. I tried really hard to get him to work with me as the local MLA. I wasn't suggesting he go to Port Renfrew to check how high the pile of logs was, but I would really like to have said that he and I were working on this together. That was good for the community and good for John Les. I told him he didn't have to do anything, just let your deputy minister talk to me about the situation. I was trying to represent people who were concerned the river was going to come rushing down on their houses. He would have nothing to do with it. "No need, I got this. We don't need any help from you." And they did sweet bugger all. In the end, nothing happened, so it didn't matter, but it was another of those examples that really stuck with me. I thought that if I ever got the chance, I wasn't going to treat people that way if they came to me in good faith and wanted to work together on something.

In 2008, I was diagnosed with bladder cancer. It was weird the way it happened. I went to my doctor because my shoulder hurt. It still kind of hurts, although not as much as before. I said, "It's painful when I throw a football." "Then don't throw footballs," he said. I went, "Ha ha, you're hilarious." He moved my shoulder around and suggested I get some physio. Then he said he hadn't seen me for a while, so we should do some blood work and a urine test. A couple of days later he called me up and said they want me to have an ultrasound. The day after that, he phoned me and said, "You've got bladder cancer." And I said, "What the hell are you talking about? My bladder is nowhere near my shoulder." But in his best bedside manner, he said, "Look, I don't know what else to say. You need to get on this right away. I've made appointments with the urologist. He's a surgeon. You see him on Friday."

I was still kind of processing this, and my family doctor added that I needed to get a scope. The urologist did the scope, which was very uncomfortable. He said, "You've got multiple polyps. We're going to have those removed, and it's going to take surgery." I said, "What if I don't do that?" And he said, "Well, you can die. That's an alternative." He also said that if I didn't do something about it quickly, pretty soon it would be really uncomfortable to take a piss, and after that it would be beyond uncomfortable. "But I'll tell you what, if you want discomfort, we'll do the surgery without anaesthetic. Maybe that will make you feel better." Suddenly I'm liking this guy. He's very matter of fact, very funny. We became quite close. When a guy's fondling your genitals all the time, and every time you see him you have to pull down your pants, and he's jamming a tube up your penis, those are bonding experiences.

I'm on the way to the surgery, and I hear about it on the radio. Carole thought I was too well known by then to keep it private, so she put out a statement. It was weird to be hearing about myself when I was trying to focus on whether or not I was going to wake up. And people on the radio are wishing me all the best before I go under, which was quite a humbling experience. Anyway, I come out from the surgery, and according to the staff caring for me, I'm very funny. I kept saying that I had to pee. I would sit up, and they would say, "Lie down, John." And I would sit up again and want to pee, and they would say again, "You have to lie down!" That was because I had to keep this chemotherapy material inside the bladder for two hours after surgery so that it would continue to corrode away at the area where the surgery had taken place. It was like a caustic stew. That all went through the penis, by the way. At last, they let me go and pee. I shuffle down the hallway to the bathroom, and I start to pee, and the pain absolutely rocks me. Ellie hears me scream, and she's going, "Oh dear, oh dear, oh dear." Now I'm thinking: "I don't want to pee. Please don't make me pee." Recovery from that took a while, but I didn't have a bag, and there weren't a lot of tubes coming out of me, so that was good. We got home a couple of days later. Big piles of flowers were everywhere. Ellie pointed to one and said it was one of the first to arrive. It was from Rich Coleman. I picked up the card and read it, then immediately let out some choice curse words. How can I hate a guy who just sent me all these flowers with some lovely words on the card? It was a nice gesture. The Liberal caucus sent something as well. It was a good example of humanity in politics.

My mom had an expression: "You're a long time dead, so don't wait around." What are you still doing in bed? Get up. You're a long time dead. It really hit me that I was closer to that with the bladder cancer than I might have thought. My mom died a year later, and that made it even more of a focus for me. Mortality is there for all of us at some point, so what do you really want to do? I vowed to myself that I was going to get up every day grateful for each one that I get. But over time that starts to fade. By 2013, I wasn't thinking about cancer at all. I was going every year for my cystoscopy, rather than quarterly. I was having the tubes and the cameras less frequently, and they weren't finding anything. Everything was clean. I just stopped thinking about it. At this point, it's more than fifteen years since the first time someone said I had cancer. I'm much closer to the end of the line, and every day does matter to me. But it's funny how I was convinced that I would never lose that feeling. Yet you do. I think it's self-defence. Your brain says you don't need to worry about that. Instead, you're gonna get hit by a bus or a sabre-tooth tiger is gonna get you, depending on the epoch you're living in. That's just the way it goes, so don't dwell on it. Just get up and do the best you can.

This was in the fall of 2008, and the election was a year later. I was thinking it would be a tough election because I was running against the popular mayor of Colwood, Jody Twa. But Colwood wasn't within the constituency, so he was a carpetbagger. He was financed by the Bear Mountain golf crowd. Stew Young, who I didn't like at the time even though our kids played hockey together, was also involved. He was the mayor of Langford and kept telling me, "You're NDP, you're not going to win, and I need more money coming out of Victoria."

When I won in 2005, I had been mostly just the NDP guy. Not many people knew who I was, and the result was pretty close. The second time, I kept thinking, "Geez, this is it. What have I really done? Have I delivered the goods, the highways, sewers and grants that my constituents want?" Governments can do these things. The Opposition can't. Later, I would say to new MLAs that your second election is the toughest one, because you're now reapplying for the job. You're asking your neighbours: "How did I do? Are you prepared to let me do it again?" Whereas the first time, people are taking a flyer on you: "What the hell, he can't be any worse than the last guy."

I wound up winning with 57 per cent of the vote, even though Jody Twa spent twice as much as I did. What was I worried about? I had dodged a bullet with cancer, and now I'd just dodged a bullet in the election. I've always felt I'm a blessed individual. So many circumstances that should have gone badly for me, didn't. This was another example of that. People liked me. That invigorated me and kept me interested for a second term of opposition. Then the idiots started picking away at Carole James.

Overall, it had been a difficult election for us. After we took so many Liberal seats in 2005, we had had high expectations. But there were a couple of bumps along the road. One of them was the carbon tax brought in by Premier Gordon Campbell in 2008. We were the first province to have a carbon tax, and I give him credit for that. I always say that only Nixon could have gone to China. That's a reference the kids might not get, but in BC it meant that only a conservative like Campbell could have imposed a carbon tax—with the able help of Carole Taylor, of course. The year before he had signed an agreement to cap carbon emissions with the Terminator, Arnold Schwarzenegger, who was governor of California at the time. There was a lot of media covering Schwarzenegger's visit, including what seemed like five hundred TV cameras, mostly from *Entertainment Tonight*. I was trying to give him a bill for the hydro energy we had sent to California in 2000, but I couldn't get within a hundred metres of him. Guys bigger than Arnold were telling me to get away from the stage. It was difficult to start a genuine conversation.

If Campbell was the first to introduce a carbon tax, the NDP was the first political party to campaign on "axe the tax." That has now come back in a big way, with Pierre Poilievre leading the charge, and it seems to have worked for him. It didn't for us. Our preferred solution was to join with Quebec and California in a cap-and-trade system, which is still not understood fifteen years later. What people understood was a tax, and they voted for the Liberals anyway. We were trying to have our cake and eat it too, which is typical of Opposition parties. How do we say we want to be better than the present government in power without saying there might have to be some pain? Campaigning against the carbon tax made us some very strange bedfellows, including former Social Credit premier Bill Vander Zalm.

The carbon tax wasn't the only problem. Few of us had been part of the NDP government in the 1990s, but in the House and on the hustings, all we heard about was the fast ferry fiasco that had been such a political disaster for the Glen Clark government. Whenever Carole stood up to ask a question, the Liberals would heckle back about that or some other NDP misstep from a decade earlier. It was total political hyperbole. Trying to hold the government accountable to the public while the government spent all their time attacking us was a weird place to be. The Liberals also had many incumbents who had retained their seats in 2005 and were difficult to dislodge. Despite all these new taxes, plus a global recession, British Columbians opted for the devil they knew. That's often what happens when people feel their economic circumstances are at risk. Campbell and the Liberals held on to their majority rather easily.

The result made me realize more than ever that we needed to be more marketable in the suburbs. However, it was really tough to convince our rump group of rural MLAs, and rural MLAs from all parties, for that matter. They all believe the city sucks out their resources. Once the trees are gone and the mill shuts down, there are no resources left, no more benefits to share. Their economies are emptied out. In government, the NDP had a program to give back some tax money to resource-based communities, but that didn't really make up for what they had lost. They'd had jobs, economic activity and municipal taxes, as well. Yet the lion's share of the money from resource industries went to the province and the federal government. That was all true. Regardless, I felt it was essential for us to have a suburban base if we were ever going to win. I started a suburban caucus. It was a counterpoint to our rural caucus that fomented most of the dissent that emerged towards Carole James a year later.

Bob Simpson from Quesnel spearheaded the dissent. He's a very smart guy, and he felt he was smarter than most people, including Carole James. He thought she had to go. As for me, although I thought the world of Carole, I had not been entirely convinced she should continue as leader after the election. But when she announced she was staying, I thought, "Okay, that's fine by me." I had no leadership aspirations. I wanted to be that faithful, loyal lieutenant you could call upon to do the hard work and be there when needed.

It goes back to what I said earlier about sports. I was never the best player, but I was always someone you wanted on the team. I was reliable. I could hit the good shot. I could play defence. I didn't whine. I could give a good speech to get people going. That was a useful thing in a caucus as well, because in the end it's supposed to be a team. That wasn't happening. There was growing dissension in the caucus over Carole's leadership. There were also those who thought we needed to be more radical, that we needed to be more bold. I can't stand the word "bold." What the hell does it even mean? But those were the sort of sentiments that were percolating within the party.

Carole had brought us back from near oblivion, but she had now lost two elections, and she no longer had everyone's support.

We worked hard to convince people to stick together. There was a vote on the provincial council, and it was 85 per cent for Carole to stay. But her supporters went a step too far. They made everyone wear yellow scarves. If you weren't wearing a scarf, then you weren't for Carole. It created some bad feelings, and I think that was a catalyst for the dissidents to say, "We're done here." Norm Macdonald resigned as chair of the caucus. Katrine Conroy resigned as party whip.

It all burst into the public eye when Jenny Kwan—who had the safest seat in Christendom [Mount Pleasant] and had been sainted by her proximity to Joy MacPhail when they were the only two NDP MLAs against seventy-seven Liberals in 2001—released an over-the-top letter calling out Carole for lack of democracy within the caucus and demanding a leadership contest. Twelve other MLAs joined Jenny and publicly declared their non-confidence, but there were others who stayed private about it. Some of them I liked and trusted, and they greatly disappointed me. Carole had one more death-grip press conference. We were called in to be totems, which is when you come in, stand behind the leader and say nothing. I told her, "Carole, I'll go wherever you want me to go, but do you really need this? We're a long way from another election. These people are going to be picking at you the whole time." There were going to be stories every couple of weeks about how rudderless we were. *The Globe and Mail* ran a particularly harsh column that called her the "Ugly Betty" of politics.

I was quite emotional about the letter and the pronouncements of the so-called Baker's Dozen. I felt Carole had been stabbed in the back. Carole deserved to call her own shot. The NDP had a tradition of multiple campaigns with the same leader. Ed Broadbent stayed on for an eternity as federal leader of the party, and Carole was only getting better, not worse. I was convinced there was no harm in her staying for one more election. Jenny Kwan said there was a lack of democracy within the caucus, but there had been democracy at the provincial council meeting. That was our democracy. That was our constitution. Those were the rules of engagement. The New Democratic Party of British Columbia had a governing council, and they had determined Carole was staying. That should have been the end of it.

As the caucus started to fray, I got pretty hot. Adrian was also steamed up, but I was the loudest. I'd be interested to see some of my quotes from that time. Probably some fairly good ones. It really disheartened me that we were unable to push the dissidents back. Carole felt she had no choice but to resign.

Adrian was forgiving towards the dissidents, after he won the leadership contest to replace her. My feelings lasted longer. Later, when I became leader, my first thought was to purge them. I told Bob Dewar, who'd come out to help with the 2017 campaign, that I'd really like to have nominations to get rid of some of these people. And Bob said, "You can't do that. Incumbency is going to be really important to us. You may not like them, but they keep getting elected." He was right. There were also fewer of them by then, and some were kind of buddies of mine. I had made it very clear in caucus what I thought of them at the time. There was no need to say anything more. I think they will always regret what they did. Some begged Carole for forgiveness, and she told them not to worry about it. She was full of grace.

At that point, resigning was the right decision for Carole. I don't know if it was the right thing for the party. I think she would have been a good foil for Christy Clark, which Adrian Dix was not able to be. Of course, we didn't know that then, since we didn't know who was going to replace Gordon Campbell, who'd also resigned. Kevin Falcon was supposed to win the Liberal leadership, not Christy Clark. Carole against Christy would have been two women running against each other. I think the contrasts between Carole—earnest and concerned, a parent of foster kids, with a lifetime of giving back to people—and Christy Clark would have been pretty interesting.

After Carole stepped away, people with fairly sizable chunks of support approached me, and I decided to enter the race to replace her. The building trades saw me as someone who understood their ethic. Big locals of the Steelworkers also backed me. Having that support meant I had enough cash to be a candidate. Was the race going to be just Mike Farnworth and Adrian Dix, two guys from the Lower Mainland running against and yelling at each other? I got a lot of caucus support and a bunch of union support, but I was still the guy from the Island. There weren't enough members to put me over the top. Adrian had already signed up thousands of new members with the help of our MLA from Surrey–Newton, Harry Bains. And it wasn't only because of Harry Bains. Glen Clark was beloved in the South Asian community, and Adrian was an appendage of Glen. I got in late, and we knew the situation in advance. But I thought another name can't hurt. I can give a decent speech. I'm not like the other bears in the circus. I had a funny line every now and then that might capture someone's attention. I became the likeable guy who was not going to win.

At the convention, if I had been on the final ballot against Adrian, I would have won because Farnworth's people were all going to vote for me. But I was third on the second ballot and dropped off. The Farnworth people came to me and said I should make a big march across the hall to their side. That seemed pointless. By then, most people had voted digitally. Only a handful of people were actually casting a vote at the convention. The result was already decided. I told them that wasn't going to work. Besides, Adrian was my friend. I'd known him for years, and he was the guy who helped convince me to run for office. I wasn't going to go to Mike and watch Mike lose, because that's what the result was going to be. I told my delegates they could go anywhere they wanted. People liked the idea of me, but I wasn't happening. Some of my delegates went to Adrian, some went to Farnworth, and Adrian won.

There's a funny story from the leadership race that goes back to my time in Ocean Falls in 1979. There was a federal election going on. It was my first chance to vote. I was on my way to a toga party, so I was wearing a bedsheet. I went into the Legion to cast my ballot. I voted for Julius Caesar. I wrote in the name, stuffed my ballot into the box, and went to the party. Years later, I'm working in Ottawa, and they have a compendium of votes for all the elections in these big honking books. I'm killing time and leafing through the book for the 1979 election in the office of Ray Skelly. He was the MP who was elected for the NDP that year for Comox–Powell River, the riding that includes Ocean Falls. I go down the list to Ocean Falls, I go across, and there it is: "Spoiled ballots, one." I circle this with a note: "Ray, I had the chance to vote for you, and I didn't. All the best, John Horgan." I leave it on his desk. Ray comes into Jim Manly's office, where I was working, and we have a good laugh about it. Fast forward to 2011, when I'm running for leader. I phone up Ray and I say, "Ray, it's Horgan. I hope I can count on your support at the convention." And he starts laughing, and he keeps laughing, and he goes, "Why the hell would I vote for you, Horgan? I'm going to vote for Julius Caesar."

As we headed into the 2013 election, we were far ahead in the polls. The *Province* newspaper had run a front-page picture of Adrian with a famous banner headline that said he could kick a dog and still win. But he didn't win. It was pretty unbelievable. One of the worst campaigns I've ever seen.

One problem was the "memo to file" that Adrian—who was then Glen Clark's chief of staff—had backdated after the fact in an attempt to extricate Glen from a controversy over a neighbour's application for a casino licence. This had come out in 1999. Adrian admitted his mistake, and fourteen years later we didn't think it would be an issue. All the veterans in the press gallery, who had covered politics a long time, also discounted the memo. They knew Adrian to be a hard-working guy, honest as the day is long. He made a mistake, no big deal. We all assumed, as Adrian did, that it had been forgiven and forgotten long ago. But the public didn't know anything about it, and the Liberals used it perfectly against us. I would be out knocking on doors, and people would say, "We're going to vote for you, but your leader's a crook. He's falsifying documents." It didn't help during the TV debate when Adrian said he was young at the time. I think that made it worse. He was thirty-five. That's not young. You're an adult.

He had also decided he would run a positive campaign. There would be nothing negative about the other guys, despite all their scandals. He believed negativity turned off younger voters. He also wanted to do everything himself, which made people reluctant to work for us. A thirty-second TV spot would take forever because he was always rewriting the script to take out anything pointing out Liberal shortcomings. That's Basic Politics 101. For a guy consumed by politics, it was so ironic that when he had the opportunity, he decided to be Gandhi. And, you know, Gandhi never ran for office, because he would have lost. It's inexplicable.

My role was to be responsible for the Island and do a few rural things, talking about forestry, mining and energy. But Adrian didn't tell me that he was going to give a speech in Kamloops where he would say that an NDP government would basically put an end to Kinder Morgan's pipeline expansion. Before that we had been noncommittal, so this was a change in our policy, and the Liberals made big political hay on the flip-flop. I'd just been talking to Ian Anderson, the CEO of Kinder Morgan, and asked him to hold off on the company's regulatory filing in Ottawa until after the election. I said we needed some breathing room to not talk about it. The next day, Adrian was killing the thing. And Ian Anderson, who's really quite a nice guy, was probably thinking what a jerk that John Horgan is, the guy the industry is wondering if they can trust.

One more thing about Ian Anderson. When floods washed out part of the Coquihalla Highway in 2021, there were hundreds of their workers with equipment two valleys over laying pipe. If they hadn't come to our assistance, we would never have got that road back together as fast as we did. They did that quietly. They didn't put out press releases saying "Trans Mountain Pipeline Saves NDP's Ass," which they could have. They didn't do that. They just quietly did their civic duty. There was a crisis. They mobilized their work teams and came to help us put the road back into shape. That's what good guys do, particularly after the way the NDP treated Anderson.

We lost the building trades. They'd been prepared to support the NDP, but it became "Why the heck would we do that? We build stuff. We need a government that wants to build stuff, and it ain't you." Our slogan was "Adrian Dix, One Practical Step at a Time." In other words, we were going to change things, but not really.

Liberal strategist Mike McDonald and Christy Clark were focused on Coquitlam, Langley and Surrey, while we were out pretending we were going to win Peace River North. The polling numbers were so much in our favour, it looked like we might win everywhere, so we would make announcements in Liberal ridings. I want to contrast two photographs that were in *The Globe and Mail* on the same day during the campaign. One was a picture of Adrian, whose bus had broken down in Barkerville, wearing a silly bowler hat. Now the first rule of politics is: Don't put on stupid hats. But there was Adrian, in Barkerville, looking nerdy. How many votes are there in Barkerville? Then there was an attractive photo of Christy stretching her leg before going on a run. And lest we forget, all those photos of her in a hard hat. My spidey senses should have been tingling at that point. Who's Joe Lunch Bucket going to vote for? The election was supposed to be a foregone conclusion, and it didn't happen. I'd been picking it up on the doorstep. There was no issue in my riding except this chatter that made me a little uneasy. The polls were all good, right up until the end, when they began to tighten.

On election night, I was watching TV in my office, and it showed something like Liberals 50 and NDP 33. I remember saying that someone was going to lose their job because they had the graphic backwards. Then underneath, the ticker said our MLA Jagrup Brar had lost. And I went, "Holy shit. If he's defeated, then this is a problem." I started phoning around: "What the hell is going on?" Adrian had been all set. Transition meeting at seven a.m. the next day, right? The wedding hadn't happened, and he was already planning the honeymoon and his fifth anniversary. This was all going to take place in the first couple of days. He missed the fact we were losing.

CHAPTER EIGHT

TAKING THE REINS OF LEADERSHIP

MY FIRST REACTION ON ELECTION NIGHT WAS: "FUCK, I CAN'T DO another four years in opposition." I just couldn't. A lot of people approached me to cross the floor to the Liberals. They didn't have any MLAs on the Island, and they said I was more like them, more like the people in their constituencies. I did consider it, because I just didn't want another four years of nothing coming to my fast-growing community that desperately needed more amenities. But it was actually a right-wing friend of mine who said, "John, you can't do that now." There were also Liberals in my community who pushed back. They said I shouldn't do it: "You are who you are, and we don't blame you for the fact our party's not spending any money here." It was more of a Stew Young manoeuvre than anything. If we can't get rid of Horgan, let's co-opt him. He was convinced the only way we'd get any money from the province was to be in government. It turned out he was right, but I had to form the government for that to happen, rather than join one that already existed.

Of course I'm glad I didn't do it, even though I might have been in Christy Clark's cabinet. But the fact I didn't totally rule it out speaks to how fragile I was at the time. It would not have been so much for me and the glory but, quite honestly, for my community. We needed schools. We needed old folks' homes. We needed all these investments that weren't coming because they were voting NDP, and they'd just done it again.

I was also asking myself if the NDP were ever going to amount to anything. It was telling that David Eby had beaten Christy Clark in her own riding. The Liberals' own leader had lost her seat, and we still couldn't form government. During the week or two after the campaign, I was seriously questioning the NDP. Jack Layton was gone. Tom Mulcair, who succeeded him, was okay with a big chunk of people in Ottawa, but it was pretty obvious his support was a mile wide and an inch deep. Provincially, we lost in BC and got thumped once again in Saskatchewan. Federally, there was no longer a single NDP seat in Saskatchewan, home of Tommy Douglas and Canada's first socialist government. It didn't look good for the long term.

Eventually, I decided I was going to ride out the last term. I would stay and support Adrian to the extent that he could be supported. The money completely dried up. Adrian was seen for what he was: a very smart, earnest, hard-working guy, but not the leader the NDP needed to get out of whatever funk they were in. Christy Clark had overcome internal conflicts, corruption, and a dubious selection process that chose her over poor Kevin Falcon to lead their party. She seemed unassailable at this point. I was wrapping my mind around the thought that this was likely the end of politics for me.

I'd like to say something more about Adrian Dix. We talked almost every day for twenty years. I was maybe his closest friend for a long time. We first met in Ottawa, two BC guys not that far apart in age. He was all about politics all the time. He was well-read, bilingual, focused and driven, and I liked that about him. I didn't have that. I was kind of a passenger at the time, just happy to be there. Adrian was a contemporary. We played basketball together at the Y. He was left-handed. He got by me once, and I said, "Oh, you're a lefty." I started overplaying him the other way, and he couldn't shoot for love nor money, but he was in good shape and fast. He was quite athletic. He played on the softball team on the Hill. He was a marathon runner. And he seemed to know every sports statistic there was—pre-Google. We would play sports trivia with each other.

Adrian didn't have a lot of friends outside of politics, but I learned things hanging around him. That's how we became friends. When we were both working, we would talk almost every day during the week. People might wonder why we remained good friends for so long when our personalities were so different. It was his absolute commitment to the job and politics, and his loftier goals, quite frankly. Put aside his quirkiness, put aside his not making the right calls when he had the opportunity, he was always in it for the less fortunate. His family wasn't lower class, but they were not that well off. His dad was an insurance salesman. Adrian didn't come from a blue-collar background like I did, but he was always working for the underdog, and I respected that so much. I also respected his work ethic. Although the sackcloth and ashes got tiresome after a time, that's how he goes through life: I can't have something my constituents can't have. His constituents love him. They think he's fantastic.

You wonder why he wasn't that guy more often. He had connections with all the multicultural groups. He championed the cause of recognizing the Armenian Genocide and issues like that. He wasn't just about the show, which I felt Christy Clark was often all about. Adrian was all about everyone else. If packaged correctly, his candidacy could have been compelling. But it was not packaged at all. That was the problem. He went on a sports show during the campaign. I thought, "Okay, good. This is where people are going to get to know Adrian." But what do you think he talked about? Did he talk about the BC Lions or the Canucks, what I or anyone else would do? He talked about wrestling. And not even about fairly recent wrestlers like Dean Higuchi or Dutch Savage, but wrestlers at the Agrodome from the 1970s. The host of the show was probably thinking: "Why the heck have we got this guy in here?" He could rattle off all the wrestlers of that era—Don Leo Jonathan, Sweet Daddy Siki and so on—but that's not who the listeners cared about. This was in the middle of the campaign, a real opportunity to expand his base. Instead, they were probably going, "What's that guy talking about? Who are these people? Why is he talking about wrestling?"

After the election, I told him to leave on his own timetable, but he could not run again as leader. He kept thinking it was salvageable. I said that it was not salvageable. Over time, I got tired of his long soliloquies. He was always saying, "This is how it will all work out, dude." And I would say, "There's one key element you're missing, and that's people. You don't have any of them in your calculation. Your political science is too much science and not enough art."

When Adrian did announce his resignation, the chatter was that the next leader would be Horgan or Farnworth. Mike was born in July 1959. I was born two weeks later. I always hang that over Farny: "I'm the younger generation, Mike, you're not." But in essence we were the same people. We represented suburban ridings. We were moderates. We had been around a long time. I felt that was not the future the party needed. We'd elected some new people, David Eby among them. Spencer Chandra Herbert had been around for quite a while, but he was still in his thirties. There were Rob Fleming, Selina Robinson and Michelle Mungall, who had just been elected in the Kootenays to replace Corky Evans. This new, younger group would be scared away by a leadership race between Mike and me. I felt a battle of the old guys would not be in the best interest of the party or the best interest of British Columbia, so I said I was out. I could see nothing ahead but acrimony, recriminations and finger pointing, and I didn't want to be part of that. I think I said at the time that we didn't need to litigate the last election, we needed to prepare for the next one, and that requires new thinking, new approaches, new people.

I left it at that and went away to Cuba, of all places, for a holiday with Ellie, my sister Kate, and MLA Shane Simpson and his spouse. I was thinking this is going to be my future: long holidays, sunny beaches, seeing the world. Then the phone calls started, with people saying, "We really need you to do this." CUPE was first out of the gate. Their leaders, Mark Hancock and Paul Faoro, said they were going to phone me every day until I changed my mind. I said I wasn't interested. Other unions joined in. So did Art Kube, who was heading a seniors' organization. Then I began getting calls from caucus members. Shane, who was on holiday with me, said that I shouldn't close the door. I told him I wasn't interested. I had slammed the door, put a big bar on it and locked it.

Ellie, of course, was delighted. She liked the idea of having my complete attention and doing things together. But January turned into February, and there were still no candidates, although Farnworth was talking about it. David Eby had dropped out because his partner, Cailey Lynch, was pregnant. I might have supported him if he'd run, but he didn't. More and more caucus members were urging me to throw my hat in. Ian Reid, my old partner from IdeaWorks, was another person telling me that I had to run: "You're the only guy who can do this." I told Ian, that's exactly the reason I shouldn't run. "If I'm the only guy, then we're in a heap load of trouble." That was my self-doubt talking. I didn't know if I had the mettle for it. I could be thin-skinned. I hate stupidity. I lash out at bullies rather than just let them continue on. And when you're as big as I used to be, that can be intimidating for people. Anger is not my go-to position on the dial. I firmly believe I'm a happy warrior. But I'm Irish and sometimes quick-tempered. I can be caustic pretty quickly, then move on with a smile on my face. That's how I would characterize it.

I just didn't know if I had the temperament for the job. Ian was convinced it had to be me. He'd been fighting cancer for eight years, and it was nearing the end for him. Carole and I went to visit him at his West End apartment in Vancouver. There was a "Do Not Resuscitate" order on the door. Then, in Ian's writing, he had added the words: "Unless John Horgan is leader of the NDP." When we went in to see him, it was tough. He didn't look like himself, but he said I was the only one who could talk to all the factions in the party and not make anyone really angry. That was Ian's last pitch. The die was cast. I was in the race before he passed away.

Ellie was quite disappointed by my decision, especially since she didn't hear about it from me. She first heard it on the radio. I had been asked a question, and I said I was running. Not long after that, some people Mike might have counted on came out for me. The next thing I knew, Mike decided not to run. When nobody else came forward, I won by acclamation. On May 1, May Day, the keys to the land of misfit toys were passed to me, and I set about trying to right the ship.

The party had no money. Brian Gardiner had been seconded to the party because, for all intents and purposes, we were in receivership. Brian's a good solid guy. He had been an MP from Prince George and had worked at the BCGEU [BC General Employees Union] for a long time. We couldn't raise five cents. The unions were the ones keeping the lights on. We had raised a ton of money for the campaign, but that was gone, and we were in debt. I sat down with Brian and party president Craig Keating and asked how it looked. Keating had a blank pad of foolscap in front of him. He flipped it around and said, "It looks a lot like this." And I'm thinking, "Oh, great, now I'm the leader, and we're broke." We owned our office building in Burnaby, and Keating said we had to sell the building as quickly as possible to raise some money. Plus, the roof was close to caving in. It was a disaster. Meanwhile, the union movement was fractured, and we were demoralized, me included.

And of course being leader meant facing another four years of opposition. I like the cut and thrust of debate, and I could give as good as I got. That part was enjoyable. But when your best day is getting above the fold of the newspaper on a story about being critical of something someone else is doing, that's soul-destroying over time.

Our focus in opposition was always about how we could make the government look bad. When you've been doing that for a decade, as I had, and you would get a question from a learned journalist that you know they know the answer to—or, alternatively, they know you can't answer because it's hypothetical—I would sometimes get chippy. I remember one day when Mike Smyth of the *Province* literally met me at the door as I was coming out of the House and started grilling me about the Site C dam. I'm going to talk about Site C later, but I had worked in energy during most of my time in government. I knew a lot about it, and I knew on issues like Site C, at that point, there was no right answer. I like Mike—he's not a pool player, I beat him several times on the campaign trail—but he kept grilling me on what was a theoretical question about a future event. And I lashed out about what a stupid question that was, with maybe a few expletives tossed in. And naturally the press gallery just grabbed onto it, cameras rolling: "Horgan's losing his mind. Awesome." That sort of thing contributed to me thinking that I don't want to do this anymore.

Dealing with the caucus was a lot easier than I thought it would be, except for one incident that's worth memorializing. Dirk Meissner, from Canadian Press, is someone I like a lot. During an interview, he asked who my top five caucus members were. I didn't want to answer, but he kept coming at me in his best Columbo style, just one more question. So I named five people. There was gender balance and there was regional diversity. I hit all the buttons. No one had a disability, or I would have named that person, too. It was a stock answer, and I was proud of myself. The next day, all my caucus members who weren't in the top five were wearing buttons that read, "I'm Number Six." Otherwise, I had a bit of a leg up because I'm an amiable guy. I make friends easily. I wasn't happy dealing with Jenny Kwan, who had turned on my dear friend Carole James, a competent, capable, pragmatic centrist with an empathy factor that's off the charts. She's who my NDP is. But I didn't push Jenny. As luck would have it, Libby Davies stepped down as the NDP Member of Parliament for Vancouver East, and that was the perfect place for Jenny to go.

We then had to fight two by-elections. One for Jenny's Mount Pleasant riding, which we were sure to win, and one in

Coquitlam, after the Liberal MLA for the riding quit. It had been Christy Clark's riding at one time, and our expectations were low. We nominated Jodie Wickens, a homemaker and autism activist. Her partner drove a milk truck. She was a wonderful person who turned out to be a really good campaigner, and she won. In Mount Pleasant, we landed Melanie Mark. She had had many challenges in her life. I can't imagine the trauma she's lived through. She was from the 'hood, and we were able to convince her to run. She won in a walk. Melanie was a young and vital Indigenous person, and a great retail politician. She was the next generation.

We took both seats when we were expected to win only one. That was the beginning of being able to say I was remaking the NDP in my own image with the help of forward-looking young women, trying to get the balance right. We were able to scoot past the equity mandate, which had been a difficult argument for us to make in the hockey rink or at Tim Hortons. Why aren't white dudes welcome in the NDP? But I was the biggest white dude in the room, and I was saying we needed to see different races and more women around the table. Jodie and Melanie represented that. When they were sworn in, fifteen drummers escorted them into the Legislature. That had never happened before, and it was powerful. Melanie is Nisg̱a'a by lineage, but she always said she was Nisg̱a'a, Tsimshian and Scottish. She's so amazing.

While I was leader, the Supreme Court came down with its landmark Tŝilhqot'in decision ruling that Indigenous title not only exists, but here's the map. This is Tŝilhqot'in territory. It was now there in Canadian law, not just in Tŝilhqot'in oral history. I phoned up Chiefs Joe Alphonse and Roger William to congratulate them. Joe Alphonse had been at an all-candidates meeting for the NDP leadership back in 2011 in Williams Lake. He was this big Indigenous guy wearing camo fatigues and a ball cap. He observed the debate, made a statement from the back of the room, and left. So I'm phoning him to offer congratulations on the decision and the fact that he had just changed Canada. And he goes, "Yeah, well, I don't know, but I'm glad you're the leader of the NDP. I don't know why they didn't pick you the first time." This guy had literally changed not just his community and not just central BC, but all of Canada, and he was more interested in how stupid the NDP was to not pick me in the first place. Of course, I agreed with him.

The Tŝilhqot'in ruling, along with the election of Melanie Mark, gave us a real opportunity to revisit a bunch of issues around Indigenous rights and title. I was all about resource development when I was upcountry, I was all about environmental protection when I was in the suburbs and in the city, and I was all about how we reconcile with First Nations. Those were issues that moved me. I always felt we could have resource development that was sustainable and share that wealth with the people on whose land it was, along with meeting the values and objectives of urban environmentalists. This was something I felt I could accomplish.

I started building alliances with Indigenous representatives like Joe Alphonse, Ed John and Stewart Phillip. They were all saying the same thing. The United Nations Declaration on the Rights of Indigenous Peoples (UNDRIP) is where we need to get to. I said, okay, but I'm worried about "prior and informed consent." Under UNDRIP, that would be required for anything that impacted traditional territory. In resource development areas, that's all you hear from industry, and that filters down to forestry and other industrial workers. Does it mean they'll say no to everything, and we won't get anything done? Well, most Indigenous people want jobs. Most Indigenous people want economic wealth. But they have never had the opportunity to pursue that. The Declaration allows them more than a seat at the table. It is *their* table. As the 2017 election got closer, it became a pillar of my campaign that I was going to bring forward the UN Declaration on the Rights of Indigenous Peoples. It was a big risk in resource towns, but it was exactly what Indigenous leaders wanted to hear.

Now that I was leader, I also had to perform in the House, which is the symbol of success. I was okay at that, but Christy Clark was better. She didn't really care very much about what she said as long as she thought it made her look good. I didn't want to say something that wasn't true, for one, and I didn't want to take a slim sliver of fact and try to make a prosecutable case out of it. I wanted a story that would resonate with people, and that's not always what comes from the research people in the basement of the Legislature. I ended up gravitating towards issues that I knew. I had great respect for Christy's wit and her intellect. There wasn't any doubt she was a smart woman, but I think she often denigrated people unnecessarily, and I know there were people in the public service who didn't like working for her.

Everything is enhanced in the House during ministerial estimates. That's when the Opposition gets a chance to question ministers on their spending plans. Often, it's an effort to elicit actual information on stuff most people don't care about. But the media always show up for the premier's estimates. Christy and I had some incidents. Now, having been premier myself and having had to endure estimates on the other side, I have a better appreciation of what she was going through. You're busy running the government, you've got cabinet meetings, you've got crises happening all the time, and then you're forced to have someone ask you questions for hours on end with a view to making you look bad.

But the media had a view of her that she relished, this cat-and-mouse game. At one point during the proceedings, after many hours, I said, "You know how I practised for today's session? By taking a pencil and jamming it into my eyeball." It was so excruciatingly painful to ask a question and hope to get a bona fide answer. That was at my core. I mean, I wasn't a Boy Scout in this, but every single question, no matter what it was, became an opportunity for her to talk about all the jobs she had created or how many LNG plants were going to be built, even if jobs and LNG weren't in the question at all. And it would take fifteen minutes to get even those non-answers. That's the back and forth of estimates. Question is asked, minister turns to officials, and they talk about the hockey game, what you are doing on the weekend, how are the kids, did you see that Netflix thing last night? Then he or she turns around and gives you a bullshit answer, and another fifteen minutes is wasted as you wax indignant in your response.

During these sessions with Christy, I was particularly uncomfortable because she seemed to relish it, and I despised it. One year her office asked our office if we could shorten the premier's estimates because Christy had some event to go to. I said sure. I can't remember what the event was, but it was better than sticking a pencil in my eye for the next three hours. The press gallery jumped on it, saying, "Oh, critical error by Horgan, giving up time in the estimates." Then Andrew Weaver, the leader of the Green Party, began beating on me by loudly complaining that he had more questions and Horgan had shut the thing down. So Christy got off scot-free, and I had somehow screwed this thing up and ended up as the bad guy. It wasn't that big a deal, but it was something that really irritated me and is still on my mind. How did I get along with Christy Clark? Not at all. Not at all.

She was a master at manipulating the message. The media were enthralled by her, and they had their view of me as not being up for the job. That further embittered my view. Having said that, there's another memory I have of her from that time. Vaughn Palmer had a local cable TV show, *Voice of BC*. I think I had more appearances on that show than anyone. He would ask a question, and I would talk for an hour, so it was easy work for him. They would also do some interviews in the rose garden at the Legislature, which was just below my window. I would yell out and heckle people as they were doing the interviews. It became a thing. I think a couple of times Vaughn had me asking questions of guests from the window, with the camera on me. One day, Christy was walking past the window with her handlers. It was a beautiful sunny day, and she was dressed in red, which often augured poorly for a crew member on *Star Trek*. I wheeled open the window and said, "Hey, Christy, if this was a *Star Trek* episode, you wouldn't be coming back from the away mission." She spun around and said, "My phaser's on stun, cuz I like you." It was instantaneous. She turned back and kept on walking. I thought, "Well, okay, good for you. I'm funnier, but that was good."

Apart from Christy Clark herself, there were other issues we honed in on, like the firing of eight health researchers by the previous Gordon Campbell government. One of those fired, Roderick MacIsaac, committed suicide. Adrian worked with his family and the other researchers to keep the story going. It was a real personal tragedy and rightly devastating for the Liberals.

I had been helped in my new job by convincing Carole James to stay. That was a big plus for me. But I lost some of my mojo when my chief of staff and longtime friend John Heaney left for Alberta. The 2015 election was going on there. Rachel Notley's office phoned and said the NDP were doing really well, and it could be a minority government. Heaney had a background in Alberta, and they asked if John could come out to help them in the last week of the campaign. He said he wanted to go and off he went. This was at a tough point for us in BC. The polls were so-so, and my attempt to recruit people to run in 2017 was not going well. In Alberta, the NDP ended up shocking the world by winning a majority. Rachel Notley was now premier. John stayed. Finally, he called and asked to see me. I knew he had a better offer. John is my friend, but this was a time when we didn't seem to be making any progress as we headed towards an election in BC.

Treading water would be a charitable way to describe it. And I was having those various eruptions with individual media representatives. Adding to that was a reputation I had for flying off the handle in the Legislature. I'm a bit boisterous and I can turn a phrase. Under Carole James, I had become one of her attack people, and I continued to be a bit of a pit bull. But deep down, on a personal level, I did not feel comfortable in that role of dumping on people every day. It was a challenge for me. After I became premier, people would ask, "How did you go from being this so-called angry man to being such an affable fellow?" Well, the truth of the matter is that I was always an affable fellow. The angry man was an act. But the Liberals were having an easier time branding me than I was at branding them.

The good news was that hardly anyone was paying attention, so their attempts to say I was this maniacal crazy man whose head shot off his shoulders if you looked at him sideways didn't go that far. The public didn't know who I was. Global TV went around with my picture, asking people, "Who is this guy?" Some said I was the coach of the Canucks, which was not a great job to have after Willie Desjardins was fired.

Anyway, Heaney came to see me and said he was staying in Alberta as Rachel Notley's chief of staff. I felt that now I was really screwed. My chief of staff, the guy who had been helping me with caucus management and being tough when he had to, was gone. We were going into the most critical time of my leadership, and I was rudderless. I asked some friends of mine, Paul Degenstein, who was the partner of Ian Reid, and Marie Della Mattia, a communications expert with ties to the NDP, for suggestions. They gave me a list of names. One of the names on the list was Bob Dewar. I said that he must be a thousand years old. He'd worked for Howard Pawley when Howard was premier of Manitoba back in the 1980s and after that with Gary Doer, when he was premier, and he was the oldest son of Marion Dewar, who'd been mayor of Ottawa forty years ago. But they gave me his number. This was in October of 2015. I didn't phone him. A year later, we're virtually into the campaign, and people in the caucus are starting to ask questions. Who are we recruiting? Who's going here? Who's going there? Where's the platform at? It was being worked on, but I didn't have a second-in-command who could really knock back any grievances that were emerging.

It was a very dark time, so much so that I phoned party president Craig Keating and said that I was going to call Nathan Cullen, who'd impressed a lot of people as the NDP's MP for Skeena–Bulkley Valley since 2004. He had not yet left the federal NDP caucus. He was young. He was new. He was fresh. I told him that if he thought he could do a better job as leader, I would be happy to get out of the way. I wasn't hung up on staying. It honestly felt to me that we were no longer just treading water. We were starting to sink. I was going to oversee another loss, and that's not why I took on the job of leader. People wanted me to do it because they thought I could win. But at that point, I didn't see any way forward.

I was at some event in the Lower Mainland, where, as Opposition leader, you're desperately trying to find a group of people interested in hearing what you have to say. I think something like ten people were there on some obscure topic, and out of my black notebook fell this card with Bob Dewar's name and number on it. I looked at it and thought, what the hell. I called him up and he said, "I thought you were supposed to call me months ago." I said I got busy. "Busy doing what?" he asked. "Busy sinking," I answered. We talked a bit. We had a lot in common. He's a sports nut. He's been successful. He was born into the NDP, and he was passionate, so I said, "Would you come and help me out?"

He agreed to come and see me, without making any promises. But first he asked me why I wanted to be premier. I said it had a lot to do with my values. Someone with my background had never done the job before, and I thought that I might be able to add something to the equation that others hadn't. It was enough to trigger his interest, so we bought him a plane ticket.

He didn't have to come out. He was retired. He had been head of Manitoba's public service union. He had a career in politics working for Pawley and Gary Doer, one of that province's most successful premiers. He didn't know me from Adam. But he did know that things had been dark in BC for a long time. We spent a couple of days together. He was kind of inspecting me, and we ended up going to this union convention at the Operating Engineers Hall in Burnaby. I'm up there giving this great speech, and I go, "I may be an asshole, but I'm *your* asshole." Huge roar from the crowd. Every time I saw Dewar for a while after that, he would say, "Oh, my asshole just showed up again." He talked to people in the caucus and other people in the NDP he knew out here, and he agreed to come on as my chief of staff.

That's when the sinking stopped. My doubts in myself were still there, very much so, but now it became more like: "We're here now. We've invested all this energy, and I've got this seasoned campaigner who is prepared to go with me into that dark night and fight the dragon." My spirits started to buoy. Quite honestly, when John Heaney left, I really didn't have anyone I could bang ideas around with other than Adrian. He was, and I keep emphasizing this, the major motivation for me being involved in politics in the first place, because he had a passion that I didn't. But he's not the guy you want to talk to about the next campaign since he's still thinking he's going to win the one we just had. Now I had that person.

CHAPTER NINE

THE FIGHT TO BECOME PREMIER

I NEEDED SOMEONE LIKE BOB DEWAR BECAUSE IT WAS ALL ABOUT THE game at this point. It's not about doing good deeds and being there for your constituency. It's about outmanoeuvring someone who's calling you an asshole every day, and you haven't yet developed a temperament for the job. The stories had begun to write themselves. If you go back to 2016, when Bob Dewar arrived, and 2017, the media had pretty much dismissed me: He's no match for Christy Clark, he's angry, they've got no money, and all these other things.

But we developed a campaign strategy that was effective. We were going to talk about things that mattered to people. We were going to talk to people about ten-dollars-a-day child care. We were going to talk in rural BC about Indigenous rights as an asset, not a liability. We were going to talk about resource industries as important to who we are as British Columbians. They're not something to run away from, as so many New Democrats have done, certainly at the federal level. That had become a dominant narrative for working people: "Well, they don't like us. They're urban environmentalists, or they're single-issue people concerned about things I'm not interested in." We were also going to have a separate ministry of mental health and addictions, although I didn't realize we were going to lean so heavily on addiction. That wasn't my primary focus. My focus was on people being given access to counselling and appropriate therapies so they could manage their mental health issues. There didn't seem to be much place for that in our user-pay system.

I was a different John Horgan because I really felt it was an end, not a beginning. For me it was, "Well, we're almost done here." I said I would do it. The election is months away and here we go. When you're in a race, it's really important to know there's a finish line. I had not yet got to the point where I thought I was going to win the race. In fact, I doubted it very much. Yet I had to demonstrate every day to the caucus, to the media and to staff that we were in the fight of our lives, and we were going to win.

It all started with Bob Dewar's arrival. Somewhere between him arriving and election day, I got the wind in my sails. We had a plan. It was achievable. We had modest amounts of money, but we were going to be able to make it work. I stopped talking about grievances and started talking about opportunities. How could I demonstrate to people that voting for me was going to be good for them, that I cared about them and their lives and the things that pissed them off? I had collected those stories from twelve years in opposition, so I was in a good position to say I knew what I was talking about.

When the writ was dropped, my mood was remarkably good. Twenty-eight days and, one way or the other, it would be over. With all my doubts and lack of tangible support in terms of the polls and fundraising, waiting for that moment had been difficult. In spite of what I've just said, I was still a bit terrified. I'd never been the front guy in a campaign before. I have insecurities like everyone else, and Christy Clark exuded confidence. Our campaign team wrapped our bus with a picture of me and a whole bunch of diverse people smiling. I didn't like walking around one side of the bus, however, because my head was too big. I couldn't stand looking at a head that big.

But once the campaign started and I was out with groups of people, they were responding to me. As we made stops, growing numbers were turning up. They weren't Trump-like crowds, but health-care workers, people looking for child care, friends I'd seen over the years as I travelled around as critic and Opposition leader. There was something building. I was on television more, and I was being recognized. I was seen as someone who was larger than life. I've never thought of myself as being charismatic, but I was being characterized as charismatic, engaging, someone fun to be around. And that was how I'd kind of lived my life, trying to be someone that everyone wanted on the team.

I got to be myself for twenty-eight days. We had a meticulous schedule. With about ten days to go, I like to say I played the Commodore, because my son's a musician. I took the stage, and a thousand people were there. Wow. The place was full. There was a single podium in this sea of people, and I got to just rip. Something was going on.

The one thing that really stood out was our promise to do away with tolls on the Port Mann and Golden Ears Bridges. Our platform had said we'd maybe cut the tolls in half or reduce them gradually over time because we were trying to be fiscally responsible. Then we heard that the Liberals were planning to cut the tolls by half. That day, we had an event in Surrey where we were going to talk about other things, and Bob Dewar said, "Change your plans. Let's eliminate all the tolls." We got our finance guy, a young man named Jon Robinson, to crunch the numbers. This was important because whenever we made a promise, the media would ask how we were going to pay for it. Every single thing. We're going for coffee: How are you going to pay for it? "Well, I'm going to dig into my pocket and pull out some money and pay for it." That was the constant refrain from the media. The government didn't have to explain anything. No one said boo about their promises. They were "government initiatives." But every single day we would announce something, and the media would demand to know how we were going to pay for it, right down to the decimal point. Well, governments pay for it through the revenue pot and by growing the economy. It's not a left–right thing.

That's been happening since the creation of a civil society. But you can't lecture the public on civic politics during an election campaign. That bedevilled us for three elections, until finally it didn't.

Jon Robinson phoned me on my way to the bus and gave me the green light. The money was there to cut the tolls. The event was at one of Surrey's big banquet halls. There was a large crowd. I announced that an NDP government would remove all the tolls on bridges in the Lower Mainland. No one knew we were going to do that. Bruce Ralston, one of our MLAs from Surrey, shot out of his chair like Rocket Man. Bruce doesn't show a lot of emotion, and if he does, it's rarely enthusiasm. I've never seen Bruce happier, more animated and with a bigger smile on his face, before or since. I knew we'd hit the mark. We had done something that was purely populist. It completely took the legs out from underneath the Liberal platform, and we ended up with a lot of seats out there that we didn't have before. It was another example of piling on populist plans, showing people that government can be a tool for good. This wasn't about scandal and personality. It was about people.

Early on, however, there was the radio debate on CKNW when I seemed to lose my temper. They had made us wait outside in our bus for half an hour before the premier arrived. I've been premier now myself, so I better understand the logistics of security, but there were Liberals outside the bus carrying signs saying, "Calm down, John, calm down." In my mind, it was all a setup, with Christy Clark in there getting another Starbucks and spending time in makeup, which maybe she was. I wasn't in a good mood to begin with. Andrew Weaver and I were jammed together in the studio, and Bill Good, the host, was very businesslike. Scribble, scribble, looking over his glasses. Then Christy comes in, and he gets up and gives her a big hug, and it's "How are you? How's Hamish [her son]?" and all that small talk. Bill says answers will be kept to thirty seconds. Right off the bat, Christy goes for a minute. By this point, I'm getting apoplectic about the unfairness of it all, thinking I shouldn't be on this stage, much less trying to compete with the Vancouver elites. Bill Good doesn't know me. I'm the Victoria guy. He'd just hugged my opponent, so I didn't feel he was giving us his best in terms of impartiality.

That was a subjective thought, and I don't want to besmirch Bill Good in any way. But as the debate went on, Christy got lots of latitude, while Weaver and I kept getting cut off. Then, at one point, she patted my arm, telling me to calm down. I snapped, "Don't touch me, please." I was thinking that if I had patted her arm, I would be toast, yet she's allowed to do that. Later, I was upset about something else, and I told her: "I'll just watch you, because I know you like that." It was a reference to her loving photo ops and that sort of thing, but as soon as it came out of my mouth, I knew I'd said something stupid. It was the worst half-hour of the campaign for me. When I came out of the debate, I was ashen.

Some of our people thought it was over. I didn't think so. I told them it's just one moment. We still have a story to tell, and we've got to go out and keep telling that story. I'd screwed up, no question, and I knew people had higher expectations of me. I also knew I was not an angry person. There were three weeks left, and from then on, I got back to being the happy warrior, that person with a smile on my face—even during those times I was whacking the Liberals upside the head. Yet it still wasn't about my personality. It was about people. We were talking about things that mattered to people.

However, I'm not taking credit for what really began turning things around. That was a woman named Linda in a grocery store in North Vancouver. Christy was campaigning there, and the cameras were rolling. Linda came up to her and said, "Hi, I'm Linda. I'm never going to vote for you." As she started to explain why, Christy said, "You don't have to. That's why we live in a democracy," and quickly walked away. Now if someone had come up to me and said something like that, I would have said, "Well, you know, I think you're making a mistake," and mentioned some of the things we were going to do. I liked to engage. But she just spun around and moved away. That's what seasoned campaigners do. They only want to talk to people who agree with them. But "Hi, I'm Linda" went viral on social media. It seemed to roll on forever, and the pat on the sleeve during the radio debate was forgotten. The Liberals also had a truck that drove around to our events. We called it the Troll Truck. They'd have signs saying, "Calm down, John" and stuff like that. Again, that worked in our favour. Their polls must have been telling them that people were liking me, and they had to find ways to counteract that, because Christy Clark's biggest vulnerability was that a lot of people didn't like her.

I was better in the TV debate. We did a lot of preparation. That was important, particularly after the radio debate. I was pretty relaxed going in, with a compelling package that I was comfortable with. The moderator asked me if I had an anger management issue. It was like the Liberal researchers wrote the question for her. My answer was something like: If you can look at the atrocities that are going on with children and family development, when you can look at communities being hollowed out, and if you're not angry, then you aren't paying attention. I didn't respond that I wasn't angry. I was frustrated that people were being left behind. That was the messaging Bob and others had developed to correct this growing story. That was the Liberals' thing. We're going to say this guy's nuts. That's how we'll beat him. I think they tried too hard, because any time anyone met me, I was far from angry. I was engaging. I was thoughtful. I was funny, self-deprecating, humble. I was a normal guy. We didn't completely stop talking about the conflicts and the corruption and the scandals of the BC Liberals. Adrian tried to not talk about the shortcomings of the Liberals in 2013. He was criticized for that, and rightly so. You need to do some of that, but mostly we went back to talking about people. That shift made all the difference in the world. That's why the tolls announcement was so important. People said, "Okay, now they're talking about something positive that matters to me."

We did normal people things like going to Burger Heaven in New Westminster for the great burger election poll. My people were petrified that if I bit into the burger, there might be juice all over the place, and I would get a bad photo. To bite or not to bite, that was the question. We actually discussed this on the bus. I said I've been eating hamburgers for a long time. I can do this. Just as we were rolling in, the Liberals had come in and bought a hundred Liberal burgers. But this was NDP-friendly New Westminster, and we were way up in the hamburger poll. I order my burger, pick it up, and there's some bacon hanging out the side. The photographers are getting ready. Just as I'm putting it to my mouth, I tilt the burger ever so slightly to avoid the bacon. The bite is without incident. Back on the bus. Problem solved. That's the kind of stuff you go through on a campaign.

We had popular issues like the tolls, child care, and getting rid of Medical Services Plan (MSP) premiums, but there were also some resources issues we had to deal with: Kinder Morgan's pipeline expansion, LNG and Site C. We'd already cast the die on Kinder Morgan, so that was easy. We knew it was not our jurisdiction, and the permits had been issued, but we opposed it because of the influx of oil tankers, and I vowed to use every tool in the tool box to get it stopped. As for LNG, I was always a supporter of natural gas because we needed it as a transition fuel. And if we could get money for the gas we were producing—rather than selling it to the Americans, who are liquefying and exporting it— that was a good thing. But we had a number of conditions: making sure that Indigenous people were full participants, that jobs were for locals, and that it was going to stay within our climate plan. It seemed to me that was saleable to normal people.

On the Site C dam, on the Peace River, which had already started under the Liberals, I said candidly that I had had as many positions on that as were in the *Kama Sutra*, because I had been the energy critic. You want to electrify? You want to decarbonize? You need clean energy. Where's a good place to get it? How about the Peace River that already has two dams on it? That was my thinking, but what I was saying was that the decision had already been made by the Liberals, and they were going ahead. Christy

Clark famously declared she intended to push the dam past the point of no return. That was a gold mine for me. I would say that she wasn't building Site C to be W.A.C. Bennett; she was using it as a political club. That's not how you build a province. I was able to use rhetoric around Site C that sounded reasonable to most audiences. It wasn't for true believers, since those who despised Site C despise it to this day. I said that if I formed government, we would look past "the point of no return," and if we could do anything about it, if there was a better way to spend $8 billion, then I was prepared to do that. But before I was prepared to say we would stop it, I wanted to know how much killing it would cost, and what were Hydro's alternatives. That was the position I campaigned on. There were certainly divisions within our caucus, but quite frankly, stopping it did not poll well.

I didn't want to say to the building trades that we weren't going to build anything. I said we were going to double our SkyTrain output. We might not build a bridge to replace the Massey Tunnel under the Fraser River, but we would put in a new tunnel. We said we were going to accelerate building a new Pattullo Bridge in New Westminster. We put together a package that allowed union leaders to credibly say to their members that Horgan was going to build stuff. He's not going to support Kinder Morgan, but he's going to do this, that and other things. What about Site C? Well, he's going to take a look at that. He's not going to kill it right away.

Towards the end, the numbers were starting to firm up. I was getting good coverage. Christy was getting terrible coverage. I had survived the "Please don't touch me" moment and life was good. On the final day, I had my friends from Victoria come over. They weren't political at all. Their only interest in politics was me. They were people I had grown up with, people I played sports with. Our kids grew up together. The ones I go to for respites of normalcy.

We're on the top floor of the Pinnacle Hotel, on West Hastings, looking out on the harbour. It was like going to Disneyland for my friends, waiting for the results to come in. They'd never done anything like this before. And then it's midnight, and we still don't know who won. All of a sudden, it wasn't as much fun as it seemed to be at the beginning, when they were thinking that if it went badly, they got their friend back, and if it went well, their friend got to be premier. Instead, there was no outcome. It was back and forth, back and forth. There were seats I was disappointed to lose. I had gone to rural areas and talked about an industrial economy, which no NDP leader had done for quite a time. We still got hit. Skeena had been an NDP seat for a long time. We also lost in Columbia River–Revelstoke and Kootenay East, where there was a high density of union steelworkers.

We waited late into the night, and it seemed clear neither party was going to get the magic forty-four seats for a majority government. The Greens had won three seats, and it appeared they would have the balance of power. At some point, I phoned Green leader Andrew Weaver to congratulate him for his personal victory and his two colleagues who had just won seats. I said we had a lot to talk about. "I know you're exhausted. I'm exhausted. But I want to leave you with two words: 'Rich Coleman.'" I'll always remember that because Andrew started laughing. I said, "I'll talk to you later." And that was the beginning of our negotiations.

CHAPTER TEN

PREMIER JOHN

THE LIBERALS HAD GONE INTO THE ELECTION TRYING TO DEFEND A sixteen-year record that was spotty, to say the least. They spent a lot of energy claiming that our New Democratic team were vestiges from a time thirty years earlier. Many voters hadn't even been born then, and that argument just didn't work for them. But we had not won the election outright—forty-three seats for them, forty-one seats for us, and three seats for the Greens. I remember it was one a.m. on election night, and we still hadn't made a statement. We had to wait for Christy Clark. She finally came out and said she had won, and she wasn't leaving. When the media asked her what she was going to do, she said she was going to talk to members of the Legislature and find a way to form government. After that, I went to our election night gathering at the Vancouver Convention Centre. We told the media there would be no questions. It was just going to be a statement about how this was not over. As I started to come down the stairs all the cameras and the microphones were pointing at me. It was quite daunting. How am I going to get through them all? Out of nowhere came Bob Dewar with his elbows up. I'll never forget it. Bob wasn't exactly a heavyweight, but he just bowled people over. I followed him right through like I was carrying a football. It was very funny.

A lot of our people were still celebrating because we hadn't lost. The media said it was too close to call. That hadn't happened in quite a while, so there was a sense of euphoria, even though we weren't exactly going to start the next day on our new vision for British Columbia. That night, I slept very well. The next morning all my buddies, my non-political friends, me and some family had breakfast at the Pinnacle, where we'd all stayed overnight. I've always stayed there in Vancouver because it's a union hotel. Then I got on the ferry to go home.

Everyone had been watching the outcome in Courtenay–Comox. Our candidate, Ronna-Rae Leonard, "Landslide Leonard," was ahead by something like thirteen votes on election night. We had to wait for the counting of absentee ballots. I had run into a woman on the ferry who said she was from Courtenay–Comox. She had voted by mail for the NDP, and she was convinced most of the absentee ballots would be for us. She turned out to be right, but if that seat had gone Liberal, they would have had forty-four seats and a majority. The Greens would not have mattered, and I probably wouldn't be talking about any of this. That's how close it was. But we did hang on in Courtenay–Comox, the Greens did matter, and something interesting was happening. Everything was different.

Looking back on that campaign, I really felt like I got to be myself. There's no other way to describe it. Politics is a lot of acting, but people sense it if you're not genuine. I tried my best to be a good leader of the Opposition because I knew it was important. But it's awful work. I had worked in government and knew how transformative that could be. The Columbia Basin Trust in the Kootenays, which I had been part of, was able to direct billions of dollars to a bunch of communities because there was a political will to do it and a government prepared to turn its promises into reality. During the campaign, there was now the prospect that I might be able to implement similar changes to benefit people. As we laid out what those changes would be, the campaign became fun. It was going from the land of misfit toys to trying to effect positive change. It was fantastic. One of the best times of my life.

We had been hard on the Greens during the campaign. I consider myself an environmentalist. The Suzuki Foundation will drop dead hearing that, but I felt we'd been addressing environmental issues all along, and the Green Party was a fledgling movement. It was a colour. It could be all things to all people depending on who they were talking to. And they went around as if they could actually do those many things they were promising when there was zero chance of that happening. Andrew Weaver and I did not get along. We were fishing in the same pond. They had all their eggs in the basket of southern Vancouver Island, and they'd taken three seats. Along with Weaver, Sonia Furstenau and Adam Olsen had been elected, both in ridings that had previously been held by the NDP. Weaver now had two buddies to bolster his arguments, and he was pretty pumped on election night. Andrew is not left or right. He's a centrist. But he knew that Green voters tend to be left of centre, so he focused on people who had historically supported us. We had been bitterly at odds with each other for four years.

Still, I was optimistic we could work something out. I felt Weaver was predisposed to supporting another guy from Victoria. He was an Oak Bay grad. I was a grad from Reynolds in Saanich. We were from our neighbourhoods, a couple of years apart. By and large, we had the same upbringing and the same cultural touch points. Despite the fact we were fierce adversaries at the time, we had things in common. When you peel all that back, there wasn't a lot of difference between the two of us. Christy Clark was from the mainland, but she really wasn't from anywhere. She had represented Port Moody, she had represented Vancouver until she lost her seat, and then she represented Kelowna—disparate communities with no similar roots. She was just the Liberal candidate for the home team.

I had also reminded Andrew during our short phone call that our platform was not so different from theirs. We were heavy on climate action. We were heavy on managing resource development in a sustainable way that left resources for generations to come while protecting and preserving those things that are so important to British Columbians. The Liberal platform was a lot different. But Weaver set up this notion that he was going to conduct interviews with the two sides and decide who to support. It would be like *The Bachelor*: Are you going to give it to Horgan, or are you going to give it to Christy Clark?

I felt Christy Clark's arrogance would be her undoing. And true to form, she sent emissaries to do the talking—Mike Bernier, the MLA from Peace River, and her chief of staff, Mike McDonald—whereas Carole James and I went to talk to the Greens. We weren't offering baubles and beads, as the Liberals seemed to be. We wanted to talk seriously about how we could form a government together. The Greens didn't want a coalition. Weaver wanted to establish the presence of their caucus. He had done enough reading to know that junior partners usually disappeared, so he wanted to be separate: throw rocks when he wanted to throw rocks, but be there for things he wanted as well.

All three of the Greens were Islanders, as were Carole and me. I think they saw the value of hanging out with the NDP more so than taking trinkets from a party that had pissed on their ideas for four years. Sonia Furstenau also had her own beef with the Liberals over a major toxic soils issue in her community. At the same time, you never know. I didn't want to overplay our hand. We met at the Grand Pacific. Carole was very much a calming influence. When Weaver would make an outrageous statement, I would get my back up, and Carole would bring it back down. They brought along Norman Spector as part of their negotiating team. He had worked for Social Credit premier Bill Bennett and had been Canada's ambassador to Israel. He was a prominent name. I think he was leaning towards the Liberals. I didn't feel he had anything to contribute, other than he wanted to be part of it.

We said, we know you're serious people. We know you have an agenda. It's not dissimilar to ours. Let's collaborate. Whereas on the other side, it was always: We are the government; you can come along, and we will give you stuff, but we are the government. After the fact, Andrew said, "They just didn't get it." For them, it was about maintaining control, and for Andrew it was about building something together. I think that was a real difference between the other guys and us. We were serious and focused and centred on people.

Near the end, there was the so-called Rugby Summit. Andrew was a big rugby fan, and there was a rugby match in Langford. I'm more a rugby fan of convenience, but this was happening in my community, so I showed up, too. I think Stew Young, still the mayor of Langford, conspired, not in a criminal way, to get us together. We were having a great time watching the game, and Dirk Meissner from Canadian Press snapped a picture of the two of us in our flowery shirts. That became a story. Horgan and Weaver meeting secretly in public.

We already agreed on Kinder Morgan, that we would go to the wall with the tools we had available, legally and through different regulations. We also agreed on banning political donations from corporations and unions. But LNG was a big hurdle. The Greens wanted nothing to do with it. I argued that if it will fit into a plan, it's a big economic opportunity. However, that was a sticking point, particularly for Weaver. We were also trying to find the right language on Site C. They wanted to kill it outright. I said we couldn't do that. We have to have a process. Those were the tough ones. But we managed to work our way through both of them to get an agreement. Towards the end of May, we announced that we now had the support of forty-four MLAs and a one-seat majority in the Legislature.

We had to wait another month to bring down the Liberals. That happened on June 29. I'd gone in to work, the usual schtick. It was a beautiful summer day. Their Throne Speech had been ridiculed by the media, who called it "the Clone Speech" because it contained so many items lifted directly from our platform and the Greens', none of which the Liberals had called for during the election. Vaughn Palmer of the *Vancouver Sun* and others in the media tried to be mischievous, asking the Greens why they would vote against something that had all the things they wanted. Of course, it didn't fly. This was our chance to vote non-confidence in the government, and we had agreed that's what we were going to do. The House was called. The vote was held. The Liberals were defeated. Although there are rules against making any noise, the public gallery was packed with cheering partisans. There was no stopping it. On the floor of the House, we were celebrating with the Greens. I remember seeing images on television of Christy leading a procession of sullen Liberals, and staffers clapping for them as they walked by. That was kind of the last waltz for Christy and her crew. I believe there are still fingernail marks on the door jamb of the premier's office from when they were trying to get her out. We were jubilant, but we didn't yet know what Judith Guichon, the lieutenant governor, would do.

We didn't have a Speaker in place. If the new Speaker came from our side, that would leave the seat count at forty-three each, and he or she would have to break tie votes. There's no denying that would have been awkward. There was still this notion that a government depending on the Greens would fall, and within six weeks we would be back in an election. That's what Christy said when she went to see the lieutenant governor: We should have another election because an NDP government can't survive. As for me, I was in my office with my lacrosse stick, throwing a ball against the wall: *thump, thump*. Our staff were in the next room watching the TV reports. The cameras, the satellite trucks, and all the media were assembled at Government House—waiting for, you know, the white smoke or black smoke to come out.

We now know what happened, but that wasn't how it happened on television. Christy made her pitch. It was a relatively short conversation, but then Christy stayed at Government House with her staff for an awfully long time. I'm still throwing the ball against the wall, and I'm wondering what's gone wrong. Are we back in an election? Finally, Bob Dewar got a call from

Jerymy Brownridge, who was private secretary to the lieutenant governor, and he said, "This is your million-dollar call. Can Mr. Horgan be in Her Honour's office in the next half-hour?" And Bob said, "We'll be there in five minutes."

We hopped into the Prius. Bob and my press secretary, Sheena McConnell, were in the back. Her husband drove, and I was with him in the front seat. We rolled up to Government House. By this time, the media were packing up. They figured there was nothing to see here because Christy Clark had finally come outside and said Her Honour was going to consider her options or something like that. Everyone was going home. That's why Bob said we had to head over right away, before the cameras disappear. I bounded up the stairs and didn't fall on my face. I felt pretty good. People said I had this big shit-eating grin on my face. I went in to see the lieutenant governor. She had consulted with experts across the country and reached a conclusion based on the agreement we had with the Greens. "Hello, Mr. Horgan. Nice to see you," she said as I came in. I sat down, and she asked me if I had the confidence of the House. I said I believed I did. Ms. Guichon then asked if I could form a government. I said, "Yes, I can." She said, "Best of luck." And that was it. It was that simple. She had two questions for me, and I had answered them. She was very pleasant. It wasn't perfunctory or anything like that. She didn't seem disappointed about it. Those were the two questions she was obliged to ask me in that constitutional moment, and I answered them in the affirmative. We were off to the races.

I always say that British Columbia has a long list of extraordinary people who have served as lieutenant governors: David Lam, the first Chinese Canadian to hold the post; Steven Point, the first Indigenous person; Iona Campagnolo, who looked so resplendent and vice-regal in her outfit; as did Garde Gardom, who was so proud to hold the position he never stopped smiling. But I continue to maintain that the most important of all was Judith Guichon, because she was the only one who asked me to be premier.

When I came outside, I hadn't yet talked to Ellie. My phone had run out of juice, so I borrowed Sheena's phone. When I phoned home, Ellie didn't recognize the number and didn't pick up. I had to leave a message: "Hey, Ellie, it's me. It looks like I'm going to be premier. I'm going to get a hamburger. I'll talk to you later." That's the nature of our relationship. She wasn't surprised by that at all. I really was hungry. I hadn't eaten since lunchtime, and by now it was half past eight. I went to get a hamburger at an Irish pub on Government Street, and I got into an argument with a guy about who was the best starship captain. I was maintaining priorities. I kept saying Captain Janeway. And he said that I didn't appreciate *Deep Space Nine*. It tells a story of the darkness of capitalism. And I'm going, "What are you talking about? It's science fiction." That's how I spent my first hour or so as incoming premier, arguing about starship captains.

When I woke up the next morning, I was thinking that the cops were going to come and pick me up. They didn't because I hadn't been sworn in, and Christy was still premier. I drove into work, loaded up boxes and did stuff like that. Everywhere I went, there were big smiles on people's faces, many of whom probably didn't vote NDP. It didn't matter. They were just happy it was going to be a new day in British Columbia.

I went by my constituency office. There was a flood of emails and a mountain of cards and flowers. It was summer. The weather was good. An election had happened, and for once the people of Vancouver Island had ended up with a result they voted for. It had been ages since that had happened. My memory is just this feeling of euphoria. There was also some feeling of dread. The fire season had just begun, and already it was bad. Our first order of business had to be finding out how to manage them.

We had a transition team in place that included Eugene Kostyra from Manitoba. He was a wonderful human being who'd been a critical player in the NDP government of Howard Pawley. Bob Dewar brought him in to help us with the cabinet. The two of them talked to everyone in the caucus, and we went over who they thought were most suited. Then I had to decide how to put them all in. The biggest risk was leaving Leonard Krog from Nanaimo out of the cabinet. He was a veteran MLA. He'd run for the leadership against Carole James, with Dave Barrett supporting him, and he'd been attorney general critic forever. I liked Leonard, but we already had four cabinet ministers from Vancouver Island on our list, plus myself. You've got the premier, the finance minister and deputy premier from the Island, and three others. We couldn't just be the cabinet from Vancouver Island. I considered Leonard a friend. I didn't know he would barely talk to me again. But I had no choice. David Eby was the next generation. There were a bunch of lawyers in the caucus, and he was the youngest and brightest, in a seat we needed to hold on to, so he had to be attorney general. Leonard would have none of that. I asked him to be caucus chair, and he said no. Then he relented and agreed. But in 2018 he resigned his seat to run for mayor of Nanaimo. He's still the mayor, so good for him. But this was a huge risk for us, because he had said he was going to quit if he wasn't in cabinet, and that would mean a by-election. We could have lost the government. As it turned out, we didn't come close to losing the by-election, but if the Liberals had not been in disarray, we might have.

There were things I wanted to do, and I made some cabinet choices early on that were pretty pivotal. Scott Fraser from Port Alberni is one of the nicest guys in the world. As the old expression goes, he wouldn't say shit if he had a mouthful of it. He had been Indigenous relations critic for a decade, and one of the things I wanted to accomplish was genuine reconciliation. Scott had talked to every First Nations leader in the province, and he listened to them, he didn't tell them what was good for them. I was very fortunate to have him as Indigenous minister to implement UNDRIP, and after him, Murray Rankin, a brilliant legal scholar who was later elected in Oak Bay–Gordon Head. Murray had spent a lifetime litigating these issues. Shane Simpson comes from East Vancouver. We wanted to make sure we did something about income assistance, but it had to be manageable within the context of being fiscally responsible, so putting Shane in at social development was very important. He didn't let me down.

I put Michelle Mungall, from the Kootenays, in at energy. A lot of people said I did that so I could look over her shoulder, but I did it deliberately. We were a gender-balanced group, and the symbolism of putting women in the so-called dirt ministries was to try and demonstrate that these are not just the domains of dudes. Anyone can manage and administer these things. And she did a very good job. At times, George Heyman could be the biggest pain in the ass you'll find anywhere, but he never let me down as environment minister. As much as he hit the table a lot about various CO_2 emissions and all that, he was absolutely fine. We told Heyman and Weaver to come up with something on climate action, and we'd try to sell it. They came up with the best action program in Canada. Mike Farnworth is Mike Farnworth. He is the kind of utility infielder you need. As solicitor general and House leader, his experience was extremely valuable. But what do you do with Adrian Dix? You put him in health and cross your fingers—and that worked out very, very well.

The swearing-in took place on July 18. We all crammed into a bus. Once again, it was a beautiful day. Government House was packed. I only teared up a couple of times, which was good. Ellie was there, of course, with our son Evan—Nate was at school in the UK—and my siblings. My two brothers and my sister had kept me on track when I was young. They had kept me out of trouble. Even when they were raising their own kids, they were still kind of raising me. To have them beaming with pride at little John standing on a stage as premier of British Columbia was pretty overwhelming. I'm crying even now, thinking about it. I couldn't look at my family until halfway through. It was pretty tough to get through that.

Carole James was a moderate like me, and she had been a leader in a very difficult situation. It's tough on a good day for a female leader: You're either too shrill or too quiet. As far as I'm concerned, she didn't get a fair shake right from the get-go. The roar that went up when Carole was sworn in as finance minister and deputy premier is one of the things I will never forget. I invited my old basketball coach, Jack Lusk. It was important for me to recognize him as an educator, but more important as a human being who invested in people, not just to make a good basketball team, but to make good human beings. And then I wanted to have a band. I thought it would be great to have 54-40 play, but we got talked out of it. Too extravagant. I remember wading into these hundreds and hundreds of people. My jacket is still on, and I'm drenched with sweat. I've got a detail of cops with me now. One of them, Greg, says he thinks we should go. He pulls me away and we get into the car. And Alexi, who's the driver, had one of those push-button sanitizers. She turns around at me in the backseat and goes *squirt, squirt*. Greg said he'd been on this detail a long time, but he'd never had to bodyguard someone he was completely unable to help, because I kept rolling into these waves of people. I never did get any of the ice cream they were handing out. I was quite miffed about that.

It was all beyond my wildest dreams. Whenever the opportunity had presented itself, I'd said you've got the wrong guy, you should find somebody better. I don't think it was lack of self-confidence. I think it was just that I always felt I was there to help other people, not to be the leader. This speaks to all those who said there was a great transformation in me from opposition to government. It wasn't that. It was a transformation in responsibility. I felt I was lifting up my colleagues, giving them room to do their thing, and hoping they would surpass me and become leaders. It was also an opportunity to reflect on all the chance events in my life that had led to this, like Bob Dewar's card falling out of my notebook at a time when things were looking very dark. I'm sixty-five now, and I've got sixty-five years of stories that you wouldn't believe about how I fell into this huge pile of horse dung and came out looking as if I'd never had a better day in my life. I can't explain it. These things just happened. But there are also consequences, and one of them is that right now, as I'm saying this, I'm in a hospital in Berlin with a tube in my throat. It doesn't always come out great, but nine times out of ten? I'll take that. I think most people would.

Going in to work for the first time as premier was weird. The Liberals had taken all the paper from the printer. They had cancelled the contracts for those big jugs of drinking water. A guy literally came in and started walking out the door with one of the jugs. In one office, they had taken all the pencils. The drawers were empty, and there wasn't a bit of office equipment remaining. It was like whatever they could do to piss us off, they did. That was Day One.

We had a group of people to start figuring things out. There was myself and Carole, and Geoff Meggs, who I'd hired as my chief of staff. Geoff had been around politics for a long time. He was Vancouver mayor Larry Campbell's executive assistant, and then a councillor himself for nine years. I had got to know him before that, when he was working as director of communications for Glen Clark. He had also co-chaired, with Carole James, our platform committee for the election. And I brought in Don Wright as my new deputy minister. He had been at Central Credit Union as their chief economist for a time and president of BC Institute of Technology. But he gave up his top spot at BCIT in 2013 when Adrian offered Don a job in his office, expecting that he would be the next premier. They were already measuring the drapes. Of course, that didn't happen, and there was no job. When I asked him to give us another chance, I said that I could guarantee he'd have more fun working for me than he would have had working for Adrian. Don had been a bureaucrat most of his life. He was virtually a career public servant, this very humble guy with a Saskatchewan smile on his face. By appointing him, we didn't frighten other career bureaucrats. Many people in the NDP wanted to fire everyone, but there's a sweet problem with firing people: You have to replace them. And finding people with expertise in niche areas like agriculture, tourism, culture, Indigenous relations and so on is not easy. They're not hanging around waiting for calls. We kept most of the public service, certainly for those first few months.

We did fire six deputy ministers based on Don's recommendations. The one deputy everyone wanted me to fire was Fazil Mihlar. He'd been with the Fraser Institute and an editor at the *Vancouver Sun*. But there were a lot of good reasons not to fire him. For one thing, he was a person of colour at a time when we were pushing equity everywhere. There were only two persons of colour among the government's deputy ministers, and we fire one of them? As it turned out, nobody worked harder than Fazil to prove himself as non-partisan. He was one of my best deputies. I could count on him to talk to the business community in a way high-ranking NDP bureaucrats couldn't—and he did it on our behalf.

Very early on, I fulfilled a campaign promise to go to Washington and try to resolve the softwood lumber dispute with the United States. The media were all saying it was an exercise in futility, that my hubris was showing to think I could solve this, and on and on. There were also a lot of comments about Leo Gerard, who was Canadian and international president of the Steelworkers union. The Steelworkers had made large donations to the NDP in many, many election campaigns. We had promised to ban union and corporate donations, so they were saying I was going to Washington to pick up one last cheque from the Steelworkers. The Liberals said Leo Gerard was my puppet master. Well, Leo had been a key player in Washington, DC, for a decade, which was extraordinary for a Canadian. He opened a dozen doors for us that would not have been opened for Christy Clark. She would have had to rely on pro forma government-to-government meetings set up by our embassy, with people dutifully nodding their heads, and that would be it. But Leo was a personal friend of Wilbur Ross, and he knew Robert Lighthizer, so we were able to sit down with the secretary of commerce and the US trade representative for long meetings and have genuine discussions about the consequences of the softwood lumber tariffs. The National Association of Home Builders said they were desperate for Canadian softwood to help build their communities, which had been hit by hurricane after hurricane. But this small lobby of southeastern US lumber barons was holding up the progress of the nation, and in fact the continent, with their political pressure to keep the duties in place.

I pointed all this out, but there was no budging them. Still, I felt it had been worthwhile. So much for this rube from BC rolling into town. Leo Gerard had opened all these doors for us, and he didn't do it as a favour, he did it because that's what building relationships is all about. That was another lesson for me: If you build positive relationships, you're going to get positive outcomes down the road.

Going to Washington also showed people working in the forest industry that we were serious about their communities and livelihoods. The industry's perception of the NDP had never been good. I remember talking with Duncan Davies of Interfor when I was Opposition leader. I mentioned value-added timber. He rolled his eyes. I said, "Don't you think that's where the industry is headed?" And he said, "Oh, yeah, but every time we hear you and your peers talk about value-added, we can smell the incense burning, and we're waiting for all of us to hold hands." We wanted to change that perception by our actions, not our rhetoric. Going to Washington helped.

I don't mind admitting I was a bit intimidated meeting with these high-powered representatives in the Trump administration, but there's always something that brings it back to reality. They had an issue with Christy Clark's edict that only BC wines could be sold in BC groceries. I remember after the meeting with Lighthizer that his undersecretary literally ran down the stairs to catch us on the street. He said that if we resolved this "stupidity over wine," that would go a long way. I said, "I'll tell you what, you resolve the softwood lumber duties, and we can drink whatever wine you want us to drink, wherever you want us to drink it." I said that with a smile on my face. That was our relationship. We were able to talk about issues that divided us. Over the long term, those things benefit you. You don't necessarily get a result at that moment, but it can pay off later on. Mind you, let's not kid ourselves, the trip to Washington was also an eye-opener. I realized just how intransigent the US administration was. There had almost been a softwood deal under Obama, and Canada said no, we'll wait. It wasn't necessarily a great deal, but it was a deal. Bad decision.

Before we went to Washington, we had stopped off in Ottawa for my first meeting with Prime Minister Justin Trudeau. We both agreed we wouldn't talk about the Kinder Morgan pipeline, which I strongly opposed, mostly because of the threat of an oil spill. The federal Liberals supported it to the extent that a year later they bought it. The major issue I wanted to focus on was softwood lumber, ahead of our trip to Washington. I wanted to make sure the prime minister, the federal trade minister, and all the apparatus of our embassy would weigh in on our behalf. We had a pleasant meeting in his office, and then we headed down the stairs to have a press conference. It was the first one for me with a national audience. I was taken aback by the number of cameras and people there, far more than in sleepy little British Columbia. And they all wanted to know my thoughts.

What happened next is a story I've told many times to many people over the years. I apologize to all those who have heard it before, but it's a good one. There are two plexiglass podiums for us, with glasses of water on a cantilevered plexiglass lift that I was unaware of. I have my hand in my pocket, something I had learned from Bob Dewar: Don't stand there like you're ready for a free kick. Be comfortable. I have a lucky coin in my pocket that the International Brotherhood of Electrical Workers gave me in 2016, and I've had good luck ever since. It was something to play with when my hand was in my pocket. The first question from the gallery is not about housing, not about softwood, it's about the elephant in the room, the Kinder Morgan pipeline. I take my hand out of my pocket to grab the podium and answer the question. And I hit the glass of water. It goes up in the air, swirling around, with water going everywhere. It seemed to take about a hundred years for the glass to start coming down. And at that moment I was thinking of Mike Harcourt, who had gone to Ottawa during the Charlottetown debates and had come back dubbed as Premier Bonehead. Not only was it not good for Mike personally, albeit totally unfair, it was not good for British Columbia. All I could think of was: Horgan goes to Ottawa and screws everything up, bumbling and fumbling. And the glass is spinning and spinning. Then it hits the ground, and it doesn't break. At that moment, I felt my luck. I was the Irish guy again. I looked down at the ground, and I looked up at the camera, and I said, "See, spills can happen everywhere." The media start laughing. And Trudeau, bless him, says, "We'll get someone to clean that up." And I was able to turn to him and say, "Of course you will, spills are a federal responsibility." That set the tone for my relationship with Trudeau and also with the media, that I could make light of a serious situation.

CHAPTER ELEVEN

ON THE JOB

LIBERAL FINANCE MINISTER MIKE DE JONG HAD SCREWED UP THE budget, leaving a huge surplus we didn't know about. That was a gold mine. We were able to get rid of the bridge tolls and MSP premiums right away and still balance the budget. I have to credit him for being so stubborn that he refused to spend a billion dollars, or whatever it was, on making people's lives better. Instead, he decided to leave it for us.

To help make up for the loss of MSP premiums, we brought in an employers' health tax. We hadn't talked about that during the campaign, but the cost to employers at the beginning was insignificant, although it has ratcheted up since then. We raised income and disability assistance rates, which hadn't been increased for ten years. And we waived tuition fees for adult basic education and ESL. I was particularly proud of that. Not everyone learns at the same rate. If you're twenty-three and you want to get your high school certificate and upgrade your skills, why should you pay for that? It was free when you were seventeen. As for ESL, all these immigrants are coming in, and a lot participate in the economy. Why charge them to learn the first language of the province they're working in? It's so self-defeating.

We also provided free post-secondary tuition for kids who aged out of foster care at eighteen. Say you're a young person, who, for whatever reason, has become a ward of the state in someone else's care. Should the state be saying, "Okay, you're eighteen. We're done with you." How many parents would do that? Given the history of horrors and terrible tragedies that have taken place over the decades under the ministry of children and family development, how could we not pay for these kids' tuition? We gave them hope where hope didn't exist. When we made the announcement in Nanaimo, it brought tears to everybody who was there.

We increased the minimum wage. That was dead simple. We also wanted to restore free transit passes for people with disabilities, which the Liberals had done away with. A no-brainer, right? But it became a real hassle since so many separate entities were involved. We ended up giving the exact amount of the subsidy directly back to those on assistance, and they could use it for transit, or not. There were a lot of symbolic issues like that, which cost a bunch of money. I don't know why the Liberals cut things like bus passes, other than sheer mean-spiritedness. These matters are now so normal, no one even thinks about them anymore. They're lost in the mists of time.

The Liberals left behind a long list of things like that, that needed progressive action. All the money lying around allowed us to jam most of them into our first six months, which really set the tone for our government. Every one of our initiatives made sense. Nobody called me a screaming socialist. Nobody said I was out of control. Carole James worked earnestly to steward our resources in our first mini-budget, updating the Liberals' pre-election budget and enabling us to tackle all these areas. People were starting to say, "Okay, they're compassionate, and they're also competent." The Liberals had been convinced we weren't going to last more than a few weeks. Instead, we did all this great stuff. It was fantastic.

Over the course of my first government, with Carole James as finance minister, we chalked up some massive surpluses that allowed us to pay down the provincial debt as well. They weren't because of budget cuts but because of economic growth and strategic tax increases. We were fortunate that Don Wright had been in government before. He didn't need to figure out how things worked. After Don left, Lori Wanamaker, who had been Carole's deputy minister in finance, became my deputy. She was a career public servant. Everyone liked her. She knew where all the bodies were buried, and she was able to move finance in a way that Glen Clark couldn't in 1996.

One of the myth-busting things we were able to do was end the narrative that the NDP can't manage money. Not only did we manage the budget, we reduced costs for people while imposing targeted tax increases to realize policy outcomes. The speculation and vacancy tax was not overly popular, except with the public. It was not merely to raise revenue. The tax was also designed to free up homes that were not being occupied. We added another tax bracket for people making more than $250,000 a year. That brought in resources to help us finance our social policy improvements. Only a small portion of the population was affected. The Liberal opposition and elements of the media tried to characterize it as some sort of huge tax grab, yet generally people thought these were good taxes. That's always the case: The best tax is one that doesn't affect me. We deliberately created that tax bracket to capture the ultra-wealthy, not in a hurtful way, but along the lines of "You're making a fair amount of money and you're not paying a lot of tax. We're going to take some of that." Not only did we balance the budget, and not only did we maintain the highest credit rating of any province in the country, our economy was growing faster than anywhere else. People weren't scared off by the NDP. That had always been the rallying call of the Right. But people were coming here in large numbers. There was opportunity.

One thing that really helped was that I had a relationship with billionaire businessman Jimmy Pattison. It started with Glen Clark being one of his top employees. Then, as Opposition leader, I went to the annual prayer breakfast in Vancouver. They've been going on for more than fifty years. More than a thousand people show up at the Hyatt and have a breakfast. The premier's there, the lieutenant governor is there, the leader of the Opposition, the mayor of Vancouver and a bunch of other people are there, and they all make a few comments. When I became Opposition leader, Adrian Dix said I had to go to the prayer breakfast. I said there's no damn way I'm going. I'm an advocate of the separation of church and state. The Legislature has daily prayers, and I never said one in my eighteen years there. I didn't feel it was appropriate. I am a person of faith, but I did not feel that was relevant to politics.

Adrian insisted that I really had to go. These people needed to see me. If they saw me, he said, they would like me, so grudgingly I went to the prayer breakfast. Jimmy Pattison always goes. He is very much a man of deep faith. You get two minutes and then they give you a passage to read from the Bible. No one knew who I was, but I used a bit of humour, read the passage and sat down. And Jimmy Pattison sent an email to Glen Clark through his assistant, because Jimmy doesn't do emails. He said, "Your guy Horgan was the best one on the stage." This was my first introduction to the business community—at a prayer breakfast I didn't want to go to. The next year I used a bit more humour, and Jimmy says, "There he is again!" So I ended up meeting Jimmy through Glen, and we talked. Then we get into the campaign, and it looks like we're going to form government. One of the other things I did as I threw a lacrosse ball against the wall while waiting for the call from the lieutenant governor was to reach out to Jimmy. I asked if he had any advice for me. And he said, "Well, you've got to keep the bankers happy. If they're not lending money, that means the economy is not going to grow." There were other bits of advice, but that was the one he ended on. However, I had learned something from Andrew MacLeod, a writer for *The Tyee*. He would always pause after one of my answers, and inevitably I would say something more to fill the silence. After Jimmy's last comment, I paused. Then he said, "Would you like me to set up a meeting?" I said that would be great. And he called all these leaders from the business community to come and see Geoff and Bob Dewar and me. I think we had four sessions of fifteen people each over the course of a week and a half.

I would not have been able to get the phone numbers of sixty people in the business community in a year. But Jimmy had phoned them and told them they needed to come, and they did. It was an opportunity for them to kick the tires and an opportunity for me to say, "This is who I am. I want you to make money." I wanted all British Columbians to prosper. I said we needed to work together and hoped they'd help me out. That was the beginning of relationships with a whole bunch of people who otherwise would not have given me the time of day. The Liberals had put the message out that we would screw up and be gone in six weeks, so they shouldn't give us any aid and comfort. But the business community is not really that political. They're more interested in their operations running smoothly. You get that by understanding who's in charge and being able to talk to them. I gave everyone my cellphone number. "Whenever you want to talk to me, give me a call." During our first few months, many of them did call me.

Fast forward to COVID for a moment. We were in an extraordinary time, and we were able to bring business leaders together in an unprecedented way because they knew they had a government and a team who wanted to help them out. We went about solving things. This was a relationship that had borne fruit over time. When we brought in changes to the labour code that under previous NDP administrations might have led instinctively to a strike of capital, they were prepared to give us the benefit of the doubt. We also changed electoral finance laws so business leaders didn't have to go to dinners and eat bad chicken to get access to government. They would have access to government without going to one more dinner, because we needed and wanted to talk to them. To this day, I think that if Jimmy had not filled that silence when I didn't respond to his statement about the bankers, I would never have been able to meet all these people and none of this might have happened.

I now had an RCMP detail assigned to me. At first I didn't want anything to do with them, but they became my dear friends. I'm getting choked up. They were supposed to work only when I was working, but when I later got diagnosed with throat cancer, I went on leave, yet they came and picked me up every bloody day. I don't know why. The last couple of days of treatment, they literally carried me into the cancer clinic. They didn't have to do that. They're just good people. Fuck, I love them today. I'll love them tomorrow.

And they can be RCMP. They can be conservative. If you sat down with Simon, the guy who carried me in, and talked to him, you probably wouldn't agree on much of anything. But at his core, he is a solid human being. And that's what I learned most of all in my time in politics: not to discount the generosity and kindness of people I might otherwise have dismissed for their partisan affiliation. I'm a partisan. I've never apologized for that. But I was prepared to listen to people. At least until they pissed me off, then I could be pretty hard on them. But first, I gave them a big benefit of the doubt.

I lived in a tiny little house on a cul-de-sac in what some might laughingly call the podunk community of Langford. When I became premier, I had no interest in changing that. Our neighbours were the same as they'd always been. It was hard on Ellie because I was away so much, but I think most people would agree that I didn't change that much. The position required that I step up in certain circumstances and be the premier, but at the end of the day, when I put my head on the pillow, it was still "How the hell did this happen?" How did I find myself with people asking me for the final say on these massive decisions? Why are you asking me? Of course it was because I was the guy in the corner office, and I had grown into it. But I don't think I became a different person.

Vaughn Palmer was perhaps the most surprised that I went from miserable Opposition leader to a happy-go-lucky premier. My message to him was simply that I was now getting the opportunity to do the things that I ran for office to do, getting good outcomes for people on tough problems requiring collaboration. Why wouldn't I be happy about that? Why wouldn't that bring joy to my day?

I ran for office in 2005 firstly because I was yelling at my TV and made a commitment to a teenager, but more importantly, I wanted to hang around with smart people again. When I had worked for the NDP governments in the 1990s, I was at a high level doing cool stuff. I was doing things that interested me, and I had missed that. I didn't realize it would be twelve years in opposition before I got that chance again. What made it even worse was that the smart people I used to work with would cross the street if they saw me coming, out of fear the Liberals would see them talking to me. It was like being ostracized. No one was leaking me stuff. Nothing like that happened. We did get some leaks, but not as a result of any relationships I had with public servants.

Once we got into government, it was great. I could phone anybody at any time and ask them a question or get them going on something. Don Wright would come down from upstairs and say, "You can't phone policy analysts and ask them questions. You have to go through the deputy to the assistant deputy to the director to the policy analyst." And I'd go: "Sorry, Don, I won't do it again... until the next time." I'd phone this person and ask them what they were working on. What's interesting to you? For me, it was satisfying genuine intellectual curiosity. At the same time, there were many things I wanted to do that I learned we couldn't do. I accepted that. Some politicians keep on driving because they think their idea is great, but I learned that if we were going to be successful, we had to amalgamate thinking. Not only that of the public service and my political appointees—Geoff, Don Wright and Don Bain, a special adviser who was effectively my Indigenous guy—but also get a sense from a broad cross-section of people. What's achievable, not just what's popular. What can you do that will lay the foundation for more success in the future?

There were a few blips. Our new minister of agriculture, Lana Popham, sent out a letter to some fish farms warning them their leases might not be renewed when they expired. We were already working with First Nations and the companies on a plan for Broughton Inlet, so the timing of her letter was not good. It was thought by some to be a very heavy-handed threat. Lana had spent time in non-governmental organizations, getting petitions signed, going to protests, that sort of thing. Having to leave all that behind and be part of government is not always an easy adjustment. She got a slap on the wrist over her letter. She took it well and became a top-notch agriculture minister. She talked to everybody. It was the perfect portfolio for her. Activism was fine, but we also had a government to run, and we wanted to do that well.

Claire Trevena was minister of transportation. She lived on Quadra Island, used to be a hippie, wanted to nationalize the ferries, make some of them free, and so on. Nutty stuff. She had been the last person I was able to contact among all those who were in the cabinet. We'd told people to stay by their phones on the day we were telling people if they were in or out, but she'd been coming from North Island and turned her phone off. It wasn't until she got to the Malahat Pass that she said to herself, "I guess I'm not in." Then it was like, "Oh, my phone's not on." She turned off the road and there were fifteen messages from John Horgan. She finally phoned me and got the news.

Although ferries were her obsession, she shed all that when I made her a minister. I had given her a tough file, and she exceeded my expectations, more than anyone else in that first cabinet. She continued to talk a lot about ferries, but ferries are always difficult. People want to get on the ferry and they can't. They're pissed off. That happens like clockwork every summer, and there's nothing you can do to fix that. You can play around the edges, throw in more money, build better boats, all that sort of thing, but you can't prevent delays and cancellations. I think she resigned herself to that. Apart from a few things she did around ferries, she began focusing on building highways, getting asphalt down—including, thank goodness, the road to Sooke. She also helped with SkyTrain since transportation was integral to that. I had appointed her for equity reasons, and she worked her ass off. I still had trouble understanding her rich British accent, but she was smart, she could take a briefing, and she didn't mess anything up.

Both Lana Popham and Claire Trevena had been part of the Baker's Dozen that spearheaded the resignation of Carole James, which so angered me at the time. I was fine with their appointments, because Carole had already turned the page. She was hurt by it personally but not politically. Nicholas Simons, who was also in the group, eventually made it into cabinet as well, although Leonard Krog did not. Carole and I both had the view that what happened was in the past. I didn't hold any grudges against them. I was concentrating on the future. As for Bob Simpson, who started it all, he ended up as mayor of Quesnel. We met regularly as part of a kitchen cabinet of Interior mayors to talk about what was going on. Bob was very helpful. Yes, he was a ringleader in the move against Carole James—he didn't like not being in charge—but that was then. We were both on to other things, and he was very helpful. We worked together because it was in the interest of the province.

One of the major issues we had to deal with quickly, just as we were preparing our mini-budget, was the so-called ICBC "dumpster fire." Nearly fifty years earlier, the Dave Barrett government had created public auto insurance in BC. Not surprisingly, the public had forgotten all about that. They had no idea what private auto insurance would cost. They only knew what ICBC was costing them. Since there were no comparators, no one was defending public auto insurance. People were saying, "It sure sucks. Maybe we should change it." There were supporters of the previous government who saw a chance for their own wealth generation by privatizing auto insurance. That's one of the battles between the two solitudes in British Columbia, and we had come in at a time when ICBC's reputation was at its lowest point. We made a commitment to change it and provide better service. Public auto insurance had to be popularized one more time.

Then, out of the blue, we learned there was a hole of more than a billion dollars in ICBC left over from the Liberals that we would have to make up from our budget. Nobody expected that. ICBC's investment portfolio had performed spectacularly poorly, and the costs of litigation were skyrocketing. Every fender bender was a potential lawsuit. The corporation had trouble providing services to people because they didn't know whether they would be sued or not. We came back to the question: Why is ICBC there? It's there for the people of British Columbia and its shareholders, the drivers of BC. They use ICBC not as a lottery ticket but as protection against catastrophic injury, and there had not been adequate compensation for those kind of injuries for generations. We were able to redress those tragedies, and we brought in customer-focused no-fault insurance policies at ICBC rather than allowing litigation on everything. The corporation wound up on a much sounder footing, and that caused us a lot less worry.

We were also able to get started on fulfilling our pledge to implement affordable daycare across the province. That really impacted people. It was something that made a link between the budget and the public, which they don't often feel. Government was doing things that mattered to them. But it couldn't happen overnight. When daycare advocates said we weren't going fast enough, we said we can't do it all. We also needed the federal government, otherwise it just wasn't possible. We needed to train more early childhood educators and create more public sector as well as private sector spaces. That was particularly critical because there was a debate about whether all child-care spaces should be publicly run. We said that would shut down a lot of grandmas who were opening up their homes at the end of the school day to care for kids until mom and dad came and picked them up. Why would we do that?

I'm particularly proud of how we managed it, because we weren't bound by an ideology. We were bound by a commitment to deliver a service. And that meant bringing in this universal institutional program in a way that was not consistent across the board. They say variety is the spice of life, and people live their lives in a variety of ways. One size doesn't fit all. Downtown Vancouver and Fort St. John are different. We had to be flexible. I remember speaking to women in the trades who had to be at work at seven in the morning, and maybe the daycare doesn't open until eight thirty. We needed someone or some family to open up their homes so these workers could drop off their young kids early and get to the work site. Flexibility is key.

Something else we did was ban the grizzly hunt. There was a strong lobby against the ban from the tourism people. I didn't see the sense in trophy hunting—Americans paying fifty grand to shoot a bear, a handful of dudes living in the bush. The guides and outfitters were pissed for sure, but it was popular with the public. It was the right thing to do, and we had promised it.

Meanwhile, we had a serious ongoing wildfire situation in the province. This was an opportunity for me to criss-cross the province, going to all the hot spots. A big challenge was that before I was sworn in, during the two weeks she was still premier, Christy Clark had been visiting various fire areas and promised $100 million in relief, no strings attached. She simply did it. We didn't know what the province's finances were. We had to figure out where she planned to get the $100 million and find a way to attach it to the Red Cross to ensure matching donations and that sort of stuff. Christy had been going around getting pictures taken with people, and I hadn't. She was still thinking there was going to be an election in six weeks. As for me, it was jarring to go to the fire centre in Kamloops and see all the fires on this massive board. It was like the one in *Dr. Strangelove*. It was unbelievable. My brother Brian was a firefighter, and he had told me that if he saw me on TV talking to people off a fire line just for a photo op, he would punch me in the face. Right off the bat, I didn't want to be anywhere other than in the background helping people get the resources they needed. The only pictures were of me in helicopters looking down at the fires. There were none of me talking to guys with charcoal all over their faces, exhausted from doing an extraordinary job.

The emergency centre was all staffed by volunteers from government ministries—from Surrey, from Vancouver, from Kamloops—huddled together in this tiny little office in Merritt. They were trying to manage vouchers for people who had been displaced from their homes and arrange any transportation they needed to get around, while making sure there were resources available to everyone. It was still a paper voucher system, if you can believe that. We couldn't transfer money directly into accounts. We were able to do that by year three, but at the beginning it was like out of the 1950s. It was inspiring to see the level of commitment from the BC Wildfire Service and the number of volunteers who reported for emergency management. It was like, holy cow, how do all these people come together? How do we evacuate large populations from their homes? Everyone was amazing.

As this was going on, we were trying to find a Speaker for the Legislature. We were government, but, with the Greens, we had only a one-seat majority. If we had to appoint one of our own MLAs as Speaker, then he or she might have to be in that situation I've mentioned and break a whole bunch of tie votes. That was hardly ideal. When Christy had called back the Legislature, they had named Steve Thompson as Speaker. I like him. He's a nice guy, and he was one of the people I had in mind to try and pull in as Speaker, but nope. The second was Linda Reid. She had been Speaker before, and she had appreciated the support I had given her during a controversy over some expensive drapes and other things she had ordered. She more or less agreed, but the Liberal hammers came crashing down on her, and that was the end of that. So we were in a bit of a bind. We thought we would make Mike Farnworth the Speaker. He would have been happy to do it, but it would be a big loss to cabinet, and we would have to try and manage votes without him as House leader. Then, God love him, Darryl Plecas showed up out of the blue from the Liberals, saying, "I hate these people." He liked the idea of being Speaker. I don't want to diminish in any way the commitment he made, because he had crap raining down on him from Liberals everywhere. He was also steadfast in trying to clean up the place. He uncovered a kind of garden-variety scandal with some improper stuff, and a controversy over a wood splitter. Despite some of Darryl's goofy press conferences, these improprieties would have been undiscovered were it not for him. He deserves full credit for that. By serving as Speaker, he also gave us the space to have a government. It all worked out perfectly for me once again. I fell into a pile of poo and came out smelling purple simply through dumb luck.

CHAPTER TWELVE

THE BIG THREE

On taking power, the Horgan government had three massive resource projects that had to be dealt with. All were fraught with controversy.

Kinder Morgan's Trans Mountain pipeline, running 980 kilometres from Alberta to an export terminal in Burnaby, was an expansion of an existing pipeline that would triple capacity and greatly increase the number of oil tankers travelling through Burrard Inlet. When Kinder Morgan walked away from the project in 2018, citing soaring costs and widespread protests by First Nations and environmental groups, the federal government bought the pipeline. The BC NDP had opposed the pipeline expansion since 2013.

During the 2013 election campaign, Premier Christy Clark promised at least three liquefied natural gas (LNG) plants would be up and running by 2020, exporting gas to Asian markets, with more to follow. In the end, out of all the LNG projects Clark had been promoting, only LNG Canada, led by Shell, was still on the table when the NDP took over. LNG Canada was potentially the largest private-sector investment in Canadian history, but the project would also increase carbon emissions, which drew the ire of the NDP's government partners, Andrew Weaver and the Green Party.

The idea of adding a third dam to two existing dams on the Peace River had been studied since 1971. Premier Gordon Campbell gave the green light to the huge undertaking in 2010, pointing to the province's future energy demands. More than 5,500 hectares of farmland would be flooded by Site C, as the dam was called. Under Campbell's successor, Christy Clark, the province aggressively pushed forward with the complex multi-billion-dollar project, bypassing BC Hydro's independent watchdog, the BC Utilities Commission. Clark vowed to push Site C's construction "past the point of no return" so that no future government would be able to undo its construction. The Green Party and most of the NDP opposed Site C.

AFTER THE TRUDEAU GOVERNMENT BOUGHT KINDER MORGAN, IT became the Trans Mountain pipeline, which was shortened to TMX. Along with LNG and Site C, these projects seemed to involve half the alphabet, and they were three big problems for us. I sometimes called them the Holy Trinity. One way or the other, we had to find agreements for all of them while most people were getting on with their lives, blissfully ignorant of our need for clean energy, the abundance of natural gas trapped in the northeast unable to get to markets, and the vexing problem Alberta had with a pipeline that affected everyone in BC.

I had campaigned against the Kinder Morgan pipeline, but it really goes back to the 2013 election. Even though I was the energy critic, Adrian Dix had announced during the campaign that we were going to stop it, without talking to me or anyone else. When that happened, as I indicated earlier, there were members of the building trades who literally put down their signs supporting the NDP and walked away from the photograph they were supposed to be part of. I'm not saying it wasn't the right thing to do—polling suggested it was—but I was Adrian's best friend, and I knew nothing about it. I've also mentioned how embarrassing it was to have to phone Ian Anderson, the CEO of Kinder Morgan, and tell him he could do whatever he wanted because we were now officially opposed to the pipeline—the day after I'd asked him to hold off of any decisions until after the election.

I'm not passing judgement on the decision itself. It was the way it happened. Opposition to Kinder Morgan became party policy and was part of my own campaign. The pipeline would triple existing capacity and make our dynamic, tourism-driven metropolitan centre into a port for the export of oil. That was anathema to most British Columbians. We vowed we would use all the tools in our tool kit to bring it to a halt. It was not so much the pipeline but all those tankers going through Burrard Inlet that concerned us.

The Greens supported our intention to do everything we could to ensure it didn't go ahead. The Christy Clark government had approved the expansion in early 2017. We didn't know then that those pipeline decisions made under the Liberals bound any future government and the Crown to respect them. Only after we were sworn in did we discover we were basically stymied. We had an obligation to protect the integrity of the Crown, which had made these decisions in good faith. That meant, if we carried out the plan we had laid out for the public, we could be sued. My heart hadn't changed, but the best and most obvious of all the tools we hoped to use—simply not letting it proceed—was not possible without significant cost. We set about recalibrating how to take it on. I had put George Heyman in charge of the environment for us. With his Sierra Club background, he was a good, solid environmentalist. He had also been head of a major union, the BCGEU. He was very articulate on these issues. We didn't get off the same page too many times.

Alberta and Ottawa characterized building the pipeline as a way to sell more oil from the oil sands to international markets.

But for British Columbia, it was a pipeline across two mountain ranges into our beautiful Lower Mainland, with an export terminal at the end. A tanker a day would be heading out, putting our pristine coastline at risk. That was how most British Columbians felt about it, and that's what we were committed to halt. We never wavered from our opposition, but we hit those obstacles I mentioned, and, as a pragmatic government for all British Columbians, we had to manage them. We gave it our best shot. We put a legal team in place and hired the venerable and respected lawyer Tom Berger. He told us, quite frankly, that we didn't have many good tools in that much-talked-about tool box of ours. But George Heyman continued to be aggressive, a bit too much so for my taste. I was worried George was going to make promises we couldn't keep. Then we got into a bigger fight with Rachel Notley, who of course was the NDP premier of Alberta at the time.

I was in Asia on a trade mission that was very important to us. If our exports are not going to the States, they are going to Asia. Natural gas was our big issue. We wanted to get LNG and a range of other matters into a trade package we could bring back to British Columbians. In the middle of it all, George announced a new pipeline regulation that, I think it's fair to say, he didn't think was all that big a deal. Well, Rachel Notley did, and the national media did, and all of a sudden there's a battle. I first heard about it when I was in Tokyo sitting with the CEO of Mitsubishi. He was giving his condolences on the passing of my brother, who had died from cancer a week earlier. That's how good these people are. Who's this in front of me and what do I need to know? They don't know me from Adam, but they want to have a personal conversation. I have to say, I was a bit blindsided by George's announcement, but I was even more taken aback by Notley's response. It had all seemed pretty innocent to me—until I got back. A pair of social democratic governments had managed to create a catastrophic event between the two of them.

The proposed changes George announced would have stopped any increase in the shipment of bitumen through BC until the impact of potential oil spills had been studied. But these were draft regulations. There was going to be consultation. It wasn't like they were going to happen tomorrow. It was an opportunity to say we were exploring another tool. Although the consequences might have been a game-changer, it was certainly not a game-changer at that point. You're inviting the industry and you're inviting the community to weigh in. This is boilerplate for the NDP: Let's talk to people and figure out the best way through this morass. But it got sidetracked.

Rachel hit the roof. She banned the import of BC wines into Alberta and threatened to cut off all oil shipments to BC. We were both long-time NDP-ers. I thought we had a relationship. I thought we were friends. One of her communications people corrected me in the media, saying we were only acquaintances, so I guessed that was the end of whatever relationship we had. I was disappointed because there had never been NDP premiers presiding over the third- and fourth-largest economies in the country. BC and Alberta could have done spectacular things were it not for the elephant in the room, the Trans Mountain pipeline. It was critical to Rachel and Alberta, and very much not critical to British Columbia. For us, there were all the downsides and zero benefit.

I was not upset at George. He was doing what he thought was right, and, quite frankly, it was what he had been directed to do: to manage a way, within our ability, to not enable the pipeline to proceed. I was more upset by Rachel's reaction. She overreacted to what were draft regulations she would have input into. But to her, it was a slap in the face at a time when her back was against the wall. She was the first NDP premier of Alberta, she was in the middle of her term, and to be able to deliver this pipeline was a key part of differentiating her from the past seven hundred years of conservative rule. I understood that. She didn't have to explain it to me. I do think we could have done a better job of managing it, and I take responsibility for that. I didn't blame George. He was doing his job.

We had thought we were on solid legal ground to stop the pipeline, until we got to government; then we learned that despite our ideas, we also had the responsibility to defend the integrity of the government of British Columbia, which had made the previous decisions. When I became premier, I did not want to be overseeing a series of court cases where British Columbians were successfully taking the government to court, all because they had been granted rights by the Crown. And the Crown was now me. The last message we wanted to send was that we were going to be reckless and draw a line in the sand. That also meant I didn't want to get into sabre-rattling with Rachel Notley. I tried to find the best way to negotiate our way out of this. It was like being at a union bargaining table. What's the best way forward: standing on a picket line or finding an agreement both sides can live with?

Rachel had a different set of dynamics. She had to try to get re-elected. I had a bunch of other variables, and her success or failure was not one of them. I had just been elected. I was certain in my path, and I knew that the BC public was on my side. People did not want to have Vancouver turn into an expanded oil export terminal. We had already seen the sinking of the *Nathan E. Stewart* tug, which ran aground during pretty calm weather, spilling more than a hundred thousand litres of diesel fuel into the waters off the central coast. The impact on the environment up there was profound, and that was just a tug and barge, not a supertanker filled with diluted bitumen. I wished Rachel well, but I had these other interests in front of me. I suggested we refer the matter to the Supreme Court for a constitutional ruling. Did we have the right as a province to interfere with the movement of oil? Rachel accepted that. I think she realized at a certain point that, although I was a convenient foil for her, I could not be what would get her re-elected. At the end of the day, she had to fight the Conservatives. Scrapping with me, with all the volunteers from British Columbia who might come and help her out, was not going to be useful.

In the end, the Supreme Court ruled against us and we lost the case. I wasn't uncomfortable with that. George was probably more ticked off about it than I was. For me it was like, okay, that's out of our way, what's next? And I have to confess that putting regulation changes in place after the pipeline's regulatory framework was already well established had not been well understood. Although not unreasonable, it might have been a bridge too far. If you're going to go through with something like that, it's good to find out if you're on sound constitutional ground rather than having it thrown out later. We said we would take it all the way to the Supreme Court of Canada. That's what we did, and we lost. In a community governed by laws, you need to abide by them, so that was the end of our tool box.

Another story about Kinder Morgan. Trudeau had just bought the pipeline, and he called Rachel and me to Ottawa. We flew all the way there and were stuck in his office, which I characterized as the principal's office, for two and a half hours, just the three of us going back and forth. I was not moving from our opposition to the pipeline. I'd got nowhere to move. I was thinking we could have done this on the phone. The meeting finally ended. It was agreed that I would speak to the media first, then the two of them would come out and beat me up. I was fine with that. As we were waiting for them to set up the press conference, I said, "Well, that wasn't so bad. My only regret is that I missed the Vaisakhi parade." Rachel said, "I missed it, too." And Trudeau turns to us and says, "You had to bring up India, didn't you? You just had to bring it up." This was after his famous trip to India where he'd been ridiculed by a lot of people for his costume changes. Even though this was a difficult day, it showed me a side of Justin Trudeau that I liked. He was able to be self-deprecating and make light of what could only be described as a tense couple of hours between three progressive politicians.

Christy Clark had seemed to promise an LNG chicken in every pot during the Liberals' campaign in 2013. I mocked their belief that this was going to happen in every community she visited. In fact, one, maybe two, was the most we could manage in terms of crews to build them, getting pipes to tidewater, the cost, and meeting contractual obligations. They created all these circumstances, phony news conferences and so on, where they would talk about LNG, how it would make BC debt free, when the chances of them actually delivering anything were remote. It was mostly fiction. I was also critical of the industry. We have this extraordinary amount of natural gas at our disposal and an inability to get it to market. They were talking about all this and not doing anything about it, so when we came to government, we set out four principles on LNG: We were all in if Indigenous people could get a genuine benefit; if workers were paid fairly; if there was no negative impact on our climate action plans; and if there would be an overall reduction in emissions. We didn't want to bring in boatloads of people to do this work. We wanted to create jobs in British Columbia.

After we had been sworn in, I went to Kitimat. It was primarily to see the new smelter. I had worked on Alcan issues in the 1990s. The company was now Rio Tinto, but Richard Prokopanko, their communications guy from that time, was still there. He showed me some faxes we had sent to each other in the mid-nineties, noting that we had been friends for a long time. We wanted to celebrate the smelter, which had cut emissions and reduced electricity consumption. While we were up there, we met with Andy Calitz, director of the LNG Canada consortium that was led by Shell. By then, Chevron and Petronas had backed away. They were tired of going to industry conferences while nothing was getting done. Out of all the LNG projects trumpeted by Christy Clark, only Shell was still in the game, but their project was a doozy. They were planning a pipeline to run nearly 700 kilometres from the Montney gas field near Dawson Creek to Kitimat, where it would feed a massive LNG Canada export facility. It would mean 7,500 construction jobs and 300 permanent jobs. Andy had an office in Kitimat, and he invited me to come and hear their story. He described where the industry in BC was going. He said it could be competitive, but government needed to shave some pennies from what their input costs were going to be.

We took that seriously, and we put together an LNG fiscal framework that was for anyone who wanted to come. It wasn't just for Shell. We said we will provide a break on provincial sales tax on the project's construction. We will let you defer it. The Greens and others accused us of giving the industry a huge subsidy. Well, it wasn't a subsidy, it was a tax break. They still owed us the money. It's complicated, but if they spent $1 billion on input costs in British Columbia, they would owe us the tax on that, but they wouldn't have to start paying it until they came on stream. That allowed them to build the project and not incur the cost of taxes during the capital phase. That seemed a reasonable concession without giving them a direct subsidy. We were not giving anything to Shell we wouldn't give to anyone else. There were a couple of other things, but they weren't unusual in an environment where government is trying to encourage private sector investment. These were concessions we were prepared to make. There would be a huge benefit down the road from something that would not have happened if we hadn't paved the way. That's the difference between a subsidy and an investment. We weren't giving anything away, because there was nothing to give. We also saw an enormous amount of income tax from the thousands of construction jobs. This was a $40-billion project, which was, to then, the largest private sector investment in Canadian history.

The contract had a lot of fail-safes to protect the province. There was a guy in finance, Doug Foster, who I jokingly called a junkyard dog, but I appreciated him. He had been in government so long, I think he had worked under the Socreds, and he kept track of every dollar spent. Everyone respected his intellect and his corporate memory, but they didn't want to run afoul of him, because in his mind every dollar spent was provincial taxpayers' money, and he was a provincial taxpayer. And Doug was on our side. He said we could find a way to do this within the regulations and within our purse. Thanks to the smart people we had in the finance department, like Doug and Lori Wanamaker, we were able to demonstrate that we could put these initiatives in place and keep the province's finances whole.

We also felt we should get credit if China bought LNG and that reduced their carbon emissions through closed coal plants. Right now, China gets all the credits for that, and we don't get any. The producers of the gas are creating emissions to reduce emissions elsewhere, but they only get charged with their emissions. Article 6 of the COP conferences has been working on a way to change that, but it's taking a long time.

LNG was a tough sell to our caucus. But it was a good test of how we were going to handle these big, controversial issues and bring people along. As premier, and as a member of the cabinet, you have all this information that others don't have access to. We had to involve caucus in a way that didn't violate cabinet confidences but gave them comfort. We also needed time for their inboxes to calm down. When governments make decisions, there's often an inundation of correspondence from the public. Sometimes it's personal, and sometimes they're form letters driven by advocacy groups. Those groups have people in the communities where members of our caucus live. Maybe someone who'd been chair of their sign crew says they're not going to help anymore because of this or that policy. That wakes them up. It's the day-to-day of politics. You want to make sure your base is satisfied—not at all costs, but enough that people have faith you're making judgements in their interest. Caucus members had to understand why we came to this decision. I think we were successful. George Heyman was one of those initially uncomfortable with LNG, but he wasn't leading any group challenging my leadership. Mike Harcourt had a group. Glen Clark had a group. And I've talked about the group that Carole James had. I don't recall any such group manifesting itself while I was premier. And, at the end of the day, when we made the decision to facilitate LNG investment in the province, George was great.

There was a time when matters got tense with our MLA for Bulkley Valley–Stikine, Doug Donaldson, over the Wet'suwet'en blockade of the pipeline route. Doug is someone I have great respect for, but he had real challenges because of his passion for Wet'suwet'en issues. That's what got him involved in politics in the first place, and first and foremost, he is a local politician. The protests proved a real challenge for him. He believed that the Delgamuukw-Gisday'wa decision by the Supreme Court, which recognized Indigenous title, should have been implemented back in the 1990s. If it had been, he argued, everything would be completely different. But it wasn't. As a minister of the Crown (Forests, Lands and Natural Resources) and also a friend of the people on the protest lines, Doug was conflicted. At one point, he paid them a visit and was on their line. That was the closest I came to having to remove someone from cabinet. It was really tough for both of us, but I think we are stronger friends now as a result. I had complete confidence in him, and he knew that. I gave him as much latitude as he needed to meet the expectations of his neighbours, who he cared for more than being in cabinet. He told me that if I needed to kick him out, that would be fine, but he could not abandon the people he knew. We managed to get through it, but it was this close. It wasn't acrimonious, it was just painful.

There was also the issue of fracking. The NDP had a record of opposing it. I had opposed it, too. But we've opposed this, and we've opposed that, and we've never come within a sniff of winning up there in the Peace, where most of the fracking goes on. A fundraising letter from someone that ends up in somebody's inbox is different than actually dealing with the consequences for all the people who work in that sector and those who live up there. The people in the Peace disagree with the people who live in Kitsilano on many issues. The job of government is to manage those things, and that's what we tried to do. No one was surprised in the caucus when I told them before, during and after the election that if we can find a way to create jobs and wealth to pay for the programs we want to deliver, we would aim to do that. We get most of our revenue from private sector investments, not from projects in the public sector.

Finally, I know I've already said this once, but let me say it again so people don't forget: LNG was the largest private-sector investment in Canadian history, and it took place under an NDP government.

Deciding what to do about Site C was another exceptionally hard decision for our government. We had been very critical of the way the Liberals handled it. They had sidelined the BC Utilities Commission and pushed ahead with very little assessment. However, despite what many people thought, and what a few of our candidates may have said during the election campaign, we did not promise to stop the dam. We promised an independent review. Then we would make a decision.

I had a good grasp of energy issues in British Columbia. When we were in government back in the 1990s, I had worked on projects for the BC Power Corporation, and I had worked on renewal of the Columbia River Treaty. I understood energy. Site C had been on the books for forty years. It was not a dam on a pristine river, but the third dam on a river that was already managed. Nonetheless, it was orthodoxy for the NDP to oppose it, largely because of the impact on agricultural land and a range of other issues that got piled on. There were those who said a sub-climate existed around Fort St. John where you could grow extraordinary subtropical fruits like cantaloupe that you couldn't grow anywhere else in BC. It was mostly nonsense. It's true there was a sub-climate, but conditions were not sufficient to feed a significant number of people, particularly with the cost of moving food to markets in the south. Almost nothing was growing there except silage. The argument that this was agricultural land that would

John Horgan, almost two, basks in the sun on the front lawn of the family home in Saanich, BC. *Horgan family collection*

In August of 1986, just back from Australia, John and Ellie bought a 1967 Buick from friends in Victoria for $17.50 and drove it across Canada, looking for suitable employment as they travelled. Eventually, both found work in Ottawa. *Horgan family collection*

Alice Horgan's four children gathered in July of 1987 to commemorate her sixty-fifth birthday. *Back row, left to right:* Brian, Pat and Kathy. *Front:* Alice and John. *Horgan family collection*

Opposite top: Horgan was elected on his first foray into electoral politics in 2005, after fifteen years working behind the scenes for the NDP. For his second campaign, in 2009, friends and family were still pitching in to help with signage. *BC NDP*

Opposite bottom: Campaigning as party leader in 2017, Horgan hit all the right notes at a crowd-pleasing gathering in Vancouver, surrounded by local candidates. *BC NDP*

BCNDP
John
Horgan

John Horgan

In what became known as the Rugby Summit, BC Green Party leader Andrew Weaver and John Horgan were spotted enjoying themselves at a women's rugby match in Langford. The next day, May 29, 2017, the two leaders announced their parties' historic agreement to defeat the BC Liberals and give the NDP a shot at government. Few thought their appearance together at the rugby match was a coincidence. *The Canadian Press / Chad Hipolito*

Bob Dewar journeyed from Manitoba to become Horgan's chief of staff when the NDP ship appeared to be sinking, and played a critical, strategic role in the 2017 election. The two posed happily together shortly after negotiation of the NDP–Green Party agreement that ensured the downfall of the BC Liberals. *BC NDP*

John Horgan was sworn in by Lieutenant Governor Judith Guichon as British Columbia's thirty-sixth premier on July 19, 2017.
Province of British Columbia

Helping organizations celebrate special days was now part of the job. Three weeks after being sworn in as premier, Horgan relished the chance to smash right through a board on Taekwondo Day.
Province of British Columbia

Marching with Musqueam Chief Wayne Sparrow, Indigenous Relations and Reconciliation Minister Scott Fraser, and Fraser's wife, Delores, as part of the 2017 Walk for Reconciliation through downtown and East Vancouver. *Province of British Columbia*

Opposite top: During all his time in politics, including his five years as premier, Horgan never lost touch with a close-knit group of friends who'd known each other since they were teenagers. They continued to get together as often as they could, as in this gathering at Shuswap Lake in 2018. *From left to right:* Horgan, Drew Finerty, Michael Allabarton, Clay Booth and Keith Bridge. *Horgan family collection*

Opposite bottom: John Horgan and federal NDP leader Jagmeet Singh took part in Victoria's annual Pride Parade in 2018. *BC NDP*

As a long-time Trekkie, the name applied to devotees of the *Star Trek* series, Horgan was thrilled when he got to meet George Takei in Vancouver, where he was on a TV shoot. (Takei played Lieutenant Hikaru Sulu.) Horgan presented him with a pin from the famous Asahi Japanese-Canadian baseball team, and the two had no problem displaying the Vulcan salute.
Province of British Columbia

Opposite top: After announcing $2.5 million in new government funding to encourage "under-represented kids" in sport on May 10, 2019, Horgan displayed some of his own skill with a lacrosse stick, effortlessly firing the ball towards the net. *Province of British Columbia*

Opposite bottom: At the seventy-fifth anniversary of Canadian troops' D-Day landing on Juno Beach, Horgan chatted with Victoria veteran George Chow, who enlisted to fight for a country that denied him the vote and other basic citizenship rights. *Province of British Columbia*

John Horgan and Carole James forged a friendship and an unbreakable political bond that lasted from James's leadership of the BC NDP in the 2005 election until her retirement from politics in 2020. Both enjoyed their appearance together at a Labour Day picnic on the lawn of the Legislature in 2019. *BC NDP*

With his public popularity at a sky-high level, Horgan was greeted with a rapturous ovation at the provincial NDP's annual convention in 2019. *BC NDP*

This was a happy moment for the Horgan family, often separated by distance, as Ellie and John sat outside on their back deck with their sons during the COVID summer of 2020. Nate (*with hat*) had to isolate for five days after arriving from London. His partner, Daisy, was not allowed to accompany him because she was not a Canadian citizen. *Horgan family collection*

John Horgan, mask in hand, watches as Health Minister Adrian Dix expands on details of BC's fall preparedness plan to confront the ongoing spread of COVID-19. Announced on September 9, 2020, the plan called for $1.6 billion in new spending to hire thousands more health-care workers and bolster existing public health measures. *Province of British Columbia*

With COVID-19 still spreading in the province, it was an election announcement like no other: no hoopla, no raft of cabinet ministers crowding the podium. Horgan stood alone in front of a suburban backyard in his home riding of Langford–Juan de Fuca to announce that British Columbians would go to the polls, despite the pandemic, on October 24, 2020. *The Canadian Press / Chad Hipolito*

Opposite top: On July 9, 2021, there was the serious announcement of a federal–provincial deal to cooperate on ten-dollar-a-day childcare, and then it was time for burgers. Horgan and Prime Minister Justin Trudeau sat down for a takeout lunch at the White Spot in Coquitlam. *The Canadian Press / Chad Hipolito*

Opposite bottom: Not long after announcing his intention to step down, Horgan hosted the country's premiers and territorial leaders at a meeting of the Council of the Federation in Victoria. *Left to right:* Doug Ford (ON), François Legault (QC), Scott Moe (SK), Andrew Furey (NL), Dennis King (PEI), Tim Houston (NS), Blaine Higgs (NB), Sandy Silver (YT) and Horgan. *Province of British Columbia*

GREAT TASTE TO GO!

Towards the tail end of his time as premier, Horgan posed with members of the RCMP security detail who were assigned to him. He formed a special bond with them. *From left to right:* Erin Harding, Simon Scully, Andrew Treskin, Horgan, Greg Haasdyk, Alexa Von Fersen and Dan Louie. *Province of British Columbia*

David Eby was sworn in as Horgan's replacement on November 18, 2022, at the Musqueam Cultural Centre. Sharing a lighthearted moment in the front row were long-time Chinese-Canadian activist Shirley Chan, former NDP deputy premier Joy MacPhail, Horgan, Lieutenant Governor Janet Austin and David Eby. *Province of British Columbia*

As he and Ellie stopped to smell the lilacs a few minutes from their stylish official ambassador's residence in the Berlin district of Dahlem, Horgan snapped a selfie. *Horgan family collection*

On weekends, the Horgans often headed out to explore Berlin. Here they are at their local U-Bahn station in early May of 2024, on the way to Krumme Lanke in the southwest of the city, on the edge of the Grunewald forest. *Horgan family collection*

Shortly before his resignation took effect, Horgan posed for one final portrait in the office he had occupied as premier from 2017 to 2022. *Province of British Columbia*

be lost forever was correct, but what would we have been able to create on that land other than canola and silage? When you take transportation into consideration, like, hey, not much.

When I was in opposition, I had gone up there with my wife. We called it the "Dam Moose Tour." Ellie wanted to see moose. I wanted to see dams. We ended up going to the Bennett and Peace Canyon Dams and to Site C. As is my wont, I engaged with people. I wanted to find out what the real deal was, because I knew the history of the NDP and I knew the history of Site C. Famously, there's a picture of me with a "Site C Sucks" sign in it. I was also aware of Hydro's unfortunate treatment of people in the Kootenays with the Two Rivers Policy, which flooded good agricultural land and forced so many people to relocate. Going to the Peace River did have an impact on me. The valley is beautiful. And as an energy guy, the more I thought about the cost, the more I thought that maybe there were newer technologies coming in that we could harness. I genuinely went back and forth on the efficacy of this investment for energy production.

But British Columbia is in a perfect spot to take advantage of our natural abundance of energy. Site C was going to be a component of that. When the Liberals first announced the dam in 2010, Andrew Weaver was there for the photo. He hadn't been elected. He was a climate scientist. He liked clean energy. Since that announcement, the dam was being purposely advanced, in the infamous words of Christy Clark, to "the point of no return." I immediately ridiculed her statement. It was absurd. You shouldn't be making policy based on "How do we prevent the other guys from stopping us?"

At the same time, I knew that if we were going to address climate change and reduce our dependence on fossil fuels, we still needed energy. We have an abundance of wind and solar, and opportunities for geothermal we haven't even looked at, plus this large megaproject on the Peace River. At no time did I ever say it was the worst thing ever and needed to be killed. We had people running for office who did say that, and I would correct those statements whenever I was asked. But the Liberals had done the project no favours by turning it into a wedge issue. That's the traditional way to differentiate yourselves from your opponents: "We're going to do this, and they're not." It bugs me on a personal level. It's disingenuous, and it doesn't advance our interests at all. Climate change is too important for that kind of partisanship.

Two weeks after we were sworn in, we asked the BC Utilities Commission to review the economic viability of Site C and recommend whether we should proceed, suspend or terminate. It had been ill-advised to undertake Site C the way the Liberals had. They were taking advice from a group of people who had wanted to do this for a very long time. They were no longer receptive to counter-arguments within BC Hydro.

Jessica McDonald was Hydro's president and CEO. She was not a friend of the NDP. She had taken ownership of Site C and was driving it on behalf of the Liberal government. She separated herself from previous CEOs at Hydro by never agreeing to meet with me. All the others did, even though it was more like, "Oh, God, I've got to meet with that guy Horgan." She would not, and it was at a critical time before the election. I wanted to be briefed on where we were at, but she was dismissive of our concerns. That's fair in some ways, because some of them were unfounded. But they were still concerns. As head of a public body, you should at least be responsive to them, so I asked her to suspend activity on Site C until after the election. She rejected that. Again, that wasn't unreasonable for her to do, but it said to me that she was not prepared to work with us should we form government.

When I became party leader, Adrian Dix took over from me as energy critic, and he was ruthless. I think he got under Jessica McDonald's skin enough for her to say that I'm not dealing with these people. It was no surprise to anyone that we would bring change to BC Hydro. I appointed Ken Peterson as Hydro's new chair. He had been head of Powerex under the previous NDP government, when they made an enormous amount of money selling electricity. That had enabled us to balance the budgets in 2000 and 2001.

Meanwhile, we were getting lots of leaks about dysfunction at Hydro from people working there. Jessica McDonald is a very capable person who has a lot to offer the people of BC. She has in the past and will in the future. But we had to deal with Site C and a range of other issues, and she was not the right person to be at BC Hydro. We let her go and started the process of review. This was not simply for my benefit because, as I've said, I had so many positions on Site C over the years it could be argued that I had experienced the *Kama Sutra* of Hydro positions. I didn't want us to be accused of putting our thumb on the scales. I wanted any decision we made to be evidence-based. We should lay it out for the public, tell them why we made the judgement we did, and not be apologetic about it.

As it turned out, the review by the BC Utilities Commission provided us with a ton of information on Site C but stopped short of making a recommendation. Instead, they laid out the implications of proceeding and the implications of not proceeding. That meant it was totally up to us to decide whether to go or not to go. The only time I've had someone come up to me at an airport and kind of shake a finger at me was just before we made our decision. It was a guy flying up to Fort St. John to work, and he was yelling at me about taking away his job. I was standing there taking it, and a crowd started to gather. He said Site C was critical to his family. I said it was critical to all British Columbians. It's not just about you. It's about all of us. At that, this guy seemed to lose hope and went away. I've always wanted to meet him again and ask, "So, how'd it go? How's everything going?" It was one of those moments. There were people with their phones. I don't know how many people recorded it. As a public official, you just have to take it. He was mad as a March hare because he thought my ideological extremism was going to take away his livelihood. In fact, I wanted to say, "Dude, I can't tell you how many backflips I'm doing to figure out how we can all benefit from the decision we make."

Before we decided, I wanted to make sure all my colleagues had some understanding of the complexity of what we were faced with. I don't mean to sound arrogant, but I was being paid for decades to think about energy issues, and electricity issues in particular. We brought in a large number of people to talk to us—energy lawyers, energy experts, even people who opposed the project. They were sworn under a confidentiality oath, which allowed them to be present for cabinet deliberations. We were preparing the cabinet for what we kind of knew was going to happen. Site C was going to be a lot harder to undo than TMX, which had not really begun in any meaningful way. Site C already had all these sunk costs and contractual obligations. It was well advanced. Bringing in these experts with their different points of view allowed us to weigh the pros and cons. And that was what we did. If it had not been a serious review, we would have been dead in the water with the Greens and many elements of the NDP. We really piled it on.

The Liberals seemed to be motivated only by getting it past the point of no return. What were the politics in that? It rings in my ears to this day. For me, it was not the politics but the policy. I don't want to sound too much like a policy wonk. I understand retail politics, too. But I think you can marry the two, and that's what I've always tried to do. Whether I was giving advice as a staffer, doing work as a critic, or implementing policy as premier, it was: "What is it that you're doing? Why are you doing it? And can you explain it to the people in a way that they will nod their heads and move on?"

We stayed away from the First Nations. That was a matter of social justice, environmental sovereignty, and rights and title. Those were separate from the question of the project's economic viability. I felt we shouldn't conflate an already complicated issue with another set of complicated issues. The West Moberly First Nations and others were already in court. We had no idea how that was going to unfold, although eventually it unfolded in a way that produced settlements everywhere.

When we announced our decision to finish the dam, someone said to me that Michelle Mungall, George Heyman and I looked as if we'd had our dog put down. That was genuine. Nobody came to this decision lightly. No one was happy about it. But there was nothing more we could have done to inform ourselves about what to do. Building Site C was not something I would have done. I would rather have spent all those billions on alternatives, because you can disperse them. You can use them for economic development and a raft of other things. But cancelling it at that point would have meant taking on $4 billion of obligations, plus all the litigation that would have followed. That would have led to a big spike in electricity rates, which flew in the face of our commitment to reduce or at least freeze them. And we would still need 1,100 megawatts of energy to make up what Site C would have produced. What's more, it would have taken two or three years to decommission the dam, at a cost of another billion dollars or so, just in time for the election. All these factors weighed on us. It came down to what was the worst or best option. And the best option was to eat our porridge and go ahead. To repeat, we would have made a different decision if circumstances had been otherwise, but they were what they were. The financial implications of cancelling Site C tipped the balance. Billions of dollars would have been flushed down the toilet, even before the lawsuits. I'm passionate about the environment, but if we're blowing all that money and saying no to resource development, how are we going to pay for all the good stuff like affordable child care that we want to do? Not just right-wingers are saying that. Left-wingers are saying that. It's me saying that.

We went to caucus at least three times over Site C. Everyone had a chance to make points and argue against it, but it got to where they were repeating the same arguments, and the group opposing it was getting smaller. The caucus wasn't unlike the public. Tell me why we're doing this. If it makes sense to me, I'll go and try to tell other people why we're doing it. When our MLAs went home for Christmas, they waited for mass membership cancellations. That didn't happen. I got more mail from people saying they didn't think I would do that and "good for you" than I did from people ripping up their NDP membership cards. I firmly believe some people join the NDP just so they can rip up their membership cards at some point over some issue they feel strongly about. The best example of public reaction was Ronna-Rae Leonard, who won Courtenay–Comox by so few votes for us in 2017. Every Friday for three years, there were people carrying anti–Site C signs outside her office. She was convinced she was a one-term MLA. In 2020, she was re-elected by five thousand votes.

Is my party now glad we have Site C? Absolutely. So are the Greens. They might dispute that, but when they plug in their hybrids...

The demand for clean energy is only going to go up. There's also the fact that when you're doing megaprojects—whether it's the Pattullo Bridge, the transit line, the dam or whatever—it's not just the result you get, it's the wealth you create for communities and individuals.

As for the West Moberly, Saulteau and other Treaty 8 Nations up there, they came to a resolution with BC Hydro, and they are benefiting, too. These are very small communities. It doesn't diminish their rights that there are three hundred people in a Nation, but it's three hundred people and there are five million British Columbians. As much as I am mindful of the consequences of our decisions on the First Peoples, whose rights and titles are acknowledged by the courts and who are now part of our legislative process through UNDRIP, we still have to make practical decisions for five million people. We also have to be mindful that we are five million people in a sea of eight billion worldwide. When I hear that if we just stop this, our climate challenge will be gone, I say, "What hubris. What arrogance." But if we can help displace other emissions, that's a good thing.

CHAPTER THIRTEEN

A PANDEMIC FOR THE AGES

On January 28, 2020, British Columbia became the second province to confirm a case of COVID-19. By mid-March, its spread was sufficiently alarming for the province to declare a public health emergency. Shutdowns and clampdowns on social gatherings began shortly thereafter. Authorities scrambled to supply preventative measures such as masks, hand sanitizers and personal protective equipment for health-care workers. At the same time, BC provided more than $5 billion in financial support for residents and businesses. The availability of vaccines by the end of 2020 was a lifesaver. But outbreaks lingered as BC experienced a series of waves from variants of the original virus. By the spring of 2023, COVID-19 had claimed the lives of more than 5,400 British Columbians. The province's public health emergency was not lifted until July 2024.

DURING MY PREVIOUS EXPERIENCE IN GOVERNMENT, THE PROVINCIAL health officer was Perry Kendall, a very distinguished-looking doctor. You could almost see the stethoscope around his neck. I knew he was retiring, but I didn't give it much thought. I wasn't in the hiring process. When Bonnie Henry was appointed as Perry

Kendall's replacement, I didn't know her from Eve, but I bumped into her outside cabinet. She was there to give a briefing to a cabinet committee about opioids. She was kind of stern with me and rather abrupt, telling me there was an opioid crisis that required an all-hands-on-deck approach. I agreed with her, moved along and wondered to myself, "Who was that?" Less than a month later, we gathered to hear from her about something happening in China. I had had an inkling of this before our actual announcement of the outbreaks. We were in Lunar New Year celebrations, and the Chinese-language media were asking if we had enough PPE (personal protective equipment). At that point, I didn't even know what the acronym meant, nor did I know why that would be of any interest to the Chinese media in the midst of Lunar New Year. I went back to staff: "What's the deal with PPE?" I was told there was a possible outbreak of an unknown virus, and a concern that we were not prepared for it.

I thought, okay, fair enough, and carried on. Then, when we got our first briefing, the pieces began to fit together. Half as many people as usual showed up for another Lunar New Year event. All the Chinese-language media were wearing masks, no one else. The mainstream media wasn't really covering it, the public wasn't aware of it, but things were happening in the Chinese-Canadian community because of their communication links with Mainland China. That was the early warning—the canary in the coal mine, so to speak.

Adrian was health minister, and Bonnie briefed us on what they knew. One of the first two cases in Canada was in British Columbia. There was speculation about where it had come from since there had been an outbreak in Washington State. We also had a briefing about the coming weekend's Rugby Sevens. It was a huge event. Sixty thousand people would be descending on BC Place in Vancouver to watch rugby for the weekend. None of them would have understood if I had said that you can't go because there's a virus going around that no one had seen or felt. We didn't cancel the event, and there was no problem, but there had also been a large international dental conference that week, which Bonnie Henry hadn't known or been consulted about, and that turned out to be ground zero for the first significant outbreak in BC.

Just after that, we had a personal experience of what might lie ahead. Despite the disconcerting reports about this deadly virus on the loose in China, the prime minister had scheduled a first ministers' meeting in Ottawa. We were literally headed towards the departure gate at YVR when a call came that Sophie Grégoire Trudeau had tested positive for COVID. Justin had to isolate, and the conference was cancelled. We turned around and flew back to Victoria. Bob Dewar, who was coming from Winnipeg, didn't get the call. He actually made it to Ottawa, then had to fly right back.

By then I was taking Bonnie Henry very seriously. I had made it my business to find out who this person was. She had been prominent during the SARS outbreak in Ontario. She was one of the most prominent epidemiologists in Canada, and she happened to be our public health officer. The more I got to know her, the more comfortable I was with her as a person and, more importantly, as a communicator. She was an empathetic physician who knew as much about this virus as anybody in the country. What good luck that she was working for the people of BC.

I also hold the view that if you have a medical issue, you rarely go to your member of the Legislature—"I've got a sore elbow. Any thoughts on that?"—you go to a doctor. But as events were unfolding and press conferences were happening with more frequency, I was watching my colleagues across the country elbowing the doctors out of the way to say, "I got this." And they would have a row of totem poles behind them who would wear their masks and stand perfectly still, staring at the cameras. They looked like geese flying south. The premier was the one in the middle, and you had no idea who all these masked people were. I assumed they were health officials or cabinet ministers, but who could tell?

Our approach was the opposite of that. I was not keen to be the face of British Columbia on every single issue. You can't be on top of everything. You can give the impression that you are, and many politicians do that, but I had a bunch of very smart people doing these jobs. One of them was my friend Adrian Dix. If you had to construct a health minister out of spare parts to be in place for a global pandemic, Adrian was it. He was pitch perfect at providing the details people needed to know. And Bonnie was perfect for the compassion and understanding of the medical challenges we faced, and what steps individuals and communities could take to protect themselves. It was very simple for me to get out of the way.

One of the first things I remember vividly was the Iranian with the virus who came via Tehran into Vancouver, with its large Persian population. The fact that Bonnie and her team were able to use their expertise to sequence the various component parts to determine exactly where the virus had originated floored me. They were also able to make virus connections to northern Italy, which was a significant location for the initial outbreak, with all those deaths that people have forgotten about. That gave me even more confidence in our team.

Now that the impact of COVID-19 has mostly passed us, I think it's important to remind ourselves what it was like. I am amazed how quickly people have returned to regular programming. People are shaking hands again, something I thought I'd never have to do. I preferred fist bumping. But people are back to normal behaviour. If they didn't have someone in their lives who was seriously affected, a lot of them think it wasn't that bad—or even that it was a hoax. Maybe it was part of a disaster movie. It didn't really happen. They forget the reefer trucks that were acting as mortuaries in New York City and the deadly impact around the world. More than five thousand people died here in BC. It's essential that we constantly remind people of the need to be vigilant in the new environment that we live in, the new normal. I'm concerned we're not doing that. I remember being criticized for saying this was "the new normal" after we had just had the hottest July ever. Well, right now [2023], we're now into the hottest

August ever, and this is going to keep on going. That strikes me as a new normal. On the health side, we have to be ready for an increasing number of challenges we've never seen before. We need to listen to our public health officials, not like sheep but as reasonable citizens taking information that is given in good faith and using it to make choices.

During COVID, the premiers and territorial leaders met just about every week for two years. The prime minister was often thrown in as well. This gave us a national perspective on how different jurisdictions were dealing with it. One of the big challenges was PPE. There wasn't enough. I remember the premier of Alberta, Jason Kenney, saying, "We've got lots of PPE. We're happy to send some to BC." He got patted on the back by everyone. Not a mask made it across the border. I guess his people said they weren't sending their PPE anywhere. Thanks very much, Jason. Not a mask, not a gown, nothing.

Like everyone else across the country, we had to really scramble for PPE, and I think we were quite effective. Peter Pokorny, one of our deputy ministers, was our procurement guy. He and Adrian were quite a good team. Adrian would say, "This is what we need," and Peter would go out and find it. There were senior medical personnel at Coastal Health who had connections back in China, so we got some that way. Taiwan also came through, although there was a diplomatic tussle over whether we could give them credit for expediting their exports. These were not traditional procurements. We didn't go the RFP [request for proposals] route. It was: We need this. How are we going to get it? And we weren't the only ones in the marketplace. That's a key thing to remember. We were driven to get as much as we could, no matter how we got it.

At the same time, we tried to keep the economy going. Bonnie was a real asset in this regard. Her personal perspective was to find ways to keep things open rather than shutting everything down. It was different in other jurisdictions. Doug Ford was yanked all over the place on shutdowns in Ontario. We made changes to liquor laws in a weekend to keep the hospitality sector open. You could go to your local drinking hole, get some booze in a bag and take it home, because you weren't allowed to go inside. Things like that were important to keep our economy functioning.

We adopted the same approach for schools. We came to a conclusion that the best and safest place for kids to be was in school. We closed the schools for a short period in April–May of the first year, then we reopened in September. We did our best to ensure ventilation was in place, and there were policies for all grades to follow. Considering how many kids there were, school outbreaks were minimal. I have a daughter-in-law who's a teacher. My son's a teacher. They get colds because you're in a room full of kids running around with runny noses, but now people were wearing masks. There was lots of hand sanitizer. Colds almost disappeared. Janitorial crews in the K to 12 system worked overtime to make sure everyone was safe as could be.

The public saw the Bonnie-and-Adrian show every day on TV, but behind the scenes, it wasn't just Adrian. I was involved every step of the way. And it wasn't just me. We also had a cabinet committee that met regularly. We made decisions. Caucus was briefed on a regular basis. I would say we were simpatico about 90 per cent of the time. There were only a couple of occasions when we had to dial things back. I think we gave people too many charts, too many trend lines and that sort of thing. Every now and then, we had to say, "We're not doing that this week. It's too much." If you give people too much information, they are not always able to absorb it. But I don't recall any time when we constrained Bonnie and Adrian from doing what they really felt needed to be done.

While they were talking about case counts and what the government was doing, in my office we were trying to fill the holes that were being created by legions of people no longer going to work. Everyone was staying home. All of a sudden, it's calm on the streets—except for people banging their pots at seven o'clock at night to show their support for health-care workers. There was a real sense of community support.

I'd never heard of Zoom calls before COVID, but they enabled me to talk to more people in the first months of the pandemic than I probably did in my whole time as premier. I could speak to literally hundreds of people in a day. Whereas, in a traditional day as premier, you get up, you drive to the airport, you go through security, you wait for the plane, you get on the plane, it's not taking off, it does take off, you go where you're going, you get picked up, you go to another place and you come home. You've spoken to fifty people, and you're exhausted. Using this new technology, I could knock off scores of religious faith groups, business organizations and social organizations by noon. I remember talking to a farmer on the Saanich Peninsula. She had just come in from outside, where she had been working on her farm. She sat in front of her computer, engaged with government, told us what her concerns were, and went back outside half an hour later feeling she had contributed to the collective good in terms of her opinions and her insights into how we could solve a problem. She didn't have to dress up, drive into town, sit in a room waiting to have a meeting, drink some coffee, have a muffin, and then go home with five hours of her life gone.

We put together an economic task force. Geoff brought in the list of California's task force, and it had, like, a thousand people. That was crazy. Our task force was ten people. It involved the not-for-profit sector, the resource sector and so on. We engaged with these ten people, and they connected with their various stakeholders. That way we were able to get information in a very accelerated fashion. I give full marks to the professional public service. We asked them to do things they had never been asked to do before. Instead of objecting, they went and did them. It was a big change from the days when, say, you weren't allowed to have a television in your bar unless it was a certain size. Could you change that over a weekend? No way. You had to have consultation. You had to change the regulations. You had to go to a cabinet committee. And it would take months for people to be able to put up whatever damn television they wanted. It was ridiculous, and that's the way government had always approached these things. We said, you can't do that anymore. We have to make decisions and have them implemented right away.

We had to shift away from balancing the budget. We wanted to give people and businesses money to make up for COVID. Easy, right? "Here, have some money." If you're in opposition, you just say, "Well, put a hockey bag stuffed with cash on the street. People can come and take their one hundred bucks or whatever, and we'll be good." But you have to have a process. You've got to make sure there's no fraud, that you're doing it in a fair and equitable way based on who needs it the most. And the government did it. Lori Wanamaker set up the program almost overnight. We gave people who qualified a thousand bucks. Horgan Bucks, they were called. It was a big chunk of money for families and singles who were impacted by COVID. Ellie was at the grocery store and the checkout person, who knew us, said, "Thank your husband, Ellie." Ellie asked, "What for?" And she said, "Our hot water heater blew out today, and we got our cheque in the mail, so we've been able to replace it." Those are the things that families deal with all the time. I was so impressed by the way it happened—as I was by the way the public service circumvented procurement processes and other procedures to get things we needed done.

We learned a lot about our health-care workforce, especially in long-term care homes. The egregious labour changes made by the Liberals had resulted in very low salaries for a lot of staff, forcing them to work at a number of different locations to earn enough money. We'd already been trying to raise their wages to close to what they were twenty years ago, then the pandemic arrived, and the most significant impact was on long-term care homes. These low-paid workers were fundamental to cleanliness, and they were working at three or four different sites. That increased their chances of exposure to the virus and of spreading it. We restricted staff to working at one location only and raised their wages. That made a big difference.

I was furious at how long it took the federal government to close our borders, but people were also demanding we close our border with Alberta, since we were doing better than they were. But how do you do that? Mobility is a fundamental right of Canadians. We would have had to put checkpoints on the thirty-two or so crossings between us. Setting up that infrastructure would have been impossible. And do we stop commerce or just individuals? Do we stop people who might have the virus and can't demonstrate they've isolated? The public kept calling for us to keep Albertans out when the bigger issue was global.

As the virus started to spread, I don't mind admitting we were frightened, but we weren't freaking out. I felt we had the best people to deal with it and, more importantly, there was a sense that British Columbians were listening. As the situation dragged on, there were protests and frustration, but there was none of that at the beginning. I believe we remained calm. A lot of that was Bonnie's temperament. I feel she set the tone. We talked about this quite a bit. My job was to be the father who came in every now and again and shook my finger. There were parties in Kelowna with young people doing what they do, and I had to say, "Come on, go home." I asked Ryan Reynolds to do a public service announcement. He agreed: "I hope young people in BC don't kill my mom." It got people's attention. Sadly, I also asked Seth Rogen, and his message was that young people should stay at home and smoke weed. Not a bad idea, but thanks, Seth. I'd first met him in 2019 at a Walk of Fame thing for him and Jimmy Pattison. I was going to leave after they did Jimmy, but the organizers said Seth was hoping I would stay, so I hung around. Man, he was stoned! The smell was overpowering. We had a good talk, and I encouraged him to invest in local weed production. Both Seth and Ryan Reynolds pointed out that they were in their forties. They thought we should ask someone else if we wanted to get through to twenty-year-olds. I said, "But you're the youngest people I know."

We were best in the country at handling the first wave of COVID-19. The second and third waves, however, were more difficult. I think there were times when we were overwhelmed by the ongoing magnitude of the pandemic. We also got to the point when people wanted to open up. They wanted to have more freedom, get on with their lives. We tried to give people that space, but we still had to bring back some restrictions. We strongly urged people to follow them in their own self-interest. We put penalties in place for not abiding by the law. We shut down a couple of home parties in downtown Vancouver. We pressed charges and so on. The revenue we got from whatever sanctions Mike Farnworth was able to concoct was infinitesimal, yet we had to have some sort of sanctions for people who flouted the law. Otherwise, the ones who were listening and doing what we asked them to do would start taking more latitude, too.

As we got into the third wave, we started seeing more and more people coming here from across the country and across the US border. The virus seemed everywhere. It became almost impossible to control. Luckily, we had our immunization program by then. It started in December of the first wave. Being able to have vaccines in eight or nine months after COVID took off was quite extraordinary. The extent of their efficacy was difficult to determine. Many people felt that if they got a vaccine, they would be immune from COVID. But no one ever said that. Vaccines did make it harder to contract the virus and definitely reduced its severity if you did get it. The stats showed very high case counts during the second and third waves, but thanks to the vaccines, the death count was no higher than when we had lower case counts.

When the vaccines came in, I was waiting my turn like everyone else. Bonnie said that she needed me to get an AstraZeneca shot. No one was getting it—they were getting the RNA vaccines—so we had a huge stockpile. My son, who was living in England, said AstraZeneca was the dominant vaccine over there. That was good enough for me.

When I was having my second bout with cancer, in 2021, my son flew back to see me. This was during the Omicron wave. He'd just had his third vaccine. He tested negative for COVID, got on the plane, landed in Vancouver, and had a random test. He tested positive. He had to stay in a basement in Surrey for a week. He'd come across an ocean and an entire country to see his dad who had cancer. I saw him for one day. He was all masked up. I was all masked up. He was as prepared as he could have been, and still he was thwarted. So many individuals had similar stories.

The restrictions in long-term care homes were particularly tough. My father-in-law died in a care home in Ontario, and his spouse of sixty years couldn't be with him. She was literally looking through the windows. That was going on everywhere. Those were the type of stories I was hearing in my constituency office. So many sons and daughters had moms and dads who were not doing well. They couldn't see them, and they didn't know how much time they had left. It was heartbreaking. It was really difficult for Adrian, as well. His partner Renée's mother was in a care home where there was a significant outbreak. He and Renée did not see her for something like a year and a half. He was living it every day and not whining about it. I don't think the public had any idea. Bonnie is an extremely empathetic and compassionate individual. She knew how this was going to break. But the last thing we needed was to open the doors to this vulnerable population and just let people flow in. It was difficult.

The Greens and the Liberals were onside during the first wave. I give them absolute credit for that. By the second and third wave, however, the Opposition was being criticized by far-right fringes for not yelling at us about civil liberties and that sort of thing. The support we'd had during the first wave was diminishing. The Teachers' Federation was also mad at us. We had meetings with them, but we couldn't change all the air-filtration systems in British Columbia schools. We just couldn't do it. Some schools were not able to be retrofitted. They needed to be torn down and rebuilt. There were infrastructure pieces that did not lend themselves to an immediate response. We had challenges with the university sector, as well. Some wanted to shut everything down, but we needed our foreign students to come in. Meanwhile, we were closing our borders. Everyone had something that was disrupted as a result of COVID.

These divisions increased the longer COVID went on. It was frustrating. We tried to talk to people. Adrian, Bonnie and I met regularly with leaders of the faith community about restrictions on their meetings. The overwhelming majority complied and found a way to connect with their parishioners. But it was still hard to tell people who were in the business of gathering regularly that they couldn't do that. Some refused to comply. They felt driven to do something different. The acrimony in the community ended up on my desk, and we had to spend a lot of time calming the waters. Overall, I think the goodwill that we built up during the first wave allowed us to do that. Was there a lot of noise? Absolutely. Were there frustrated people? No question about it. I don't want to diminish in any way that fear, that anxiety and that frustration. However, I think a majority of British Columbians said, "Okay, we're in this together, and we'll figure it out. You guys haven't steered us wrong, so we're going to stick with you." Even as we got into the more challenging components of the later waves, I believe people hung together. But we'll see what history writes about it. We'll see how people look at it five years from now.

It's not as if there were no disagreements among us, either. We had them all the time. Adrian would say, politically, we couldn't do something. And Bonnie was saying privately that we had to. Public servants would also weigh in on the implications if we decided to do something. We had to try and reconcile all those things, and the buck stopped with me. At the same time, the buck had been in many pockets before it got to me. We were always assessing and reassessing our progress. As for Bonnie, she sometimes got peeved at the briefings, answering all these questions from the media until they ran out. Every day. Every day. She was not a professional communicator or a polished politician. She would get irritated and say, "I've answered that question already." Although many people wrote us about how delighted they were with her, it wasn't about performance, it was about informing people where we were and where we were going—together. On days when there were issues we really wanted to lean in to, I would be sent in. Bonnie didn't have the clout to do that.

Adrian seemed to have been rehabilitated in people's eyes. Remember, he had been leader of the party and voters had rejected him. Now they saw his work ethic, his commitment and his passion for making sure people were being well served by the government. His stock rose. I was happy about that because I'd known him for so long, and people now saw the extent of his selflessness. That was not always evident in the political sphere, but it was evident when he was the face of public health with Bonnie Henry. As the pandemic stretched on and people got tired, however, a bit of the shine started to come off Bonnie and Adrian. They were suggesting things to me, and I would say, "No, we can't do that. What are you talking about? Don't be silly." But they kept coming up with more restrictions. I mean, I think the world of both of them, but we got to a point in COVID where for me it was: "No, no, people are done." Adrian wanted to keep ratcheting it up. It was hard at times for us to hold him back. Once, I had to really yell at him. He was going ahead with some closures without telling me. I shouted at him: "You don't run the goddamn government! The next time you try and shut something down without talking to me, you won't be a minister anymore!" That was pretty hard to do, because Adrian is my dear friend, but I needed to give him a clear wake-up call.

We did an internal inquiry that examined our response, pinpointed shortcomings and recommended improvements we could make. I didn't support having a commission of inquiry. Having an independent person sit down and pass judgement on the decisions of public health officials was not in their interest, nor in the interest of figuring out how we go forward from here. There was no handbook for what we went through. The one pandemic handbook we had was written thirty-five years ago, and it was theoretical, so we chronicled the COVID pandemic inside government, and now we have our own updated manual.

Looking back, nothing could have prepared us for COVID. I don't know how many times I said "unprecedented" during that period, but it was a lot. Don Wright likened it to constructing an airplane in the air and preparing to land, but there was no runway. That was really what we were doing. How could we prepare for something when we had no idea what was going to happen next? In some cases, it required blind faith. There were many dark days. We simply had to get up and try to do better the next day. COVID wasn't leaving. Wringing our hands would have changed nothing about the spread and mutation of the virus. Mutations were what I most dreaded. I had nightmares about them. But I don't think we missed the mark too many times.

CHAPTER FOURTEEN

WORKING WITH THE GREENS

THE CONFIDENCE AND SUPPLY AGREEMENT (CASA) WE SIGNED WITH the Greens that brought us to government was an unprecedented document in BC politics. I don't think that's appreciated enough. CASA was a framework for governing, a way to keep the Greens with us by reaching agreements on a whole range of issues. I suppose it was also a bit of a shield against those in the public who would ask why we weren't moving faster on something. We would say we have to work with the Greens. What can we do? I'm being a bit glib, but it was a balancing act. We also had to manage personalities. Despite our collective focus on others, politics is ultimately a bunch of people who sometimes get bruised feelings, get anxious when they're not getting their way, and like to lash out. Andrew Weaver was less like that, but others in the Green Party were saying they needed to attack the government, even though the Greens were now part of government. For hardcore Greens, that was a hard sell. I think it was also a hard sell for hardcore New Democrats.

It wasn't easy to reach the agreement that brought down the Liberals, but we had no idea of how much more work it would take to manage CASA for the next thirty-nine months. We started by forming a bipartite consultative committee made up of Carole James and George Heyman for us, and Sonia Furstenau and Adam

Olsen for the Greens. They would meet once a week, or more if needed. CASA was our guiding document. We shared bills, pieces of legislation and things we were contemplating so there would be no surprises. That was big. We made sure the civil service and ministry offices recognized that the Greens needed to know what was going on and be given a chance to provide feedback before going ahead with something.

To administer CASA and provide bureaucratic support, we put together a secretariat headed by a career public servant, Donna Sanford. Furstenau and Olsen were first-time MLAs, and she had long sessions with them, explaining how government worked and that they couldn't just kill projects. She facilitated meetings. She brought political staff and the professional civil service together to make sure we were all hitting on the same points, not in a duplicitous way, but in a way that would help us enact the will of 60 per cent of the voting public. The Liberals said it was some sort of political stunt. It was not that. We were trying to institutionalize and operationalize an agreement we came to as a result of the people's choice, which was to vote you, the Liberals, out. If there was a hero during our first term, Donna Sanford would be that hero, because she took most of the flak.

Andrew Weaver and I were the other component. We had meetings at least once a week. They were heated at the beginning, because we had issues. By year three, however, we were just hanging out, shooting the shit. Geoff Meggs, who sat in on them, would do his emails and say, afterwards, "Well, I'll never get that hour back." Over time, Andrew and I became friends. I wouldn't say we were bosom buddies, but I grew to respect him, and I know he grew to respect me. I consider him someone I will look up when I get back home. There are some people from my caucus I won't look up.

This was not a coalition government. It wasn't about agreeing on everything. It was something different. We could still go out and criticize each other. We had our list of issues that were part of the agreement, but either of us could do things outside that list.

Confidence ensured that we would be able to marshal sufficient votes to approve legislation. Supply ensured we would be able to pass budgets to spend the money required to provide services to people. Supply was key. Appointing Carole, who was finance minister, made sure that the core values of the Greens were consistent with where we wanted to go in terms of the budget. George Heyman was quite happy to be part of the subcommittee. As a former labour leader, his negotiating experience was critical. It wasn't easy bringing along three other people and satisfying them. The Greens wound up voting against some bills, but usually those bills passed with support from the Liberals.

Crucial to our agreement was the "no surprise" clause. If we were going to bring something forward, we would talk to them. If they were going to bring something forward, they would talk to us. That was essential to the work we were doing. House management was also critical to keep government going. For that we had Mike Farnworth, the longest-serving member on the government side and one of the nicest guys you'll ever meet. He gets along with everybody. He was tailor-made for managing a minority Parliament.

Of course, we had big challenges over TMX, LNG and Site C. They were more than just letters of the alphabet. They were massive energy projects that had a significant impact not only on BC's economy and the people of the province, but also on our relations with the Greens. They were constantly being asked if they were going to bring down the government over them. But Andrew felt we were living up to our commitments. We had never said we would not proceed with Site C. The same with LNG. He kept hitting us over it. He didn't hold back—and that wasn't manufactured—but he did see the bigger picture, and that did not involve defeating us over LNG. He was always of the view that it would never proceed anyway. Kinder Morgan was less of a hurdle since we mostly agreed that we would do everything we could to stop their pipeline bringing raw bitumen into the heart of BC's major metropolitan centre. In all three cases, we were open with the public on why we came to our conclusions. Unlike the previous government, we didn't use these initiatives as a political wedge. We wanted to use Site C and LNG to build a stronger economy that would produce the revenue we needed to meet all our social commitments.

What trumped Site C and LNG for Andrew was our commitment to a climate action plan with specific, legislated targets. He is not a blind ideologue. He knew the power from Site C was going to be green, and we were going to need lots of it. He also knew that multi-billion-dollar investments were hard to say no to, so again, he wasn't going to bring us down over these projects. But we had to prove to him that they could be managed within our climate action goals. And we did. We committed to cutting our emissions by 40 per cent by the end of the decade, even taking into account what would be produced by LNG. When Andrew saw we were serious about climate action, he worked hand in hand with us to create CleanBC, which is what we called our plan. Many of his initiatives, many of his ideas, are part and parcel of what's in our climate plan today, and I consider it the most aggressive and doable in the country.

I did have one very heated conversation with Andrew. He had held a media event claiming the mayor of Fort St. John, Lori Ackerman, had told him that I had told her, before the Utilities Commission's review, that we would not cancel Site C. He implied the decision had been predetermined. I called Lori. She confirmed he was making that up. It hadn't happened. I unloaded on him with both barrels. I really let him have it. Thankfully, it was over the phone. He's a big guy, and two big stubborn guys yelling at each other is not going to accomplish anything. I got it out of my system, and Weaver apologized for mischaracterizing Lori Ackerman's remarks. That was the first and only time we had a real donnybrook, but it was a good one.

That blowup and the time yelling at Adrian Dix were the only two occasions Geoff heard me lose it. So, as to the notion that I was Angry John, it happened only twice in five years. Both were for good reasons. I had to shake Weaver up enough for him not to bring the government down, and, as I explained earlier, I simply needed to give Adrian a loud and clear wake-up call.

The Greens prevented us from bringing in card check for unions trying to organize a workplace. If a union could sign up 55 per cent of the bargaining unit, they would be granted certification without a vote. That prevented employers from intimidating their workers in the lead-up to a certification vote. But card check was a challenge for the business community, and many pundits thought it was a damaging issue for the NDP because it seemed to tie us too closely to unions. Adrian had beat around the bush on the issue, but during the campaign I came right out and said we would do it. I made that clear at a meeting with the *Vancouver Sun*'s editorial board. I was sliding through all the questions with good, easy politician language until Mike Smyth asked if we were going to bring in card check. Rather than skate around it, I just said, "Yes. Yes, we are." When I got back to the campaign office, our staff was worried: "Is this going to be awful?" And it was not awful at all. Smyth wrote a column in the *Province* about it. Nobody noticed. Nobody reacted. However, we couldn't pass card check until our next term because Andrew Weaver opposed it.

When we had met with labour in 2017, they had been iffy about supporting us. It was hard for the leaders of the building trades to go to their memberships and say "Vote NDP" when their members read in the papers every day that we weren't going to build this pipeline, we weren't going to build that bridge, we weren't going to build anything. Of course that wasn't true, and the building trades eventually came out for us. Having Andrew Weaver with his arms crossed, saying no to card check, enabled me to deepen our relationship with labour. That allowed me to meet with every union president and remind them how important it was to have an NDP premier, someone you could call for little things before they became big things. They never got that with the Liberals. They were frozen out. Union leaders could tell their members we weren't screwing around.

We also created Community Benefits Agreements, which made sure union-negotiated conditions were in effect on large public sector projects. They were not simply for unions, but for all British Columbians working on these projects, even if they were non-union. We made a point of calling them "community" agreements so you can talk to non-union people and say, "As part of these agreements, we're going to train your daughter and your son and your neighbour to be tradespeople through their apprenticeship programs." They get that. It's about building a community, and that makes sense.

We followed through with our commitment to the Greens to hold a referendum on proportional representation, which we too had promised. It was BC's third referendum on the question. I voted against proportional representation in 2005. It sounded stupid. This was my first election as a candidate, and representation by population, or first past the post, worked for me. It was what I knew. In 2009, there was another chance to vote for proportional representation, and that time I voted for it. Anything had to be better than perpetually allowing the Liberals to win because of huge constituencies with hardly any people having the same weight as constituencies with tons of people. I felt that was wrong. However, I have to say I wasn't overly enthusiastic about it. I didn't try to convince people at the doorstep.

For our referendum, I had wanted a simple yes or no. Do you want to keep what we have, or do you want to go to a fairer system that makes sure every vote, no matter where you live, is worth the same? I gave the job of drafting the question to David Eby as attorney general. He relied mostly on staff. He came back with a ballot that was very hard to understand and sold it to cabinet. Weaver was okay with it, so I let it go, and we had the vote. I campaigned in favour of proportional representation with as much vigour as I could, even though I didn't like the way the question was fashioned. It failed, and that was the end of that. We had followed through on our commitment.

I would still like to see proportional representation. People with my type of personality can find a way to make PR work as long as the party lines are not too rigid. The NDP is basically a loose coalition to begin with—people with this point of view and people with that point of view, all coming together. It made sense to me. Plus, with my advancing years, I would not have to deal with it more than once, so I thought, why not? I was having so much fun that changing the players I was dealing with would not have been that big a deal. I already had to talk to the Greens, and sometimes I had to talk to the Liberals to get things done. The Greens voted against LNG, but there was no way the Liberals were going to do that. However, I wasn't surprised people rejected PR, and I don't mind admitting that the huge majority we won in the next election under our traditional voting system was quite satisfying.

Near the end of our mandate, Andrew stepped down as leader and began sitting as an independent. When that happened, the dynamics of CASA changed dramatically. It was no longer as strong as it was. We had completed most of the CASA commitments we made. In fact, we were starting to talk about CASA 2.0. But Sonia Furstenau was now a candidate in the Greens' leadership contest. That meant she was going to be as outspoken as possible to gain the support of the Green membership. That's politics. You want people to support you because of your ideas. Leadership candidates for any party, including the NDP, would do the same. But the upshot was that Sonia became progressively antagonistic outside the Legislature and inside CASA. She became difficult to deal with. Nothing was good enough. The Greens would not allow things to move forward. It was all backing up. Andrew hadn't shied away from drawing public attention to what he believed were hypocritical positions I had taken. That was fair game, because he was not going to bring down the government. He didn't stand in our way. He was just highlighting our shortcomings. I had built a relationship with him, and suddenly there was a candidate running for his job who was being obstructive, so that was a challenge.

During debate on our 2020 budget, without any advance notice, Sonia rose in the Legislature and tabled an amendment. We had met with her literally the day before, and she had said nothing about doing this. If she had, we might have entertained her amendment, because that was the nature of our relationship. But she had not discussed it through CASA or with Carole James, who was both our finance minister and one of our CASA point people. It was a complete surprise, and a budget bill amendment threatened the government. We figured out a way to resolve the situation, but it was a sign of things coming apart.

The other event which finished it off for me was the Greens' opposition to a bill we wanted to bring forward that would allow hospitals to detain and provide medical treatment to young people for up to seven days following a drug overdose. That really, really bothered me. I understand, on the surface, that it rubs many people the wrong way, but there were other voices in the community, and I was more concerned about them. On these very challenging social issues where lives are in the balance, people say you have to do something—until you propose something, and then they say, "Don't do that. Do something else." What, for goodness' sake? Well, you know, free heroin for everyone and, okay, we can have safe supply. I get that. But there are those who were advocating having dispensers on the side of the road, like old cigarette machines, handing out narcotics to people. That's insane. Our bill was directed at young people already in a hospital setting, and they would stay there for a week at most. I don't know how any reasonable person could oppose that, but the Greens did, and I was very disappointed, to say the least. The bill fell off the table, and I moved on. There were so many other matters we had on our agenda, but by then our partnership was pretty well in ruins.

Notwithstanding how it ended, CASA worked for more than three years. I think back on how we formed government with the NDP caucus and the three Greens, Andrew, Sonia and Adam, working together. We were so optimistic and hopeful, and, as it turned out, with good reason. CASA was a success. Critical to that was making transformational change through collaboration rather than using blunt objects. It was hard work. I don't want to minimize that. All those endless meetings. Notes would be prepared, then further meetings were held. We set out to make changes, and we made them in a collaborative, transparent and open way. We found those points of commonality in a minority Parliament to deliver an agenda that was not our agenda but the agenda of the people of BC. Despite the difficulties, I found it exhilarating to be part of a minority government. It required all of us to be bigger than ourselves.

CHAPTER FIFTEEN

A COVID SNAP ELECTION

I'VE TALKED ABOUT THE SERIOUS PROBLEMS WE WERE HAVING WITH our Green partners once Andrew Weaver was out of the picture. Sonia Furstenau's attempt to amend our budget bill in the Legislature was a serious tipping point. Carole James had already decided to leave politics, because of personal health issues, when she had to deal with someone who, disingenuously, had said she had no problems, then the next day, with great bluster, tried to amend the budget. We were in the middle of a pandemic, and it was becoming increasingly clear that the government needed a new way forward. We didn't need a government that included having to talk and cooperate with an aspirant for leadership of another party while the guy who spearheaded the original CASA document was heading for the door. Andrew had been a strong leader and often ran counter to his colleagues.

When Andrew said he was leaving, that was when I first started thinking about calling an early election. It wasn't like the press releases were ready or anything like that. But the circumstances may not have been better. I don't mean electorally, I mean our ability to actually conduct an election, because we were still in the midst of COVID. There was no guarantee that a year later we would have been in any better position with regards to the pandemic. Of course, I was mindful of the fact we were way up in the polls, but I also knew that elections are difficult on a good day. You can have bozo eruptions from candidates and all sorts of stuff. Everything has to go your way.

We had no idea what it would be like campaigning during COVID. Something like that had never happened before in BC. It's one thing to say we're going to have an election campaign. It's quite another to do it. There were countless moving parts. We didn't know what we didn't know. What I did know was that I had a functioning government that was getting results for people. I find it ironic that the media criticized us back in 2017 when we moved the fixed four-year election date from May to October. I had always advocated that. By October, the public accounts are in, and you can no longer pretend the books are balanced or in deficit. You have an official record of what happened in the previous year, and you can campaign on that rather than "Here's my budget, vote for me, and you'll get everything you want," which had been the case for the last six or seven elections. The media asked why we added six months to the fixed election date instead of taking six months off the date. Interestingly, if we had done that, it would have put us into an election exactly when we had it.

As it was, we faced a barrage of criticism for calling an election a little over three years into our term. We were accused of being cynical and opportunistic, taking advantage of the pandemic and the fact we were twenty points up in the polls. To which I plead guilty. But with some caveats. We knew we had had consistently good polling numbers, but we didn't know if they would stand up. Carole James wasn't running again. Shane Simpson wasn't running again. Claire Trevena wasn't running again. Doug Donaldson and Judy Darcy weren't running again. They were all very capable cabinet ministers. In fact, I made only one change in my original cabinet, when Jinny Sims stepped down over some accusations about an immigration case that were later determined to be unfounded. So, yes, I do plead guilty to saying we have a massive lead in the polls, an inexperienced Opposition, and now is the time to go. But there were other reasons to go, as well, and they were more important to me. The exceptional times we were experiencing required more than an ordinary response. At the end of the day, I felt confident it was the right decision. The critics were right that we were having an election during a pandemic, but we put checks and balances in place to ensure we could maximize participation as much as possible through mail-in ballots and a host of other initiatives.

We had led the country by allowing Dr. Henry to be the major point person communicating how we were going to get through this. Her approach was to keep everything open to the extent we could. Remember social distancing? Historians can grapple with this, but as chief medical health officer she did not see the pandemic as an impediment to participation in an electoral process. We needed a stable government that had the confidence of its public to deliver on what was to come, whether it be more shutdowns of whole sectors of the economy, more people staying in place for long periods of time, or uncertainty about the health of our loved ones. This was an extraordinary time, and our relationship with our political partners had been broken.

The media and our opponents didn't see it that way, but the time to renew the government's relationship with its people could not have been better. We had been given the public's trust in 2017. Asking for a renewal of that trust was appropriate. As it turned out, the public felt that way, too. Besides, we weren't the first to hold an election in Canada during the pandemic. There had already been elections in Saskatchewan and New Brunswick.

It did feel weird campaigning with a mask on. There were no mass rallies, no door-to-door canvassing, and there was a huge mail-in vote. We were mindful of the possible health implications of bringing people together. Yet, in my mind, having the election when we did was important. We needed the ability to govern based on the events of the day and the growing COVID case count. The totals were relatively flat at the beginning. They started going up during the last week. Then, in the week right after the campaign, the case count numbers took off. In terms of public safety, had we waited another month, an election would not have been possible. It really was the perfect date.

During the campaign, I stayed at the Pinnacle Hotel in Vancouver. It's not the Pan Pacific, but it's well located, it was a union hotel, and everyone knew who I was. I liked going to the Pinnacle. When we formed government, my press secretary said to me, "Oh, good, we can stay at the Pan Pacific." And I said, "No, we're not going there. We're staying right here." It's my place. I went back there a couple of weeks ago for a BC Lions game, and I was hugging everybody. It was fantastic. I was with my son, and he got to see all the regular people there. In 2019, I was driving with my RCMP detail down Hastings Street, and I noticed a picket line in front of the Pinnacle. I stopped the car, got out and started talking to the workers about the hotel. There's always one or two elevators being serviced, the carpets are from the seventies, and all that. So I'm addressing the group and saying that I don't stay here for the elevators, I don't stay here for the carpets, I stay here for the people, and you deserve to benefit from that. Not only is it a place where I stay and where people know me, but now they know I have their backs, by standing on the street corner and declaring to the owners of the hotel: You should treat these people better. I'm a bit off-topic, but the Pinnacle played a key role in the election.

We were staying on the eighteenth floor. There used to be a revolving restaurant at the top. It became our media centre. We rented out the whole floor and literally ran the campaign from there. Other parties were putting up green screens for their backgrounds. We had a real backdrop of Burrard Inlet and Grouse Mountain. I would do Zoom calls from there. I would do press conferences from there. I'd go up to the roof, do the morning agenda, go down to my room, do some reading, come back up, do some stuff, and then go out on the road for a couple of events. That became the campaign. We couldn't have predicted it, but the Pinnacle became the perfect spot. We didn't have to go across town. We didn't have to rent another place. We just went upstairs.

The whole campaign team stayed at the Pinnacle rather than being spread all over the place. When we called the election, we had no idea we would have a studio right upstairs that was not only functional but beautifully run by people who were rooting for us. I have no idea whether management was, but the staff certainly was.

Doing most of the campaign from a studio at a Vancouver hotel was also the best thing we could have done for climate change. Rather than getting in a private plane and flying somewhere to speak to sixty people who were already going to vote for me and maybe listen to people who weren't going to vote for me, who were yelling at me and calling me a dickhead, it was: Here's our message, here's what we're going to try to do, and you can vote for us or not. It's up to you. In fact, we're going to make it easy for you. You can stay home and put your ballot in an envelope and mail it in.

The TV debate was much different from the first time, against Christy Clark in 2017. Then, my staff had prepped me for hours and hours on end to be ready for anything. This time I was prepped by Paul Degenstein, who was a friend and Ian Reid's life partner. He's a very creative guy from Regina. During our preparations, I got frustrated about something and he said, "You don't have to worry about any of that. I just want you to look in the camera and smile. That's all I want you to do. That's what people like. They like that guy. They don't want you to be grave. They don't want you to be concerned. That's 'COVID John.' I want 'Happy John.' Whatever the question is, whatever the circumstance is, I want you to look in the camera and smile." In 2017 we had been up against a great campaigner. I really had to be on my toes. Now I was debating Sonia Furstenau and Andrew Wilkinson. Paul just said, "You go, boy. Have some fun. Look in the camera and smile." That was quite a change from 2017. People were saying, "I like that guy. I don't like the NDP, but I like that guy Horgan. We're in a global pandemic. He seems to be running things okay. Let's give him a chance."

On election night, we won the largest majority in the history of the NDP in BC. We pretty much swept the suburbs, winning in ridings like Langley and Chilliwack, where we had never come close before. I had asked the public whether they wanted me to stay the course or did they want to choose one of the other options. I thought that was as fair and as open as I could be, and the outcome was a positive one for my government. I go back to Ronna-Rae Leonard, up in Courtenay–Comox, who won that unlikely narrow victory in 2017 that gave us our minority government. This time she won easily. That's what happens when you're given an opportunity, when you're able to break the stereotypes that have been created over decades, not just in British Columbia but across the country. You know, "Social democrats are compassionate but incompetent bumblers who will wreck everything they come across. We need used car salesmen—no disrespect for used car salesmen. We need all these alleged business people who hate government. Let's vote for them to run the government." It doesn't make sense at all.

Having a majority was going to be a big change from the past three years, but there were things about minority government I was going to miss. One of my strengths is my desire to make the table as big as possible, and Andrew, Sonia and Adam had been willing partners in an adversarial system, at least until near the end. I was able to sell my team on the need for compromise. During our minority government, I was also able to use Andrew, and he was able to use me. He used me as a foil at times, and I used him on card checks. It benefited both of us, but that was at an end. When you have a massive majority, everyone—your opponents and your allies—expects you to just plough ahead.

CHAPTER SIXTEEN

MENTAL HEALTH AND THE OPIOID CRISIS

THROUGHOUT MY TIME AS PREMIER, WE WERE DEALING WITH THE terrible opioid crisis, which seemed to get worse and worse no matter what we did or didn't do. I think I mentioned that my first encounter with Bonnie Henry was a random meeting outside the cabinet chamber, and the only thing she wanted to talk about was opioids. As we continued in government, although I had never sat down with the provincial coroner or had any discussion with her, I knew that every month we were going to get another report on the number of opioid-related deaths. Unfortunately—and I want to make sure that I don't misspeak here—the body count became more the issue than the social challenges we were dealing with. Many people who have not been affected by a loved one having an addiction, and, heaven forbid, succumbing to that addiction, don't believe this happens to their neighbours or to their friends. They think it's a Downtown Eastside problem and these are "junkies." That's not a term anyone I know uses, and in fact it's not true. A large number of the people dying every month are construction workers prescribed opioids for workplace accidents. The prescription ends and they end up finding another way to feed their addictions. This is about stigma. It's about how do we talk openly and candidly about addiction, and how do we manage it.

I remember being at a first ministers' conference, and two of the premiers—not that it matters, but you can probably guess who they were—were saying that apparently they're just giving away free drugs in British Columbia. Caroline Cochrane, the premier of the Northwest Territories and the first woman at the table since Rachel Notley, was a social worker who understood addiction. She came from the second-smallest jurisdiction at the conference. But here were these two dudes talking about junkies and free drugs. She told them point blank that most of the addicts in her community and Yellowknife were not junkies. They were construction workers. She just ripped a strip off them. And I thought, "Good on you, sister." She was horrified that the leaders of two Canadian provinces should be so dismissive about a problem that was clearly beyond the individual capacity of citizens to manage. We have a collective responsibility to make sure we are doing our level best to have programs for harm reduction, for rehabilitation, for law enforcement and for prevention.

We were the first government in Canada to have a ministry of mental health and addictions. In my opinion we ended up spending too much time listening to the "free opioid, safe supply" crowd. Not that I disagree with safe supply, nor do I want to leave the wrong impression, but I created the ministry to deal more with mental health, and it got completely consumed by addictions and the opioid crisis.

My vision was to have a dedicated minister for both addictions and mental health. If you go to your local emergency room and your arm is bent in three directions, you get treatment right away. If you show up with anxiety or depression, the reaction is: I don't have the skills to address this. You need to talk to somebody else. Here's a name. We need to have heath-care workers to help these individuals. That goes back to the Canada Health Transfers and the need for more funding to provide more services. If we are going to create a health system to meet all the challenges of opioids, other addictions and the mental health crisis, we need more people. The only way you're going to convince someone to stop what they're doing is by having someone there to help them every step of the way. And it's tough. But you don't give up.

We've had a hundred thousand people coming to BC each year for the past two years. There should be incentives in place for them to consider being a social worker, a health-care worker or a mental health officer. I know, in Victoria and Vancouver, they've been trying to pair mental health workers with law enforcement. Sadly, a law enforcement officer on a mental health check was killed in Burnaby a year or two ago. She was actually the daughter of a dear friend of mine from years ago. It was such a tragedy. A young police officer. Mental health was her mission, her calling. We also needed more psychologists and psychiatrists so that when people presented themselves with, say, an enormous anxiety they can't shake, they would get help. That was my number one objective. We never got there. Adrian was responsible for the health-care budget, and Judy Darcy, who was the minister for mental health and addictions, was responsible for the programs, with a very small budget. That was a mistake. We should not have separated them out.

I don't want to fault Judy Darcy—she worked her tail off—but we didn't manage to get the balance right. We did some stuff trying to destigmatize mental health. We worked with Clara Hughes, a wonderful person who had struggled with mental health issues. She's incredibly candid about it, and what an athlete—the only Canadian to win medals in both the Summer and Winter Olympics. She is so positive. We also worked with Corey Hirsch, the former Vancouver Canucks goaltender and mental health advocate. I wasn't oblivious to the addictions problem. But mental health was a key component of what we were supposed to do. People were crying out for help and not getting it, whether it was anxiety, depression, bipolar disorder, autism, you name it. We weren't putting enough resources into training people to assist this huge segment of the population. They needed care, and they're still not getting it as far as I'm aware.

We have primary care clinics with social workers in them, but not nearly as many as we should. Much of the money and all of the emotional energy went to the opioid crisis. And every thirty days the coroner would broadcast how many British Columbians had succumbed to overdoses. That made it an easy story to cover at the end of every month. What's the number going to be? Government, what are you doing about it?

I went to the Powell Street fire station on the Downtown Eastside one day and talked to the crew there. There were six calls during the hour I was at the station. None were to put out fires. They would go and revive someone. And in many cases that person would be ticked off because now they had to go get high again. It was a form of madness. We brought forward a whole host of harm reduction initiatives. More than anyone else in the country. We assumed that if we were giving a sufficient number of people the drugs they needed, the market would collapse. But the market didn't collapse. During the pandemic, it expanded. We thought restricted borders would reduce the importance of fentanyl. It only created a massive fentanyl industry domestically. It seemed as if every time we tried to be one step ahead of this scourge, we were pushed back again.

We needed the federal government to participate as well. We worked very hard on the decriminalization piece, on safe supply, on making sure that all four pillars of dealing with the drug crisis were adequately represented. But we lost track of the enforcement piece. I don't mean enforcement against addicts, who were just trying to find a fix, but on those who were preying on the vulnerable. We didn't push hard enough on getting the criminal element out. People not directly exposed to addiction watch television and see the pushers and organized crime, and they wonder why we aren't doing something about that. And I say, "You're absolutely right. Why aren't we?" The fact of the matter is that our law enforcement is laser-focused on trying to break up organized crime, but it's hard to make a difference. You have to keep chipping away at all the elements. You have to make sure that harm reduction programs are not only robust and successful but are also understood by the community where they are being introduced, because a lot of people take them out of context.

I've talked about wanting to have involuntary care for minors who are hospitalized for a drug overdose. Depending on the circumstance, we would have kept that individual in a hospital setting under medical supervision. Maybe that would have been enough to clear the head, enough to get a treatment program going. Parents loved the idea. It would not have been in a bloody jail or in a withholding rights setting, but in a health-care environment. It wasn't like we were going to keep you until we decide to let you go. It was defined. It was going to be managed, not by politicians, not by advocates, but by health-care workers. It was not incarceration. But everyone lost their minds, and the Greens torpedoed it. They then had the audacity to say we were not doing enough. But when we offered to do something like that, they opposed it. I can be critical of the Green MLAs all day long, but I have to say there were also people within the NDP and some within the Liberals who took the same view.

In the Legislature, every time there was a coroner's update on overdose fatalities, it became fodder for Question Period. Whenever that happens, you're no longer genuinely talking about the need for policy change. You're talking politics. You're trying to diminish your opponent rather than trying to find a solution. Did it become politicized? It did. Man, it did. Good luck with that. When we were in opposition, we did it too. But when I had the opportunity, I called on the legislative health committee to address the crisis in a non-partisan way. I welcomed members who had been talking about the issue. Niki Sharma was the chair when we set it up. Sheila Malcolmson was also on it for us. She had been a Member of Parliament in Ottawa, so she came from an environment where any committee you set up is an inquisition designed to besmirch someone rather than solve a problem. They're all about lambasting ministers. No one talks about people who are suffering. But for us, if the Opposition parties thought they had a better idea, we were ready to hear it.

Two months later, they issued their report. Solutions were proposed. Government accepted the recommendations. Not long afterwards, another coroner's report came out. The death toll was higher than the month before, and the hyperbolic partisanship returned. It's really sad. I don't have an answer. We can't provide the perfect silver bullet. I will say that we went through safe supply a lot, and that makes complete sense to me. If we can take the poison off the street and replace it with something that won't kill you, while still meeting your addiction, then we should do that. If you're an addict, you're looking for one thing only, your next fix. Wouldn't it be appropriate for governments and the health-care system to work together to ensure that people in this situation don't end up dead? But the advocates could not agree on how best to do that. It all seems pretty simple on the surface, but it's been impossible in practice.

As for decriminalization, we worked hard on that and eventually all the key stakeholders, including police chiefs, said they fully supported it. We wanted decriminalization to be a province-wide issue, because people were dying in Kamloops, they were dying in Kelowna, not just in the city of Vancouver. We had to fight with Vancouver mayor Kennedy Stewart, who saw himself as czar of saving the world without much idea of what he was talking about. He characterized himself as using his connections in Ottawa from his term and a half as an Opposition member with the NDP. Meanwhile, we were dealing directly with the health minister and with Trudeau. Trudeau didn't want to do it. As it turned out, he was right. No one anticipated the open drug use and how big a problem that would be. It turned into a bit of a train wreck. I also wonder if the harm reduction train is also coming to a halt. Even very committed physicians are reluctant to prescribe opioids. There is a clutch of advocates who are like, "We need to give crack pipes out in vending machines." Wild harm reduction stuff. "Give everybody what they need and everything will be fine." Well, no, they're not going to be fine. They're still going to die. "Oh, they won't be stigmatized. They'll have their dignity." What dignity is it for someone bent like a question mark lying in the gutter on Hastings Street? My efforts in all these matters were pretty much unsuccessful.

There's also the matter of housing. At the time, the closing of the Riverview mental health facility and bringing patients back into the community made complete sense to me. But if you're not going to put community supports in place for them, it's going to fail. And, boy, did it fail. We need more Riverviews but doing different things in different ways than they did up to the 1970s. Enough time has gone by. Let's have a genuine discussion about what treatment looks like. How do you deliver that in a setting that protects the individual and protects the community as well? People in some cities are terrified to walk down some streets, and that's not fair to citizens. It's not fair to the people who live on those streets.

We have to get back to some semblance of eliminating the criminal element—the big players, not the addicts—and that means really charging up law enforcement. But when we were trying to do that, it was a time when there were all these cries to "defund the police." It was very difficult to address the root cause with some of our base saying, you know, "We don't need any police." I had the best of intentions at the beginning of our government, and right through the first few years, but by the time we had a majority, I just pushed it all away. Geoff had to spend way more time on it than he wanted to, but we weren't making any progress. My personal intervention was not going to make a difference. The minister still had to respond every month to the growing number of fatalities. In Question Period it was always about how insensitive we were, and then people forgot about it until the next month's total would come out. I don't know how others felt about it, but that's how it felt to me. Did we do enough? Clearly not. But there was no shortage of effort by people on the ground and by people in government.

CHAPTER SEVENTEEN

JUSTIN TRUDEAU AND ME

AND OTHER POLITICIANS I HAVE KNOWN

I GREW UP IN THE ERA OF JUSTIN'S FATHER, PIERRE ELLIOTT TRUDEAU. I was an undergrad at the time. Trudeau was a progressive. He was dynamic. He had beaten Joe Clark in the 1980 election, which was kind of the first wakening of politics for me. I was taken by the fact that I was working with the son of the first prime minister I was ever aware of. I was not aware of Lester Pearson. I wasn't aware of Diefenbaker. I was aware of Pierre Trudeau, so there was a bit of that star factor with Justin. He's got a beautiful head of hair. I mocked him about that. And he had the good sense not to mock me about my absence of hair. We had a solid relationship right off the bat. In all my engagements with people who had a different political perspective, whether they be municipal politicians, other premiers, federal ministers or the prime minister, I always felt it was not just my responsibility as head of the government of British Columbia, but as someone who built a career out of trying to collaborate with people with different points of view, to try and build friendships. I'd have to say we hit it off. We had challenges along the way, but he saw electoral advantage in British Columbia. The Tories do well here, the New Democrats do well, and the Liberals, when they are successful, do well in BC. When they are not successful, it's calamitous for them. He saw me as someone who had deep roots in BC. That was something he could take advantage of, and of course BC was also a chance for him to visit Tofino and friends and family that he had out here.

They are not as deep as mine, but he has roots in British Columbia, too. He taught school here. He worked here. BC has a special place in his heart. I know politicians always say they're this or they're that. I remember Christy Clark once saying that in her heart she was Filipina. Well, no, she wasn't, but politicians take these hyperbolic approaches and try to become part of the local fabric, no matter how bogus. But Justin Trudeau was genuinely part of the local fabric because of his mother's family. I didn't have to tell him what the issues were in British Columbia. He understood them in a way previous prime ministers hadn't. There have not been a lot of British Columbians who have played a prominent role in our national government. Other than Kim Campbell, Trudeau is as close to a British Columbian as we have had.

One of the things we connected on was salmon. That was something I was very passionate about. I wanted to make sure the federal government didn't ignore this iconic species that has had such an impact on the landscape, our wildlife, and the people here going back thousands of years. When I mentioned salmon, he lit up and began talking about going to the Capilano fish hatchery with his grandfather as a kid. That's not to say other political leaders won't be able to learn the issues out here, but Justin had a physical connection to the land and the people of BC, and we have not had that in our history. It's a shame.

He was well versed on substantive issues. I think it's unfortunate that he was cast by his opponents and by the media as this kind of glib, superficial fellow. Although there are likely many situations and issues he may not be fully conversant on, I can't imagine even walking a day in the shoes of a prime minister, with all of the cleavages and diversity in Canada. Just the Ottawa–Montreal axis is tough enough, much less the Maritimes, the North, the Prairies, Alberta and the West Coast. I was never going to be that critical of him.

I've often told the tale of the spilled glass of water at our first meeting in Ottawa. It's a story I never tire of. Not only was it funny, but I think it endeared me to Trudeau. Whenever he came to BC, we always tried to get together. I took advantage of our relationship to ensure that when there were issues with federal connections or components requiring federal funding, he was listening to me, and we were seeing results. I worked hard to cultivate that relationship.

Of course, we had big disagreements over the Kinder Morgan pipeline after the government bought it. To be honest, I don't think that was Trudeau's first, second, or even third choice, but he and his team felt it was a requirement for national unity. It was not in the best interests of his climate initiatives. It was not in the best interests of his collaborative federalism approach, because we were very much opposed to it. And there weren't too many others across the country who cared one way or the other. But Quebec was excited about the pipeline going west since they didn't want any pipeline going east, and Alberta wanted it in a big way. It may have been the right call for Canada. It was not the right call for BC. But he made it, and it did not affect our relationship.

We had several meetings while sharing a meal. One was lunch at the White Spot in 2021. It was all about child care. The federal government wanted to have a national child-care program before the next election. They saw we had had success with our ten-dollars-a-day initiative and were laying the groundwork for a lifetime of learning that would start from infancy rather than kindergarten and go all the way to adult education and apprenticeship programs. They wanted to follow our lead. We were already there, but other provinces were kind of territorial. They didn't want the feds intruding into their jurisdiction. I didn't disagree with that, but I also knew that an influx of federal money would allow us to move even faster on our own initiative.

Trudeau and I announced our agreement on child-care funding at the Lafarge Lake park in Coquitlam. The organizers of these things said we should have a picnic, and I said, "What are you talking about? He's busy. I'm busy." I was happy just to have had the announcement. We ended up getting a bag lunch from White Spot and having hamburgers at a table outside. The photographers loved it, but it wasn't just a photo op. We had a real conversation about child care, besides how good the burgers were. It's not like we spent tons of time together, but when we did it was genuine. We were friends.

Trudeau and I had another gastronomic summit after I became chair of the Council of the Federation. We'd been hammering away at Ottawa over health-care funding. Trudeau said he was coming out, and we'd talk about it. I had just had surgery. I was all bloated up, looking like a bag of hammers. We had a press conference, and the plan was for us to go out for dinner. But people had heard that Trudeau was coming, and there was a protest at the Legislature. My press secretary called the federal entourage as they arrived at the airport to give them a heads-up. The innocent on the other end of the phone said, "Oh, what's the subject?" My press secretary said, "I don't know. It's Victoria. It's a protest. It's every subject. Pick one." They came, and there was yelling and screaming and drums beating and so on. We had our media session at the Legislature, and instead of going out for dinner, Trudeau and I went up to the private members' lounge in the Legislature. We got a couple of six packs of beer and a couple of pizzas, and we spent three hours talking about where do we go and what do we need to do. There was no staff, just us. I don't think anyone's ever talked or written about our Pizza Summit. We talked about whatever came up, soup to nuts, cabbages and kings. But I kept bringing it back to health care. Health care, health care, health care. That was easy to do, because I had a big slash on my neck, and I was going to be getting radiation. I wasn't worried about it, but I was worried about my energy. When I took over the Council of the Federation, I didn't have cancer. Now I did.

Justin eventually agreed to set up some sort of framework for discussing health-care funding. He would appoint his health minister, Jean-Yves Duclos, Finance Minister Chrystia Freeland,

and the minister of intergovernmental affairs, Dominic LeBlanc. Sadly, nothing really came of it. When we were together for our beer and pizza, he had seemed genuine. He had understood the problem, and he wanted to fix it. But nothing happened. Having been a premier, I knew there were always a bunch of problems I was aware of, wanted to fix and wasn't able to, and not because of lack of effort or sincerity. Something like that may have affected Trudeau's failure to follow through on his commitment, but to be honest it felt like a set-up.

So there were these frustrations, but overall I enjoyed being with Trudeau. He has a theatre background, so some of it may have been feigned, but I have a pretty good bullshit meter. I liked him, and I think he liked me. We didn't see eye to eye on a lot of things, but he knew we were champions of carbon pricing and climate change initiatives. Those were issues he wanted to bring forward. He didn't have a lot of allies across the country. When I was first sworn in, there was a Liberal premier in Nova Scotia, a Liberal premier in New Brunswick, and Liberal premiers in Ontario and Quebec. When I left, there were no Liberal premiers in any of those places. He was running out of folks to talk to. Rachel Notley was also gone, so there were Conservative premiers across the country, except for BC and Newfoundland. That limited the number of people he could have a serious conversation with. I benefited from that. British Columbia did as well, because we needed to have a federal government focused on our interests. We made progress. A host of things got done: the child-care initiative, funding on rapid transit, significant ocean stuff, and an icebreaker, which is supposed to be coming.

That was critically important to me on a personal level. As a maritime province, why are we not building more vessels here? Why does Halifax and Davie Shipbuilding in Quebec continue to get the lion's share of shipbuilding contracts? We have worked hard to get commitments to build vessels staggered in a way that would allow us to maintain and grow a workforce in the shipyards of Vancouver and the Island.

At the same time, we signed a lot of things with the federal government that didn't happen. I think it's important to mention that. For instance, we wanted to electrify the gas fields. If we were going to export LNG, we needed to reduce emissions at the wellhead. The fastest and best way to do that is to electrify those processes to reduce domestic emissions. That would help us in both the short and long term. The federal government agreed. We signed an MOU (memorandum of understanding), and to this day, I don't believe a thing has happened on it. That was typical of their government in other areas as well. But it was atypical to our relationship.

I also had a good working relationship with Erin O'Toole, the leader of the Conservative Party at the time. I was NDP, but I wasn't critical of him. I saw him as a moderate. I met him a couple of times, and I was very impressed. I told him I would never vote for him, but as long as he was focusing on the needs of British Columbians, I would be right there with him and be supportive of his efforts to build his team out here. After he lost the election and was being thrown off the boat, I phoned him up and encouraged him to stay on: "You're a normal human being. The world needs more normal human beings. Try to resist those who want immediate gratification and keep trying to build relationships across party lines, across the various schisms, sector by sector." These are the people we need in public life: people who understand that total victory is not on, regardless of their ideological perspectives. Victory comes when you bring as many people as possible to the end result. That's good politics. It's also good policy.

After Rachel Notley lost in 2019, I was the only NDP premier in the West. At the Western Premiers' Conference, there were three right-wingers and me. That wasn't a problem. I'm comfortable with most people. Jason Kenney and I got along pretty well. Geoff and I met with him and his chief of staff quite early on. The Western Premiers' meeting was in Edmonton, and we went a day ahead of time so we could, you know, deal with TMX, deal with the wine boycott, and were they going to turn off the taps. Just kidding about the last one. Rachel Notley had threatened to do that. I would still have preferred her as premier of Alberta, but you deal with what you have. Jason Kenney had just won a majority, and we wanted to make sure we started with as clean a slate as possible. After his years in the cabinet of Stephen Harper, he seemed to be one of the best politicians to arrive in that office in a long time. Who knew that his collapse would be so colossal? It certainly didn't feel that way at the beginning. When we were sitting down for our meeting, I was more at risk than he was. We had a minority government, while he had a very comfortable majority. He was bilingual and totally consumed by politics. He didn't do anything else but politics. We wanted to get in there and get a sense of how this was going to work out. And we did. We also had some laughs, although a couple of times I would tell a joke, and he had this way of pausing before he laughed. It was almost like he was processing it. Is Horgan being funny? Social cues were sometimes lost on Jason.

Scott Moe and I got along ridiculously well. He's more right-wing than Jason Kenney. He's against the carbon tax and he's anti-tax in general. But, again, my approach was to find things you agree on and focus on them. Try to avoid the issues where they have chips on their shoulders.

Doug Ford and I first met at a premiers' conference in New Brunswick. He had recently won the election, and this was his coming-out party. At the time, Rachel Notley and I were still fighting, so we were very much a hot topic among the media. Then Doug arrived. Literally, like being drawn by a magnet, all the media rushed towards him, leaving us totally alone. As we stood there together, I remember saying to Rachel: "You know, we could be dancing naked in the garden, and no one would notice." Doug had a very narrow view. He represented Ontario, but it might just as well have been Toronto. I'm sure he's expanded his interests, but in the beginning, it was all Toronto—or rather Scarborough,

Scarborough, Scarborough, with Etobicoke thrown in. But we got along. After a few months, he said to me, "I'm sure glad the NDP in Ontario is not like you. We'd be in deep trouble." I would get texts from him. One day I got a message from him that he was in cabinet and needed some advice. Could he call? And I thought, I've got to keep this. Who would have thought something like this might happen? Once again, I hadn't changed my values one bit. I was just always of the view that we need to find a way to get through stuff. I found myself sitting at the head of the premiers' table with a bunch of people with different points of view, and we still managed to work collaboratively on the issues that we shared.

I like Jagmeet Singh. I'm proud to be part of the first federal party to elect a visible minority as their leader. And, as a turban-wearing Sikh, he's very visibly a minority. I give him full marks for his courage and his intellect and his passion for people. But the federal and the provincial NDP are two different animals. I remember being on a panel for the federal election in 2021, and this person from the Ontario NDP attributed Jagmeet Singh's lack of success to the policies of the John Horgan government. I was listening to this person from Toronto I'd never met, not set eyes on before, talking about something she knew nothing about, having no idea of what it's like to run a government. If she had looked more closely at the results, she would have seen that the only place the federal NDP held their own was BC. For the Toronto-based NDP, which has been driving the federal party for some time—Jagmeet is from Brampton—it was a complete misunderstanding of what role New Democrats can play in government. Upon becoming leader, Jagmeet called me and told me he was thinking of running in Burnaby. I responded, "Why would you do that?" He said that people were saying he needed to get a seat in the House of Commons. And I said that I would tell him a little story.

When he was first elected leader, Jack Layton did not run for a seat in Parliament. He travelled around the country talking to people. Eventually, he oversaw the largest clutch of federal NDPers ever elected. Fast forward to Tom Mulcair, regarded by many as one of the most effective Opposition leaders in the history of Parliament, and he got whomped. I asked Jagmeet, "Why are you rushing to get into the House of Commons to follow Tom Mulcair when you should be following Jack Layton? Go and talk to people. You're not going to increase our vote out here if you move to BC, because we're already doing pretty well, particularly in the Republic of Burnaby." I said the NDP needed him in Toronto, in Brampton, in the suburbs, to tell the story of social democracy there. He disagreed with me. He ran in Burnaby, he was elected, he got to the House of Commons, and there was no impact. No one pays attention to the House of Commons except the people in the press gallery. My only criticism of Jagmeet is that he is following a songbook that is not going to work for social democrats. We need to be on the ground talking to people, understanding what the issues are, not simply hectoring the government but offering alternatives.

We disagreed on LNG, but I knew the challenges he faced and that he was going to oppose it. I made it pretty clear, there are people in Burnaby who will disagree with you on LNG. At the same time, there are likely people in Brampton and people at the Council of Canadians who will think better of you if you stand up for their fundraising initiatives. However, if you want to change the public's view of the NDP, you have to change what you're saying and how you're saying it. Continuing to say, "I'm against, I'm against, I'm against" will not get you a single building trades worker. If you keep on saying the NDP stands against whatever is going on, people will keep on saying you're a great Opposition party. If you want to form government, you've got to start talking as if you can form the government. Having said all that, I have enormous respect for him. I'd vote for him tomorrow if he was on the ballot. So that's the end of that.

CHAPTER EIGHTEEN

2021: *ANNUS HORRIBILIS*

From late June to early July of 2021, BC experienced extreme temperatures that shattered all previous records. Labelled a "heat dome," the excessive heat claimed the lives of 619 people, most of whom were older adults living alone with compromised health due to chronic diseases. In mid-November, the southwest of the province was deluged by two days of extraordinarily intense rainfall, which meteorologists called an "atmospheric river." The resulting floods and landslides devastated communities and farmland, washed away roads, forced more than 3,300 people from their homes, and claimed five lives. The year was also BC's third worst wildfire season to date, sparked by severe drought and record heat. All told, more than 1,600 fires consumed nearly 9,000 square kilometres of land, and 181 evacuation orders were issued. On June 30, in the midst of the hottest day ever recorded in Canadian history, the town of Lytton burned to the ground. Two residents died.

AS WE HEADED INTO 2021 WITH OUR MAJORITY GOVERNMENT, WE HAD no idea what lay ahead. It would turn into a terrible year, both for the province and for me personally. BC was hit by two unprecedented—there's that word again—climate change disasters, months of devastating wildfires, and I was diagnosed with throat cancer. All of these events took a toll.

The heat dome was the first to hit us. We were accused of not being prepared. But, you know, it's interesting, I was in my house in Langford and something was going on that I'd never experienced before. We'd lived in Australia, for goodness' sake, yet I'd never felt anything like the heat that late June weekend on southern Vancouver Island. I reached out to the ministry of health and asked them if we were ready for these high temperatures, because I found that I was struggling with them. I didn't know I had cancer at the time, but I'm a relatively healthy middle-aged guy, and I was finding it hard to cope. What was happening in the rest of the province? What was happening in emergency rooms? What was happening with the paramedics? I was assured that everything was good, which was a relief to know. Two days later, of course, we found out six hundred people had died.

I could be critical of our response, but I'm not. To what end? No one had experienced anything like this. No one had expected the atmospheric river we had later in the year, either. No one expected a pandemic. These things had never happened before, so how could you be critical of people who were stretched to the max? For a variety of reasons, we don't have enough people in the health-care system to deliver the services people expect. We had taken steps to try and increase recruitment and retention of everyone from care aides to specialist surgeons, with little effect, so I'm not going to be critical of anyone.

It's true we didn't have a province-wide emergency alert system in place during these events. Mike Farnworth had been trying for a long time to get one that worked, because they are not always effective. Sometimes they are, and sometimes they're not. We have one now, but it took time to get there, and it's a little bit different than everyone else's. But it's like the mask mandate: If you're looking for silver bullets to solve complex and vast problems, you're not going to find them.

The heat dome was tragic, beyond imagination. And I misspoke by saying "fatalities are a part of life." When you speak as much as I do, occasionally you're going to say something that's going to clang. I will regret forever saying that sometimes people die. I'm saddened there are advocates who just want to keep punching me in the face over that: "Oh, he was horrible. Look what he said." Well, you know, I've said ten billion words, and you can pull out a lot that were stupid, but it doesn't change how absolutely heartbroken I was, and I could feel it happening. My elbow was twitching. I could sense something was going on that was totally new and different.

We didn't know how much of a crisis it was until it was over. It took twelve hours for the system to understand what had actually happened. Many people didn't come to the hospital, they died at home. The total might actually be higher than six hundred because there were people who had other ailments that led to their deaths. But the fact is, as I keep saying, the system had never experienced this before.

How I reacted to it as a politician was unfortunate, but not relevant. What's important is that now I'm listening to radio broadcasts, watching TV news, looking at the internet, and people are being reminded what to do when it's really hot. Check on Granny. Make sure the people in that walk-up who don't have air conditioning are okay. The government now has a program to get air conditioning into places where people can't afford it. Some say there should be a maximum temperature that rental units and houses can't go beyond. I don't know how you implement that, but we're talking about it. We weren't talking about it two years ago. I wasn't even thinking about it two years ago.

During the heat dome, the town of Lytton burned to the ground on the hottest day it had ever experienced. Residents believed the fire was set off by a passing freight train, although neither the Transportation Safety Board nor the RCMP were able to pinpoint the cause with certainty. The people of Lytton are still not at home. There are reasons for that. It was an industrial town.

There are toxic contaminants all over the place that have to be cleaned up. A majority of residents didn't have insurance, which we had to figure out. And I remember saying that when we rebuild, we have to rebuild with a view to climate change because Lytton is always the hottest place in BC. Always. Let's rebuild Lytton to prepare for these types of events because they are going to keep happening. But there have been all these roadblocks, which have delayed rebuilding Lytton to whatever it's going to be.

On top of that, there were Indigenous issues. Lytton is where the Thompson and the Fraser Rivers come together. People have been there for thousands of years. It's not just a matter of digging a little deeper, putting down some foundations and starting again. There are archaeological values there that have to be respected. But having said all of this, I just couldn't believe how long it was taking. I kept turning to Mike Farnworth: "What the hell's going on? Why are we not doing something?"

It was one of our worst wildfire seasons ever. The fires started in the spring and went right through the summer and into the fall. They seemed to be burning everywhere in the province. Thousands of people were evacuated, and many homes elsewhere were lost, in addition to the town of Lytton. I remember thinking: How long can this go on?

Then there was the atmospheric river, which was very bizarre to me. I have lived in Ocean Falls. It gets fourteen feet of rain a year, so there's an atmospheric river there all the time. At one point, I went back to Ocean Falls to talk about First Nations issues. When I arrived, it was raining. When I left, it was raining. And living on southern Vancouver Island, it's a rainforest out in Sooke and Port Renfrew. We get a lot of rain. I was accustomed to that. But I wasn't accustomed to the rain we got during the atmospheric river in November and the floods that resulted. The consequences to farmland and our roads and infrastructure were staggering. We were not prepared for something like this. How could you be?

Mike Farnworth, who was in charge of emergency preparedness, was also minister of public safety and solicitor general. There is now a specific minister for emergency management. Bowinn Ma was the first. Before I left, I was talking to cabinet about the need for some sort of Marshall Plan for climate change in British Columbia. Take the issue of dykes. When I was in opposition, every time I talked to a mayor along the Fraser River about maintaining and raising the dykes, they would say they didn't have the money to do that. The BC Liberals had downloaded responsibility for that onto the municipalities. There was no plan in place. I kept saying this was the ideal time to start thinking about what we were going to do about that. The fact that nothing has really come of it is disappointing to say the least.

People keep saying there are no longer any votes in advocating measures to combat climate change, but there have to be. After heat domes and atmospheric rivers, and after successive wildfire seasons, everybody understands there's something different going on. This is not our grandparents' Kansas anymore. This is a new place, a new normal, however you want to characterize it. Governments can't continue to carry on the way they have in the past. They have to start doing new things for the future. COVID had already showed us that we didn't have enough people to protect and care for vulnerable populations. Whether in care homes or in four-storey walk-ups in the Downtown Eastside, we didn't have the infrastructure to protect people. During the heat dome, it got to be thirty-five degrees at three in the morning. We need to do something about that, too, rather than just say, "Oh, wasn't that unfortunate?" Because it's going to keep happening. Governments have got to get their head around that, and the only way they will do it is if the public says, "Please do something."

These weren't the only challenges we faced in 2021. We had to make another big decision on Site C. Costs were continuing to escalate and there were geotechnical issues. We had a new minister, Bruce Ralston. Our previous energy minister, Michelle Mungall, had a baby, then a second baby, and decided she'd had enough of politics. Bruce was the Renaissance man of the cabinet. He was very well read and an expert on his own file and on everyone else's as well. With my background in energy, he knew he had to sharpen his tools, so he was always ultra-prepared. He told us about the geotechnical challenges of the powerhouse for Site C. It was a massive infrastructure project, the largest of its kind on the Peace River. My first reaction was that after forty years of assessments, you would think they would have had it right. But technology means they can now determine infinitesimal movements of the earth.

When Bruce told us there were significant technical issues, you could see the reaction from those around the table who had been there for our first decision: "Will this never go away?" I've already talked about fires and floods and pestilence and all the rest of it. Now Site C was back because advanced technologies had discovered these geotechnical issues. Of course, thank goodness they were discovered. But fixing them involved drilling a swack of boreholes to stabilize the infrastructure, and the estimated cost had ballooned to $16 billion.

We had to reassess our original decision to go ahead. There were now fifty-seven members of caucus. Many of them were new and had to be brought up to speed. We went through the same process as we did on our first go-round, although we didn't bring in the energy and resource economists that we did before—or the environmentalists, for that matter. We brought in geotechnical experts to explain to us in minute detail why we needed to increase the capital cost to get a better outcome. Bruce was as prepared as any minister could be. He was grilled over and over with technical questions, and he had the answers right on the table. Everyone was apprehensive. It was another opportunity for those opposed to Site C to say, "I told you so. You should have stopped when the cost to cancel was $4 billion. You would have saved another $8 billion." When we announced our decision to proceed, however, despite the added costs, Bruce didn't get a single question in Question Period. It didn't come up.

And despite the mega-costs, as I keep saying, those 1,100 megawatts of clean energy will be dispatchable twenty-four hours a day, seven days a week, twelve months of the year. The value of that in an energy-constrained marketplace is enormous, even if getting there has been one of the province's most challenging public policy questions. Whoever writes the book on Site C will need multiple volumes just on our period, much less all the previous work done by Social Credit, by the Harcourt and Clark administrations, by Gordon Campbell, and then finally by Christy Clark.

One of the experts we brought in the first time around was Mark Jaccard, a recognized expert on sustainable energy. He can be arrogant, but he's smart. Although he, too, had had more than one position on Site C, he's a true climate guy. He looked at the landscape of British Columbia and said there was nowhere else we could find firm power at that price. The longer you wait, the more expensive it will become. And the dam may yet come in at $20 billion. But I don't think there's any doubt that at the end of the day we will all be better off having that energy, particularly in an era of climate change.

Yet another difficult situation was Fairy Creek, up by Port Renfrew and in my own riding. More than a thousand people were arrested as part of a huge, prolonged protest against the logging of old-growth forests. This was a long-standing issue which came home to roost for us, and it frustrated me no end. I was thinking that we had made all these old-growth decisions thirty years ago, but the kids of today said, "Well, I don't care, man. You need to make new decisions for my generation and generations to come." They weren't necessarily wrong, yet I continue to hold fast to the idea that communities, workers, governments and Indigenous people have to have working forests. The plan has always been to harvest these areas in a sustainable way. During the campaign, I said that many old-growth stands are worth more standing than they are lying down. That's absolutely true and remains true today. But it doesn't mean we have to stop everything tomorrow. There was some photo of a truck driving down the highway with one massive cedar log. That's manna from heaven for protestors. Even if the tree had been cut down in 2020, before regulations to protect special trees took effect, as a fundraising tool such a photo was priceless.

It was all very well for me to say the amount of planned harvesting, which was driven by First Nations, was infinitesimal in the grand scheme of things. The pictures of enormous cedar logs on the internet, with people saying, "Send us money and we'll stop this," and Hollywood personalities saying they were going to go and lie down on the road, resulted in thousands of people coming to protest. They said they were doing it in the name of the First Nations. It didn't matter that Indigenous leaders from the area asked them to please go away. They said they were staying because one Indigenous guy said they could be there. Money was flowing in from around the world. They wouldn't reason, they wouldn't negotiate, they wouldn't do anything except stop everything. It didn't matter that right beside Fairy Creek were Carmanah and Walbran, two huge old-growth areas that were protected long ago and will be there for all time.

We put a process in place not unlike what we did for Site C. We invited the more thoughtful ringleaders to sit down with us and our experts. Let's determine just how much old-growth forest is left. Let's not leave this to chance and speculation. Let's draw some maps. Let's figure it out—which is what we did in the 1990s with Clayoquot and other watersheds. And we got good results. The people who participated were confident they weren't being hoodwinked by "deep state bureaucrats" who were only involved in forestry because they wanted to denude the hillside. They, too, are passionate about the environment and our forests. They go to work every day trying to have an industry that will create wealth but also an industry that will be sustainable over many generations. I felt there was a sense of trust between the environmental groups, internal government representatives and the minister. We tried to get to a place where people were comfortable.

Garry Merkel, a member of the Tahltan Nation, chaired our old-growth advisory panel. He was on the side of the environmentalists, the First Nations' side and also the industry's side. It's tough having separate components. With Garry, we were able to have all sides represented in one person: "I'm Indigenous, I'm a forester, and I'm also someone who lives in a community. I'm the whole package, and I understand how we can get through this." His leadership was pretty important. I think it stifled some of the more shrill voices in our caucus and within the environmental movement. When you can have someone of Garry's calibre saying that these are the steps we need to take and government is moving in that direction, it's a big plus. Having everyone at the table is the only way to resolve this. But some of the people invited to sit down with us refused because it might curtail their fundraising activities: "I'm not going to make money saying that I'm sitting down with the government right now, but if I'm saying, 'I'm lying in a ditch on a road in the middle of a forest,' people will send me money."

We put out a white paper on the future of the forest industry. We also agreed to defer old-growth logging in a number of areas pending further study. I think it's safe to say we went further than I intended to go but not further than we needed to go. In the meantime, we had also agreed to a request from the First Nations to put off the logging of old-growth timber at Fairy Creek for two years. But that still wasn't good enough for many of the protestors. People kept yelling at me. And when I look back at that time, what really pissed me off is that much of what happened at Fairy Creek was initiated by some teenager in Washington State who used Google Maps and saw there was a road into this green area. I'm not making this up. He was seventeen when he started it, and I kept wondering, "What the hell do *you* have to do with forest policy in British Columbia?"

I've always felt that the best way through any conflict is to find a resolution that meets the interests of as many of the conflicting components as you can. We set out to do that, and we made progress, but when I would lay out, the minister would lay out and the public service would lay out what we were doing, and here is the data, it was still not good enough for some. I got very exasperated: "Not good enough for who, and who made you king?" They didn't want a single old-growth tree to fall. I would prefer that, too, but it's not practical. In one sense, the protestors were correct that not all was right in the kingdom. It's a different world from the solutions we came up with thirty years ago, and the forest companies never lived up to their commitments. Yet it's not all broken. Some of the decisions made in the past were good decisions. They need to be maintained. The challenge for government is that your regulatory regime needs to be robust enough to not only meet the commitments of the past but also be able to follow new commitments that need to be made for a new future.

At the end of this *annus horribilis*, while we were struggling with all these issues, I was diagnosed with throat cancer. This was my second cancer. And it's funny, my bladder cancer was diagnosed by accident, after I went to the doctor for a sore shoulder. I had no outward symptoms. Had I not gone in with my sore shoulder, the cancer would have advanced for who knows how long, so I was lucky. It was similar with the throat cancer. I had a lump in my neck, which I still have to this day. I asked Dr. Bonnie Henry what she thought about it. She said she couldn't give me any medical advice, but that I should see someone, you're not supposed to have lumps in your neck. So I went to my GP. That started the process. Eventually I had what's called an ultrasound biopsy. I'd already had a PET scan, but they hadn't been fully transparent with me. Interestingly, that PET scanner had actually been opened by us in Victoria so that people didn't have to go to Vancouver. When I went for my test, I said hi to the woman there, and she said she had met me when we opened the facility. I said, "Well, I want you to know that when we did that, I didn't expect to be lying inside it."

The PET scan had discovered that behind the lump in my neck—my throat—was cancer. I had noticed over time that I was gulping a lot. I thought maybe it was some sort of nervous tic from giving speeches. I found it extremely difficult to stop having this gulping sensation when I was about to go on for a press conference. Kim Emerson, the former reporter, had been giving me some advice on presentation when I was in opposition, and he asked me why I kept gulping like that. I said I had no idea, I just needed some water. But it turned out be a manifestation of the throat cancer going back to 2015 and 2016.

They told me there was good news and bad news. The good news was that the lump in my neck was benign. But the cancer behind that was a problem. After the ultrasound biopsy, I ended up having surgery to remove my lymph glands, with radiation to follow. Meanwhile, we'd been through these extraordinary times in the province. The atmospheric river happened between surgery and radiation. I was largely consumed with my personal situation, but it did not prevent me from wanting to be involved in every aspect of what we were doing. I was continuing to text. I was talking to Geoff and talking to my deputy, Lori Wanamaker, every day, trying to make sure that there was at least the perception I was still involved in government. Other than the anaesthetic and the radiation treatments, which were brief but intense, I don't think I missed too many beats.

I had in mind that I could plough through it. The prognosis was good. But there was still COVID, there were still climate issues, there was still an opioid crisis, and all the things the leader of the government needs to focus on. It was at that point I first had the thought that maybe my time was up. Not because of cancer, but I started to inventory our horrible year, then I went back to the year before that and the year before that, and I started casting forward to what was ahead. I mean, I was sure it couldn't get any worse than 2021, but maybe it would. I started questioning and doubting my ability to continue to function at a high level and provide what people expected of me. There was now a seed of doubt about whether I should run for a third term.

I went through thirty-five radiation treatments, and they were tough. I shed forty pounds. After the thirty-third treatment, I was violently sick every twenty minutes. But there was nothing to vomit. I hadn't eaten in a week and a half. It was just bile. It was the worst I'd ever felt in my life. At the next session, the oncologist said it was unusual for me to react that way. He thought it might be a response to the morphine I'd been prescribed, but he didn't want to rule anything out, so we did a test for COVID and suddenly all the health-care workers were in full PPE just in case. They would come in, see me, then take it all off and put it in a receptable to be burned. When I went in for my second-to-last treatment, everything had plastic all over it except where I was going to lie down. And I was thinking, why not have COVID, too? That's a nice way to end. It turned out I didn't have COVID, but that was my frame of mind.

We were into January by this time. What's 2022 going to be like? Can't wait. Let's get started. Two weeks after the last treatment, I was back in the office. Stupid, really stupid. But I felt I had to. I've looked back at photos they took at the time, and my thought is, "Who let me out of the house?" But I felt good. I'd lost a lot of weight. I'd had a beard prior to the radiation. All the hair came off. It just kept falling off where the zapping had happened. I had a suit on that I hadn't worn in ten years. I had a mask on because COVID was still around. I went up to the microphone to address caucus. They were all happy to see me. They hadn't seen me for a while. And I said, "The suit's from 2014." I took off the mask and said, "The moustache is from 1984." All my other hair had abandoned me, but the moustache stayed. I figured, what the heck, I'll keep it. Obviously, this had been a transformative, life-changing experience for me, as these things generally are.

The support I received and felt went through the roof. There were stacks and stacks of cards from well-wishers across the country. One guy really stood out: Tony from Salmon Arm. He had the same diagnosis I had, but he'd started treatment a month ahead of me. He was able to predict how I was going to feel at various times—these things are going to happen, then afterwards you're going to feel this. I called him the Ghost of Christmas Yet to Come. He was representative of all the good wishes I was getting. There was no partisan stuff. And this support continued after I got back.

CHAPTER NINETEEN

INDIGENOUS ISSUES AND RECONCILIATION

I HAD PLAYED LACROSSE WITH THE SAMPSON KIDS, AND TOM SAMPSON was Chief of the Tsartlip Nation when I became an MLA. One day, he and I were walking through a part of his territory where a golf course and resort were being built—Bear Mountain it is now. It was a massive, sprawling development in my community, and he was showing me some sacred sites. There was one particular spot he wouldn't show me. I said, "Why don't you tell people where these are so we can put them on the map?" He said that if he told people where they were, everyone would go there. There was a cave with a pool, which was a cleansing pool that had been used for thousands of years. It was part of their highway, and they would stop at the sacred pool. Well, the developer blew it up and filled it with old tires and cement.

Chief Sampson and I had been friends since we were kids. We used to put quarters of oranges in our mouths and make our teeth orange between periods in lacrosse. And as we poked around, he commented: "Can you imagine what our moms would think? Here you are, an MLA, and I'm the Chief of our people, and we're walking through the bush, and I'm showing you all these cultural touchpoints." Then he stopped and said, "Oh, here's a white man's cultural artefact." And he picks up a golf ball. I'll never forget that. He's showing me burial cairns—they didn't carry the dead back to their villages, they buried them right where they were—and beside that is a stupid bloody golf ball. There's a clash of cultures right there, if there ever was one. I've tried my entire life to bridge that.

I spent my formative years in government as an analyst and adviser for resource-based issues. In British Columbia, you can't talk about resources without talking about Indigenous rights and title, and our thinking as a government had evolved on whether they exist. Indigenous people had been bringing forward court cases for a hundred years. They all said the same thing: "This is our land, we never ceded it, and we want it back."

The Harcourt government changed our approach. Technically, the Treaty Commission had been started under Social Credit, but treaties were first given flesh under Mike Harcourt, and then by subsequent governments. I was a product of that. By the time we came to government, however, there had been twenty-five years of treaty-making and only three or four treaties, despite millions of dollars spent on lawyers who would have to be paid back at some point. First Nations were at the tables in good faith, but they were saying this wasn't getting them anywhere. As Opposition leader, I had sat down with Grand Chief Stewart Phillip, Terry Teegee and Cheryl Casimer. I told them I was a big champion of treaties. And they said, "Well, you're a real dummy, because they're not working for us." And I said, "No, no, we're going to change the mandates. We're going to get outcomes." And they said, again, "No, we're not going to get outcomes. You seem a nice guy, Horgan. Why are you so stupid?" It was a sobering meeting.

I went back and talked to Indigenous representatives in my own community. I talked to other leaders I'd met. They weren't the big hitters, but they all said the same thing: The UN Declaration on the Rights of Indigenous Peoples (UNDRIP) was the way to go. Scott Fraser had been the NDP's critic on Indigenous issues for most of our time in opposition. He said they were right. We had to embrace it. We talked about it in caucus. There were people saying it would slow things down, it wasn't tenable, and it wouldn't work. I said the only thing that will work with Indigenous people is changing what we've been doing up until now, because that hasn't got us close to where we need to go. This was not part of the treaty process. It was separate.

UNDRIP acknowledged the extent of Indigenous rights and title and committed the government to involve them in all matters that affected their territory. I announced that if we were elected, we were going to implement it. The business community said this was madness, it was crazy. At the same time, they were also saying we needed to solve these problems with Indigenous rights and title. Investors don't like uncertainty. They can go elsewhere. For us, enough was enough. It was a big deal to promise it. It was an even bigger deal to do it.

Once we became government, I put Scott Fraser in charge. Having been our Indigenous critic for many years, he knew much more about Indigenous communities across the province than anyone else in our group. He was also a lovely guy with oodles of patience, which you need when you're dealing with Indigenous leaders and their communities. You don't just sit down and say, "Where are we?" It's more like, "How did we get here?" That's important. It's cultural. It's paramount for both sides of the table to first hear the stories.

Throughout this process, we were working with First Nations to actually create the legislation. It wasn't something we simply pulled out of a hat. This was a collaborative process with the Assembly of First Nations, the Union of BC Indian Chiefs and the First Nations Leadership Council. The federal government was also involved. Jody Wilson-Raybould was a prominent Indigenous leader from Vancouver Island who also happened to be minister of justice at the time. We struck a really positive working relationship. At some point, we were having a cabinet meeting, and we had invited Jody to speak to us about what Canada was going to do on the Declaration, because we were preparing to table legislation in the coming session. I was sitting at the head of the table. When Jody came in, I gave her my chair and moved one seat over. I looked on one side of me, and there was Melanie Mark. On the other side of me, there's Jody Wilson-Raybould. One of my colleagues took a cellphone picture of this, and I cherish it to this day. I'm sure that's never happened before. A white dude giving up the chair of a cabinet meeting to an Indigenous woman who is the minister of justice for Canada and then moving to sit beside the minister for advanced education, who is also an Indigenous woman.

It struck me in that moment how far we had come from the constitutionalist days of Mel Smith [BC's leading constitutional adviser until 1987], who argued for years against any additional rights for Indigenous people other than those in the BNA Act. It was a symbol to me that we were on the right track. I was ready to collaborate with Jody and the federal government to do this together.

Indigenous rights had not been extinguished in BC, as they were in other jurisdictions, so we really needed the UN Declaration. Jody and I were both in agreement, although the prime minister not so much. I'm not saying Trudeau wasn't supportive, he was, but then a funny thing happened. Jody disappeared from the cabinet, and then the Liberals, and so did the federal zeal for implementing UNDRIP. For all of Trudeau's professed support, there was no tangible outcome. When the feds fell away, we had a gut-check moment. Do we wait for them to get interested again, or do we just proceed? We chose to proceed.

It was well received by Indigenous communities. There was a significant ceremony when we tabled the bill in the Legislature. Grand Chief Stewart Phillip, Grand Chief Edward John, Regional Chief Terry Teegee and Cheryl Casimer of the First Nations Summit all addressed the Legislature. For them to be sitting at the clerk's table was unprecedented.

I want to say something here about Gordon Campbell. I appreciated his reversal on Indigenous rights and title. Early on in his government, they had brought forward what, in the opinion of many, including myself, can only be described as a racist referendum on minority rights. And it was a failure, a public relations disaster. To their credit, Campbell and his team did an about-face and accepted that they had to alter course, given numerous crystal-clear rulings by the courts on rights and title. They took up the challenge of expanding the economy to include Indigenous people. That change of position made it easier for me and our team to bring forward the UN Declaration on the Rights of Indigenous Peoples, and to have it passed unanimously in the Legislature. Andrew Wilkinson, who was then leader of the BC Liberals, had to twist a ton of arms in the Liberal caucus. Not the real Liberals, all two or three of them, but the conservative crew, who were, like, "We can't possibly do that. We'll be roasted back home." I give full marks to Wilkinson. He brought them along, and we had a unanimous vote on UNDRIP, which was really important.

Then we set about implementation, and that's where the challenges came. I don't want to dump on the lawyers at the attorney general's ministry. They were quite rightly saying, "We can't do that. We can't show randos"—as the kids say, meaning you can't show so-called random people—"draft legislation before it's been introduced in the House." That's counter to the foundations of responsible government. We had to change how we shared information and talked to each other. And there were issues like, if we're making a change to the Highways Act and it has no Indigenous impact, why are we having to consult with researchers at the Union of BC Indian Chiefs? That's a legitimate question from government. It will take time. The key is trust. That's something that always needs tending. There was trust when we introduced the bill, and there was trust when we started bringing forward specific legislation. One of the first test cases was how to take the principles of UNDRIP and transform our environmental assessment processes. That was an issue that George Heyman worked very hard on, and it was fundamental to investment choices.

On the matter of whether there was now an Indigenous veto, which concerns many people, I took comfort from Terry Teegee.

He said the words "free, prior and informed consent," which are part of the Declaration, were just that. We don't have a veto, but we need to know what you're doing on our territory. If we disagree with what you're doing, we can make it very difficult for you. That's different from saying you can't do it until I agree with you. I know that many who oppose the Declaration always pull out that clause about consent. Well, it's just a clause. It's big, but it's not a showstopper in my mind. I agreed to proceed only when I had a commitment from the Indigenous leadership that they felt that way, too. If you go back and read Terry's comments in the Legislature, he was pretty clear as a leader of Indigenous communities with the Assembly of First Nations that their interpretation was that UNDRIP did not give them a veto.

The easy route is not always the best choice. First of all, if we hadn't made the difficult choice we did, we would have been in litigation all the time. I maintained then, and I still do, that a dollar spent on litigation is a dollar wasted on reconciliation. Will there be obstacles? For sure. But I think we will all be better off down the road because we have started on that reconciliation journey. It's not a weekend, it's not a month, it's not a year. It's forever. We are cohabiting. I'm not going back to Ireland. My ancestors came here and we're staying. But we need to be respectful of the fact that when we arrived, whenever that was over the past two hundred years, whether from Asia, from Europe or from countries south of us, there were Indigenous people already here. They were well established, with traditions, with cultures, with economic foundations, and we need to be respectful of that history. We need to make sure that our future is collective rather than separate.

No Indigenous issue roiled the Horgan government more than opposition by Wet'suwet'en hereditary Chiefs to the building of the 670-kilometre Coastal GasLink pipeline through traditional

Wet'suwet'en territories, which covered close to a third of the pipeline route. Twenty pipeline benefit agreements were signed with elected band councils all along the way, including five elected councils who were part of the Wet'suwet'en Nation. But a number of their hereditary Chiefs did not agree. Supporters began blocking a forest service road, which construction crews used to access their work sites. Protestors defied court injunctions that ordered them to stop blocking the road. In early 2020, after the RCMP launched a major operation to dismantle the blockade and make arrests, sympathy blockades of roads and rail lines erupted across the country, causing a significant disruption of the economy. COVID, injunctions and some negotiations eventually led to an end of most of the protests, but two years later a midnight attack on one of the construction camps resulted in millions of dollars in damages.

We also had to deal with the ongoing Wet'suwet'en protests and blockades over the LNG pipeline. Early on, before the blockades, we had gone to Smithers to meet with the Wet'suwet'en. Six months later, I went to a smoke feast up there, along with some cabinet ministers, to hear from the Office of the Wet'suwet'en. That's the organization representing their hereditary leadership, and we wanted to kickstart reconciliation discussions with them. We also spoke with elected band representatives. Their primary grievance was that the Delgamuukw-Gisday'wa decision had not been fully implemented. It would have been easy for me to say this wasn't a problem for my government. It was a problem from thirty years ago that was not dealt with by Harcourt, by Glen Clark, by Gordon Campbell or by Christy Clark. But it fell on us to deal with it. In good faith, I went and sat with the leadership on these two separate and distinct occasions. Later on, we brought in people to help us through this, like Miles Richardson, the well-regarded Indigenous leader from Haida Gwaii who himself had led protests to stop logging on Haida territory. We sent in other Indigenous facilitators as well, people familiar with the challenges of hereditary leadership versus elected leadership, which one could argue better represented the will of the community. We encouraged the Wet'suwet'en hereditary leadership to get a common position from their people. We weren't prepared to just listen to them when there were other voices that had been elected who were saying something completely different.

It was a governance challenge within the community. It was for them to solve, not us. We felt we had put in place the tools to allow them to do that. We provided capacity funding for that to happen. Then COVID came along, and the community meetings came to a halt. We were saying they needed to have community meetings, but meanwhile you couldn't have community meetings because of COVID. I am not apportioning blame to anyone, but circumstances prevented the Wet'suwet'en and the numerous clans from gathering to figure out what it was that they all wanted, not what a handful of militant people wanted. It was clear what the militant people wanted: nothing. They wanted no intervention. Most of the clan chiefs seemed to be supporting this, but it was easy for them to say it's not going to work because of these militant people.

I go back to Fairy Creek. There are people in the impacted territory who don't want to see logging. They are not a majority. I'm a democrat, and at the end of the day, we all have to be democrats. That's not to say we disregard other forms of governance, similar to the Wet'suwet'en, but we have to incorporate them in a way that also meets the needs of five million people, not just five hundred. It is going to take time to lay the foundation for that in the UN Declaration. It can't be retroactive. It has to be forward-looking. There was no way I could stop the pipeline, even if I wanted to. We had already found that out with TMX. Once contracts are entered into, permits are issued by government—and I am now the government. I can't say, "What the hell was Christy Clark thinking? What the hell was Gordon Campbell or Mike Harcourt thinking?" That doesn't change the fact that when you're the premier, you're responsible for all the contractual decisions that have already been made and all those coming forward on your watch.

I felt we had demonstrated extraordinarily good faith on Indigenous issues around rights and title. There were existing court rulings that supported hereditary rights, but there were other foundational issues that, as a democracy, also seemed to be relevant. I thought they should ask their communities what they wanted, rather than just assuming they knew. The government was caught in the middle. We had the best intentions in the world, intentions that far exceeded those of others who had come before us. That did not change two hundred years of history. But it's interesting that the Trans Mountain pipeline, which we opposed, was supported by some Indigenous communities. Some even wanted to buy it. As for the Coastal GasLink pipeline, there's a First Nations equity stake in that pipeline that will be a stream of revenue for as long as natural gas is still a viable option. There are benefits to be had along with the costs, and that's rarely mentioned.

I was very disappointed at the way it unfolded, with all the protests and blockades up north, rail blockades across Canada, protests, arrests, and an exceptionally violent attack on a construction camp. The most outspoken of the Wet'suwet'en leaders seemed to get anything he said in the media, but it was harder for us to respond. I thought I understood what they wanted, and I tried to communicate that I was going to do everything I could to meet their expectations. But that didn't seem to matter. It really ground me down.

When the protests arrived at the Legislature and the doors were blocked to our public institution on the day of the Throne Speech, and we had to sneak the lieutenant governor into the building through a secret passageway, that was kind of the end for me. I was always challenged on the Wet'suwet'en hereditary issue, because I just didn't believe the hereditary Chiefs were genuinely looking for a solution. It seemed to be only obstruction, and you can't function that way in a free and democratic society, which we are. As a social democrat, I come from protest. I've been in more protests than I can remember. I know protests and dissent. I get that. But the transition from activist to administrator is challenging for everyone, particularly for social democrats or greens or progressives. We're in the business of resisting "the man" or saying, you know, that the majority isn't listening to the minority. But my responsibilities changed when they swore me in as premier. I had to do things that maybe I would not have done if I had been on the other side of the line. I made a conscious decision, and I've talked about this with other New Democrats across the country. If you want to yell at the building, great, but if you want to change things, you've got to get inside the building. If you want to make policy changes that will affect people's lives, like child care, sufficient social assistance premiums to keep people alive, mental health, ensuring communities can grow and prosper and thrive together, you have to sit down to figure it out. You can't do it on the lawn yelling at the Legislature or lying on the road, stopping a truck. I'm not suggesting militancy isn't an important part of our process, but it's not the only part. If people choose to do that, that's their business. I chose to get inside the building and try to make real change when I had the opportunity.

As I said, the Throne Speech protest was a turning point. It led to significant despondency on my part. I was the first premier from Victoria in years. All these past premiers did most of their work out of the cabinet office in Vancouver. I went to work at the Legislature every day because it wasn't that far from my house. And every day, there would be a bunch of people banging drums. It was driving me crazy, but it didn't change my commitment to Indigenous rights and title, nor did it change my commitment to making sure that the needs of five million people were being met in the context of trying to change our past by having a better future. I still maintain that we are on the right track. But it won't happen in a weekend, and it won't happen by wearing a black mask. If only you do this, everything will change? Well, it won't.

Around the same time, people claiming to be environmentalists supporting the blockades were lying on my driveway, knocking on my door, telling my wife that I was a war criminal. That's intimidation. That's thuggery. Ellie looked out the window for a long time after that to see if anyone was driving by. It only happened twice. There was no harm. They were a hapless group of people. But that doesn't change my view. I don't think you should try and intimidate your neighbours because they have a different point of view. My whole perception of protest, my whole perception of minority views, has been tainted by that. I will never forgive those people who made my spouse uncomfortable in her home when she had nothing to do with it.

Even with all the protests and blockades going on, we continued to try to find solutions. At one point, there seemed to be an agreement. Carolyn Bennett, the federal minister for Indigenous relations, was involved. Our own minister, Scott Fraser, went up and signed a document with some of the hereditary leaders. But there were many different clans, and they all had different leadership structures. They were all valid governance models that had been in place for generations, but heads of the clans didn't always agree. People didn't always agree who the head of the clan was. The matriarchs got tossed out, and some hereditary chiefs, who were men, came in. How did that happen? I haven't commented on their internal workings before, because it wasn't my place to say, but there were intractable problems that didn't have easy solutions, despite the best efforts of a lot of people with a lot of goodwill, including people on the ground, not just the government.

This wasn't the only matter where elements of the First Nations gave consent but which environmentalists were anxious about. I'm thinking of Hydro projects, fish farms, and logging in some communities. They are always going to be a challenge, but we did not shy away from them. I was frustrated by the protests because I felt we were making progress on all of the issues that people were concerned about. It wasn't fast enough for them, or it wasn't to their liking. It's kind of like, well, I like the Blue Jays, but you know what, I really like the Expos, too, so what am I going to do when the Blue Jays play the Expos? Well, I'm going to bang my drum and yell at the building. Maybe that's a bad analogy, but I was frustrated that our best intentions were not enough.

You're not going to get anyone more focused on Indigenous rights than Miles Richardson. He was not there to make it easy for the company or the government but to help find a way forward for the Wet'suwet'en. The desire of the majority of the people in the territory, I would argue, was for an end to the protests. This was when there were allegations of Mohawk warriors coming from the East to foment dissent in the community. The local matriarchs were saying this was not their way. These people are from somewhere else. We don't want them to promote and fight our battles. We need them to go away. That was covered briefly by the media, but then it was overtaken by trains being stopped and the blockade in Cornwall.

I continue to be relentlessly optimistic, but it would be misleading if I didn't say that I became despondent at that particular time because of my passion for Indigenous rights. How did I become an enemy here? That's a personal observation, not a premier observation. It saddened me. I found it difficult to go to work when that crew was out front. At the same time, I did have a lot of people bolstering me, and I'm grateful for that.

CHAPTER TWENTY

OUTTA HERE!

AS WE HEADED TOWARD THE SUMMER OF 2022, IT BECAME OBVIOUS TO me that maybe it was time to leave, despite all the support I was getting. I famously dropped the F-bomb in the Legislature. I had a big smile on my face when I said it. I thought it was comical. It was almost imperceptible, but it was on Hansard, and if you could read my lips, you knew what I said. All of a sudden, it was like, "Oh, my goodness, angry Horgan is back." So I took a bar of Irish Spring soap, stuck it in my mouth, took a picture, sent it out on the internet, and I apologized to the Legislature for my language. But it was another sign for me that perhaps my time was done.

I consulted Ellie about my decision, and only Ellie. We went to a friend's place on Gordons Beach and watched the otters play. They were river otters, and they would come out every morning, play around and just have a blast. We would watch them, and we would laugh. I thought, we need to do more of that and less worrying. In a year-end or wrap-up interview, Ellie explained it in a way that was really quite perfect. She said that even when I wasn't away from home, I was still thinking about what had to be done next. It was like twenty-four hours a day. You try to shut down just for a bit, but you never really shut down. It's always in your mind. People would say they were going to leave me alone—except for the emails, the text messages and the phone calls—other than that, they're leaving you on your own.

Geoff Meggs and I were joined at the hip. He knew more about the difficulties than I did, because his job was to keep the difficulties away. I still have his resignation letter. I'm going to accept it one of these days. If someone has to fall on a sword because of a misstep by the government, the role of the chief of staff is to be the first one out the door—not me, but him. Thankfully, we never got to that place.

We started talking. It was the end of the session, and we had a caucus retreat on the 27th or 28th of June. I was thinking: "Well, I can continue on for a year, but that won't give the party and the province time to adjust to a new approach." I thought the best decision for all of us was for me to go sooner rather than later. Geoff started doing all the work that had to be done to make sure there wasn't a huge shock. But we didn't want to let too much out of the bag.

You always say you're going to run, until you decide you aren't. The minute you say you intend to step down, you're a lame duck leader. And there were still things I wanted to do, like the first ministers' meeting that would be taking place in two weeks. But I had made the decision, and I couldn't lie, I couldn't pretend. If someone asked me directly whether I was going to run for another term, I couldn't say yes when I knew that wasn't true. Ellie had already been disappointed back in 2014 when I had told her I wasn't going to run to be leader, and then I did. This time, when I told her I didn't intend to run again, she asked, "Are you sure? Am I going to hear something different on the radio?" I was thinking about all this when Gregor Craigie, host of *On the Island*, the CBC morning radio show in Victoria, asked me if I would lead the party into the next election. It was on the Friday before the next cabinet session. I didn't want to lie to the guy, and I didn't want to tell him anything without having a chance to talk to cabinet and the caucus, so instead of answering the question, I replied with a lot of blah, blah, blah.

But the die was cast. It was hard to do, because I treasured doing the work. I was also grateful for my popularity, but that didn't affect my decision-making. After I made the announcement, I was in Palm Springs and someone recognized me. He had a big smile on his face, and he said, "Your timing was perfect." And I thought, okay, it was the right thing to do. If I'd stayed six months longer, a big policy issue or yet another calamity might have come forward, which would have been a bridge too far for me. I was already throwing F-bombs at the Opposition leader, and my tolerance for stupidity was getting shorter and shorter. I didn't want to despoil all the work we had done as a party and as a movement. We had gone from four consecutive terms in opposition to two electoral victories in a row, with the prospect of a third. I didn't want to wreck that. That was more important to me than having some sort of victory lap. That would have meant staying on when I knew I was leaving and doing a bunch of things for myself rather than for the people.

The regular functioning of government requires the head of cabinet to be fully engaged. During my time as premier, I wanted to give everything I had for as long as I could, and it had become pretty plain to me that I didn't have that much more to give. I looked around at the fifty-six other New Democrats. I saw many in their thirties and forties, with mountains of energy. My mortgage had been paid off. My kids were out of the house. It was just Ellie and me. Beyond the obvious, like climate change issues and the swirling up and down of the economy, I didn't feel I was as connected to the real challenges people face as my colleagues were. In terms of energy and perspective, I felt they would be better placed to take them on. David Eby, who replaced me, has two small kids, one just going into school, one a preschooler. There's someone who understands the importance of child care and a work-life balance. I was past that. I don't mean I was living high on the hog. I was a comfortable middle-class guy in a middle-class community, but also someone who was running out of enthusiasm to do the work that needed to be done. I was available to talk about things if required, but after five solid years, I had run the course.

I felt that the time to go and to start this generational change was while we were still popular. We weren't getting bad forecasts from finance or anything like that, but it was pretty clear that as our megaprojects started to wind down, there were going to be some significant challenges. I mean, look at the forest industry. The leaders in the forest industry could care less about British Columbia. They want to take as much profit out of the land as they can and invest it in the US, Sweden, anywhere but in British Columbia, and then they blame us for their decisions. That's an obvious challenge for us. So we needed a renewal, and it had to start with leadership that would then shape what that renewal would look like. I'm not a TikTok guy. The tools of this generation are not my tools. I had all these young staffers freaking out about the latest thing on Twitter, and I'm going, "I couldn't give a sweet damn about the latest thing on Twitter." I was still a happy warrior, but I was becoming a grumpy happy warrior.

There was something else that demonstrated to me that I had lost the thread, and that was the Royal BC Museum. I grew up in Victoria. I'm a student of history. I love the museum. I've been there a billion times. Carole James's mum would leave her at the museum. That was child care then. I was all in favour of capital improvement for the museum, so when the museum and tourism ministry people came forward and said that this is what they were going to do, I said, "Go ahead and do it." When they also said they were going to close the museum for eight years to do it, and it was going to cost $800 million, I regret not putting my thumb on the scale. I should have said, "What???" I didn't do that, because they said there was no alternative, and it had taken four years to get to that point.

I remembered being briefed on the museum ten years earlier by the CEO, Pauline Rafferty, when I was in opposition. She said there were critical challenges with the building and the collections, and the archives were below sea level. Our historic archives and the documents that define who we are, that help us with Indigenous issues, all the things that make up our treasure trove of artefacts, were at risk. That had been a decade ago, and I'm sure the problems of the museum went back much further than that. I asked the museum administration, as well as their board and the minister responsible, to bring me a plan to replace it. Carole James and the finance ministry would make space in our capital plan, which they did.

We kept waiting and waiting and waiting for something to come back. Since I hadn't been following it chapter and verse, when it finally did come back, I assumed they had exhausted the consultations and all that kind of stuff. I put my faith in the people who made the decisions that this was the right way to go. We made the announcement, and the loudest noise came from the people of Victoria, and they were not happy. I thought, "What's wrong here? What am I missing?" That was another factor in my decision to leave. If I was not reading the room right on something I'm so passionate about—that I thought everyone else would be passionate about—then I'm no longer up to it. I'm a step slower than I should be, and someone else should be doing this work.

Having realized that we'd gone astray, it wasn't hard to go before the cameras and say that I had screwed up and to put most of the project on hold. I've always felt that if you screw up, fess up. Everyone knows you're not perfect. If you continue to deny the evidence before you because you don't want to admit you're wrong, people are not going to believe you anyway, and they will think less of you. It had become a talking point in Question Period. It was the museum this and the museum that. The Opposition claimed I wanted to create a legacy for myself. They called it the Premier's Vanity Project. That was outrageous enough, but what I really did not want was for the hard-working people at the museum and the hundreds of thousands of people who support what goes on there to cringe every time they heard the word "museum." I didn't want them thinking, "Oh gosh, they're driving ahead with something nobody wants."

We should have figured out that closing for eight years was too much. Quite frankly, I was so passionate about it, I was blinded to it. I thought, eight years, okay, I guess that makes sense. We were going to have travelling pop-up exhibits and move them around the province. We were going to invest more money in local museums. It was going to be a net benefit to our shared heritage, and it would allow Indigenous people to repatriate some of their artefacts, plus provide some resources for them. The capital budget included moving artefacts from Victoria back to Tŝilhqot'in, back to Tahltan, back to Ktunaxa territory. Some of these artefacts had been stolen from them. Other First Nations said they didn't have the capacity to care for their artefacts. Instead, they said they would like an area where they could come and practise their cultural activities with their artefacts, which we would keep for them.

When we decided to change our mind and hold off, Aileen Machell, my acting director of communication, argued that Melanie Mark, our minister of tourism, who had been front and centre at the original announcement, should be at the second announcement, too. And I said, "No, it's my responsibility." Melanie had been tagged with the whole cultural uproar around the museum's Old Town. People were already sniping at her over that, about wanting to keep this exhibit of pioneer Victoria. It had been there a long time and people loved it, but there was no mention of colonialism or anything like that. My objective was not to have Melanie stand beside me. The mistake was not hers, it was mine. I was the one who had said, "It's taken too long, let's get going on this!" I wanted to be the one responsible for backtracking.

The museum was starting to achieve the status of the 1990s fast ferry fiasco, which the NDP had been hammered over for years afterward. Was this something we wanted to ride the next two years? There was nothing Melanie could do except look like someone hanging her head beside me. I wanted to say that the reason we were suspending the project was because I did not want this outstanding institution to be tarnished by politics. That wasn't on Melanie Mark. That was on me. Our communications person kept arguing that she should be there. They were good arguments, but I still felt it was not the right thing to do. We had the press conference, and it was all about me. Afterwards, Aileen said, "You were right, and I was wrong." I was proud that she felt strongly enough to not just let it go. She had been filling in for our regular communications person, who was on maternity leave, and she'd never been in a situation like this before. I was the premier, but her boss, Geoff Meggs, had told her to go back and disagree with me again if she felt strongly about it. And she did that when she could have just let it go. That was good for her and good for me. I had listened to her solid arguments and didn't change my mind, when others might have.

We did not stop the entire project. A brand-new facility for our critical archives is being built. In addition to its obvious heritage value, there's the economic importance of keeping track of records and understanding who did what when, and who owned the property, and why they were dislocated. There are also huge cultural opportunities, but that was lost on everybody. People kept fighting about Old Town. Local journalists like Les Leyne kept asking, "Well, what about Old Town?" And I thought, "That's your biggest issue when we've got seven and a half million artefacts? You're worried about a diorama with a fake horse and a phony cannery with some bird poop? Meanwhile, we can't bring big exhibits to the museum because there's only one elevator and it's not big enough to start with." It was a state-of-the-art facility in 1960. We are light years past that, and we keep bringing stuff in with nowhere to put it.

The good news was that a component of the project was to construct a new facility for research and the archives, and that's being built. I'm very, very happy about that, because it solves half the problem. The archives can be moved to a location above sea level, in a brand-new modern facility. There will be appropriate air conditioning and all the other necessary aspects to protect the artefacts. That relieves the pressure, and we will still have the place where people want to go and look at the horse and the fish and the Old Town and go back and forth in the replica of the HMS *Discovery*. It'll be great.

On my last day, the swearing-in ceremony for the next premier, David Eby, took place out on Musqueam territory in Vancouver. I've talked about my RCMP protective detail, whose job it is to protect whoever the premier is through thick and thin, and that during my cancer treatment they were there every day to drive us to the cancer clinic. That was something they did not have to do, God bless them. However, the moment a new premier is in place, I'm just John from Langford again, no more protective detail. And I found myself wondering, "Are they going to leave me way out there, standing at the side of that dusty road, waiting for an Uber or trying to find a bus or some other way to get me back downtown?" As I was getting out of their car for the last time, they gave me a bus pass. It was pretty funny. And they did give me a ride back to the city. They were the greatest people. They became my friends, my colleagues. I worried about their kids. I worried about their challenges. They are trained not to talk while they're driving around a VIP. Well, it didn't work with me, because I never shut up.

At some point after I stepped away from politics, I was approached by the prime minister with the proposal that I become Canada's ambassador to Germany. My older son, Nate, who currently lives in the UK, studied in Germany, in Freiburg. He's fluent in German and interned at the Bundestag for six months. I suggested that if the PM wanted a Horgan in Berlin, my son Nate would be better. But Trudeau seemed to think, despite my complete lack of language skills, that I was the right choice. It's funny because I had actually written the foreign service exam in 1984. I never heard back until the prime minister called me. When I told him that, Trudeau remarked that they don't throw anything away in Ottawa. My exam must have fallen behind a file cabinet or something. At any rate, I was pretty excited. It was an extraordinary time in world events.

The government in Germany was Social Democratic. Maybe the Canadian government was purposefully sending a social democrat to be our representative in Berlin. Stéphane Dion was down the road as our ambassador in Paris. Ralph Goodale was high commissioner across the Channel in the UK. That's a formidable group of relatively progressive former politicians. As a student of history, looking at the views of Canada around the world, one of the things I go back to is that they ebb and flow. If you're an Opposition politician, whether Liberal or Conservative, you condemn the government for their ineptitude on international issues. I would argue, however, that people still look at Canada as that great arbiter of moderation. That's what I certainly plan to pursue in my remaining time in public life. I've been able to work with anybody. I think that's the sort of thing the prime minister saw in me and hoped to bring forward to the position of ambassador. My grasp of the basics of energy politics and energy policy in the context of Canada will also be one of my strengths. I understand the instability that Russia's invasion of Ukraine has caused and our challenges in the Middle East. Energy is going to be a significant issue, not just for Europeans, but for citizens everywhere. If we are in a position to work within the confines of our climate policies, Canada has a significant role to play.

And there is Canada's role in international trade. I think we swing below our weight class, and we need to change that. I'm a homer, born and raised in Victoria, but I did my undergraduate degree in Ontario with the idea of getting a pan-Canadian view. I've criss-crossed the country many times, for recreation and when I was heading up the Council of the Federation. As I've said, Doug Ford was one of my best buddies. Many people may be horrified by that, but for me, it's about taking an opportunity when it's given to you. In the case of the Council of the Federation, there were thirteen people sitting around a table with an enormous opportunity to do positive things, whether they were left, right, or indifferent to political direction. I plan to take this appointment to elevate opportunities right across the country.

CHAPTER TWENTY-ONE

LOOKING BACK

AFTER FIVE YEARS, I WAS A DIFFERENT PERSON FROM THE GUY WHO became premier in 2017. I had a better understanding of the complexity of the world we live in. I had a better understanding of how difficult it is to effect changes that seem so simple in opposition. How many times did I say in opposition that you could do that with the stroke of a pen, and how many times did it have no impact? That really sticks out in my mind. I'd like to think I'm a better person because I was able to listen to people. As premier, I was able to have access to different perspectives. To learn as much as I can every day has always been my life's mission. If you're confined to one perspective and only talk to people with that perspective, your ability to grow is limited. As premier, people would talk to me. When I was leader of the Opposition, not many people really wanted to talk to me. One person who did was Janet Austin, who became lieutenant governor. She was chair of the YWCA at the time, and she wanted to talk about child care. I remember saying to her, "You know, there aren't many people on the Vancouver Board of Trade who really want to spend time with me." And she said, "Well, I'm not a partisan. I know that the more people who understand this challenge, the better off we will be." That was refreshing to hear. I think I have a broader worldview because I've been exposed to other people and always had space in my heart for other views.

There are many things I miss about not being premier. It's a funny thing, but I would always get tired by the end of the day. I'm an older guy, and we'd be on the road, pre-COVID and post-COVID as well, going to events and doing all these things, and then there would be the final event of the day, starting at eight p.m. And I'd go, "I don't want to do that." And my press secretary, Jen Holmwood, and others with us would give me a look and say that it would be okay once we got there: "You'll be fine." And then I would always be the last one to leave, because I'd get there and get pumped up by the energy of the people and the opportunity to just hang out with them. I miss that more than anything. I just miss people, and the energy that I got from them. I'd literally be sweeping the floor, talking to the janitors on the way out: "I'll see you next time." And then I'd go, "Oh, I'm exhausted. Why are you guys making me do this stuff?" And they would roll their eyes.

Did I leave the province a better place? I've talked about the museum. I didn't make that better, but I did make the archives and collections a little better. I didn't have the impact on mental health that I wanted to, but we made some progress. We made strides in reducing costs for people in some areas, so more of their discretionary dollars could go toward housing, food and other things that were being battered by inflation. Doing away with tolls for people who had to travel in the Lower Mainland was profound. So was reducing child-care costs for people who absolutely need to have care for their children. And so was moving away from medical services premiums. All these things we did had a significant impact.

Without Andrew Weaver and our Confidence and Supply Agreement with the Greens, none of them would have happened. I don't bet, but in this case I would bet a thousand dollars that Christy Clark and the BC Liberals would not have removed the tolls, would not have introduced child-care initiatives, would not have waived tuition fees for adults, and would not have increased disability and income assistance. Nor would they have raised the minimum wage, as we did. We made sure there were annual increases in the minimum wage, after a decade with no change at all. It was even more regressive under the Liberals, because there was a training wage. I remember my son getting a job in a restaurant, and he was paid something like six bucks an hour. He thought that was great. I asked when he was going to get minimum wage. Oh, in two hundred hours. When is that going to happen? Five years from now, because I'm two days a week for three hours. It wasn't a salary. It was servitude.

Now, having said that about the minimum wage, we do need to watch it carefully. We tied it to inflation, and there was a massive spike at a time when businesses depending on minimum-wage workers were just coming out of COVID. Then they were also smacked with paid sick days, which I'm proud we put in place during COVID. We told people to stay home when they were sick, but many of them couldn't afford to do that because they had an economic imperative to go to work. Otherwise, they would have trouble paying their rent or buying their groceries. These were good, significant changes, but they had an impact on small businesses. We need to ensure they are not being crippled by them. At the same time, however, an even bigger challenge for small business was finding people to fill those jobs, especially after COVID. The only way they're going to do that is to compensate people. The economics are pretty straightforward, and most businesses understand that. If there is a scarcity of employees, how do you combat that? You have to increase wages. Nothing is ever easy.

George Lawson, a New Democrat for a billion years, was critically important in my thinking on disability assistance. He was the provincial council delegate for Vancouver–Mount Pleasant, the poorest constituency in BC. He would come to every council meeting, and he would make a speech, which was challenging for George. He had difficulty putting his thoughts together, but he became a symbol to me of how important that issue was. Here's a guy who was completely participating in his community through a political party, and he was being pulled back every year rather than being lifted up. Raising disability rates right off the bat pleased me no end. We continued to do that over the course of our surplus budgets. The former government had always said they didn't have the money. How do you not have the money for the most vulnerable people in your community when you have the money to give tax breaks to the wealthy? I know that sounds like rhetoric, but it's reality for people who are living on the poverty line. You can criticize me all you want for saying that those who have more should give more and those who have not should get more. It's common sense. If you can't help people when you have the opportunity, then you've wasted that opportunity. These are NDP issues to be sure, but they are also community issues.

People say I went against the brand of the NDP by approving huge resource projects. I don't agree. I was always drawn to the NDP because I thought we were all the things I've been talking about: the party of workers, the party of small business, the party of farmers, the party of intellectuals. Go back to the CCF and the League for Social Reconstruction before that. They were designed to bring together all those who were being marginalized by the wealthy. Historically, it made complete sense to me to be a social democrat. It also made sense economically. It made sense to the capitalist in me to say that if we are lifting everyone up, everyone is going to benefit. The more people who have money in their pockets, the more they're going to spend in the stores of my community. I don't know of a single minimum-wage earner who's taking their surplus and spending it in a tax haven. They're spending it at the corner store. Or sadly, these days, they may be spending it on Amazon. Everyone's doing that, and the corner store is suffering, not because we're increasing the minimum wage but because it's hard for these small businesses to compete with massive global companies like Amazon.

But those resource projects we approved boosted the economy, and the thousands of jobs helped a heck of a lot of workers and their communities. That was good for everyone.

Eliminating MSP premiums was a tough one. There was no shortage of people saying we couldn't do that. "Where are you going to find the revenue?" Well, from economic growth, where else? Rather than reduce them, the Liberals actually kept increasing the premiums. They wouldn't boost the minimum wage, but they raised MSP premiums every year by the amount of inflation in order to pay for our health care, which is supposed to be free. A lot of people had employers who paid their MSP, so they didn't have to worry about it. Well, what about the 40 per cent who didn't? Contractors, people working on their own, small business owners—they all had to pay their own MSP premiums. People cheered us for doing it. It was one of the largest tax breaks in BC history.

If you can find that formula to reduce costs and continue to provide services, which I believe we did, then you are going to be successful. I don't say that in a self-serving way. I've never understood why anti-government types would run to be part of a government: "I hate government. Vote for me, and I'll get rid of it." Well, why don't you just ignore it? I have no problem with you being anti-government, but don't try to become part of the government then sit there for decades and claim that you hate government.

There are a whole range of issues governments can put in place to change people's lives, with little cost, that can elevate people so they play a greater role in our discourse and transform how we look at each other. For example, we did a lot to combat racism, which really reared its head during the pandemic. There were images of people pushing elders of Asian descent to the ground for reasons known only to the persons doing it. These images were being beamed not only across British Columbia but around the world. We needed to take a stand on that, and we did.

I also look at the success of our equity policies in terms of the candidates we are putting forward in campaigns. In 2020, we elected more women than men—that had never happened before—along with candidates who were Chinese Canadian, South Asian, Indigenous, Filipino and LGBTQ. The diversity of the community was now reflected in its government. That didn't happen by accident. It happened by deliberate choices the NDP made as a group. Our goal was to change the face of politics and the people who were participating. Why would women want to become involved in politics if you're not providing them with child care, if you're not providing them with access to resources? Historically, men have had well-financed traplines to pay for their campaigns; women have not, so we put in place programs and initiatives to help women be successful, rather than just allowing them to run for seats they would never win. We said that this is an NDP area and it should be represented by a woman. We made that party policy. I said before that this was a hard sell at the hockey rink, but the result has been the most diverse group of people in the Legislature we've ever seen. We elected the first South Asian Speaker of the Legislature. South Asians now turn on the television and someone who looks like them is overseeing our primary democratic institution. These are big deals. They are symbols. They are vehicles to change how people interact with each other. We brought back the human rights commissioner—a double-edged sword to be sure—but it's a commitment we made, and I'm glad we did it. It's important to have a way for people to express their discontent at how they're being treated in the community, along with helping people at the lower end of the economic spectrum.

Housing—affordable housing—was a big problem that we worked hard at when we were in opposition. Our housing critic, David Chudnovsky, did a really good job exposing the challenges of speculation in the marketplace and how that drove up the purchase price of homes. We didn't do a lot of work on how we were going to build homes for those who had no expectation of buying one and couldn't find a place to live. Municipal councils, rather than the province, were making decisions about land use. I understand their fierce response against the province telling them what to do: "We're responsible for land-use planning. We're building our communities. We have to deal with Board of Variance meetings and planning meetings with angry neighbours. Don't you, as a legislator, tell us our business. Help us with our business instead." We tried to do that.

In our first term, Selina Robinson was not solely minister of housing. She was also the minister of municipal affairs and responsible for TransLink. I felt that if we had one person looking at where we were building the housing, where we were building transportation links, and how that was affecting municipal governments, then we'd be in a pretty good spot. I specifically bundled all those responsibilities that way to try and find a means to cajole municipalities to make faster decisions. But Selina, who had been a councillor, and other municipal representatives came back with the response: "Don't you think they're already trying to do that?" I don't know too many councils, other than a few on Vancouver Island, that are literally trying to oppose the development of housing. How do we help them ease the burden and not have them overwhelmed by developers who just want to build single-room or one-bedroom condos? We need to start building two- and three-bedroom units. Families need more than a bachelor suite. They need more than living in someone's basement. We tried having one minister handle it all, but the issue was too enormous. Other municipal issues also got in the way.

We put out a target for building new homes. It was a large number. I would advise future governments to try and avoid that, because it's impossible to verify either way. If you're successful or unsuccessful, your opponents will always say you're unsuccessful by putting forward their own numbers. Todd Stone, the Liberal MLA for Kamloops–South Thompson and a former minister of transportation, was a particularly effective critic. He would take one sliver of information and make a thesis out of it. The information was completely irrelevant to his point, but he did it in an effective way. He looked good and he always got coverage. It was frustrating. Rich Coleman bought SROs [single-room occupancies], but that was transforming stock, not creating stock. We needed to create lots of new housing just to maintain the status quo. We were actually building quite a bit of new housing. Then immigration numbers exploded, so we had to build even more.

Our target was 114,000 units. That didn't mean our government was going to build that many—the economy was going to build them. We were going to enable it to happen. But we didn't communicate that effectively. The perception was that we were going to build them ourselves. Todd Stone manipulated the situation. He would say that we had said we would build so many units and BC Housing had only done this many. They never talked about all the housing stock that was on its way. That's why I think housing targets are an illusion. What's your barometer for success or failure? You can set any number. We had a lot of staff and cabinet members who had been on municipal councils, and we were still flummoxed by it.

We bumped up the speculation and vacancy tax, which some people like to talk about as a disaster. If you Google "speculation tax," you will find way more stories about how awful it is than you will about people going, "Oh, that's a good tax." But 99 per cent of the BC economy is not affected by it, and the tax had a lot of support. Something like 18,000 or 19,000 units that were previously vacant became available for people.

We had a number of initiatives like this, and we still didn't make a dent in it. I'm not critical of Selina or David Eby, who took it on later. Not much of what we did seemed to work. I continue to think that it's not just throwing pasta against the wall to see if it sticks. You have to keep trying different ways, different methods.

I am not an ideologue. I would call myself a passionate partisan when it comes to the underdog, when it comes to those who need assistance and aren't getting it. I really encourage people who have much in their heart to find a way to do that. There are countless British Columbians who make sacrifices for others. That's not political. I think it makes the world a better place. I'm also a populist. But when people talk about populism these days, they associate it with the Right. I reject that. Tommy Douglas was a populist, and he was very much on the Left. Jack Layton was a populist who was also very much on the Left. I believe that populism has been ill served by those on the Left. They have not embraced the notion of populism. If you're going to affect people's lives, the best way to do that is to engage with them. That's what populism is all about. It's not being on a ship by yourself deciding what's happening to the people on the island without ever getting off the ship. Get on the island and talk to the residents about what they need and how they believe it can be best delivered to them. I think social democrats have lost sight of that in many jurisdictions. Political parties have to make better choices. The challenge we have on the Left is that we are having difficulty separating activism from administration. A few too many people believe that their role and function is to secure a seat in the Legislature or Parliament so they can rail against something.

The federal NDP has significant challenges. They're fishing in the same pool as the Liberals. There is only so much space on the dial for the various perspectives in the community. I support proportional representation because I believe it would better reflect all views in the community. Alliances would have to be constructed after an election. The NDP itself is a coalition of labour, community advocates, environmentalists and other activists, but we have always precluded bringing in entrepreneurs, people who can see the sun where the rest of us tend to see showers. It's by creating those coalitions that you succeed. Brenda Bailey comes from the private sector. We were able to recruit her to run as a member of the NDP. She was elected and became the minister of jobs and investment. She's passionate about both social issues and a vibrant economy. We need more people like that. Ravi Kahlon was a key member of my second cabinet. He is a former banker. Bowinn Ma is an engineer with a business degree from the Sauder School of Business. This is not your grandparents' NDP. And it has to continue to be that way.

We need to see more people who reflect the diversity of our economy. If we don't talk about the economy, we will be left in the dust. That's the future. We can't be just the party of "no." When you're in opposition for an eternity, you have to try and find a group of people who will listen to what you have to say. Unfortunately, too often it turns out that they're mostly people who want to stop something rather than people who want to build something. The reality is that most people want to build something, and they weren't seeing that in the NDP, at least until recently. I think that will be the salvation not just of the federal party but of social democrats across Canada. Become the party where people can see innovation and opportunity rather than obstruction and intolerance to other points of view.

Our good positions on social issues, equality and affordability don't happen if you don't have a robust economy and a vibrant community. When we allow the Right to be in charge of the economy, it always boils down to tax breaks and tax cuts, which do a disservice to so many people. If you characterize it appropriately, you can sell people on our belief in a strong economy. It's not about messaging and wordsmithing. It's about values. We have to talk about creating wealth in a sustainable way that is mindful of all the challenges we have with the planet we live on. I've said it repeatedly, and I think I'm right: BC is filled with New Democrats who don't know it yet. The only way to convince people that their values are your values is to show them, not just talk about it. Of course, you can only show them if you have the opportunity to form government.

For us to have political success, we needed to demonstrate to voters that the mythology that we couldn't run a peanut stand was just that, a myth. When it came to fiscal matters, we had to be better than our opponents all the time, and we needed to instill that discipline in a fractious group of people—which the BC NDP has always been. If we were going to be successful in not just standing outside the building yelling at it with picket signs, but inside the building effecting policy changes on issues like harm reduction, environmental policy and reforming the forest industry, we had to accept that you can't do that with a protest sign. You have to be at the cabinet table. That requires a discipline that goes beyond the right-of-centre view when it comes to fiscal management and beyond the left-of-centre view when it comes to social policy. You can run left or you can run right, but I believe the trick for governments right across the country is that when you govern, you'd better do it for everybody. Most people just want you to get out of their face, make sure their kids can go to school, their parents find a place to live, and that they don't have to spend too much to get by every day. Those are the things that motivate voters, not creative slogans, not rapier-like wit in the House of Commons. For me, the reason why the NDP has been successful in BC in the last few years is that we've taken that ground. Those who are on the Left will say, oh, your centrist views are anathema to us. Well, maybe that's because you're outside yelling at the building. We're inside trying to effect the changes that you're talking about. And until recently we've been able to do that very few times over the past fifty years.

When I inherited leadership of the NDP, we were flat broke and deeply in debt. We had very few prospects. We had challenges recruiting candidates. Who wants to spend their time in opposition? We turned that around. People often ask me what I was most proud of as premier. I can't really pick out one thing, but perhaps I'm proudest of the fact that I had the opportunity to be premier and I didn't fall completely on my face. I had the chance, the honour and privilege to do the work, and people more or less thought well of me. It means something to me that I was still one of the country's most popular premiers when I resigned. That speaks to the people I had around me. I did very little of it myself. I had solid help from elected and unelected people who supported me. There were also people who didn't support me in the beginning but who came to support me.

I've always said that, as individuals, we are an amalgam of all the people we've met in our lives, the good and the bad. People who were extremely odious and harmful to me on a personal level helped shape my views in the sense that I didn't want to be like that. I had to find a way to not merely dismiss them but to manoeuvre around them and maybe bring them along a little bit. There's always something you have in common, even with folks who are odious.

Given my doubts and a healthy dose of humility, taking on the party's leadership was a big challenge for me. The fact that I had success was a direct result of not thinking I was the smartest person in the room. I was always looking for backup, for reinforcements. It's wrong to say I never had an original idea, but I've stumbled upon a lot of other people who have had good ideas, and those ideas had been collected and amalgamated from other ideas. A good example was the transformation of the treaty process into something different. Cracking the nut of Indigenous self-government, rights and title had been vexing BC for generations. There's still a lot of heavy lifting to come, but I think we found a way to break out of that. It wasn't based on my ideas. It was due to other people's ideas, plus my gut feeling that we could achieve that kind of breakthrough if given a chance.

Over the years, there has been a big change in the media, and not for the better. In the 1980s, when Brian Mulroney was the prime minister, the news cycle was twenty-four hours. Now it's twenty-four seconds, and there are fewer and fewer people chronicling those events. When I came back to Victoria from Ottawa, Premier Harcourt had to contend with at least four separate individuals from the *Vancouver Sun*—Justine Hunter, Keith Baldrey, Jim Beatty, Vaughn Palmer and maybe someone else. That was from one newspaper. Then there were all the other print, radio and television people, with everyone competing to break stories. That doesn't happen anymore. It's all about getting clicks. There are a number of members of the BC press gallery who are long in the tooth, and good for them. But the assignment of the coming younger generation is to fill content rather than break stories. They have multiple platforms. They are constantly trying to get something out into the soup. Meanwhile, the public pays attention to almost none of it. There is simply too much stuff out there.

I would suggest that politics is now a little bit about getting clicks, too. You can see it in their campaigns. This is the issue we're going to drum the government on, and we're going to keep pounding on this same issue. We're going to do mailings on it, we're going to do fundraising on it, and so on. That completely loses touch with the people you're actually trying to reach. If you're wanting to incite fire in the belly of the base, fair enough, but if you're going to change people's minds, you usually don't do that by just kicking the government. The challenge for politics is, how do you connect with people again? Is it rallies? I don't think so. For me, it's about building relationships. And you don't do that by direct mail, you don't do that by standing on a stage, you do that by talking to people and listening to them and hearing what they have to say.

I was with Jack Layton during his last campaign. My job was to be the guy with the microphone at the town hall meeting and make sure we didn't give the microphone to someone who was going to ask an outrageously stupid question and slow everything down. My job was also to get him out of the room and onto the bus, because we had to get to the next show. This one time, Jack and I were meandering through the crowd. We were just at the door to jump onto the bus, and there was an elderly woman in a wheelchair. Her elderly husband was behind her. I could see the people inside the bus. They were reaching their hands out to grab Jack and drag him in when he spun around, squatted down and spent half an hour talking to this couple. I didn't intervene in any way. I agreed with Jack that he needed to recharge his batteries by having a human conversation with human beings so that he could go to the next place and relate to people rather than just reading the script, giving the message of the day, getting the clip for the news, and then going to bed and flying off to the next town. I believe that is the politics of the future as well. Policies really matter, but the nuances between Left and Right are so blurred these days that you have to convince people to have confidence in you. Do I trust this person to use their good judgement to make the best choice out of a whole bunch of bad options? You need to connect with people to do that.

When I look back—and this may surprise people—of all the decisions we had to make as government, I think LNG was the toughest. In those early days, there was still an opportunity to grind the whole thing to a halt. That would have been met with enthusiasm by the base of our party. We also had to put together an incentive package that I knew Andrew Weaver was going to go nuts about. In fact, there was a chance the Greens could vote us down over it, and we'd be in another election. The possible consequence to the government was in the same league as the "Sorry, Leonard, you're not in cabinet" decision. But did I support making more money from our natural gas and creating jobs in the North rather than giving it to the Americans so they could liquefy it and make all that money, which is what we were doing by piping it to the Gulf Coast? For me, that was a no-brainer. It may seem simple now, but at the time it was anything but.

A word about climate change, which threatens our continued existence. We are up to forty million Canadians now. That's among a population of eight billion in the world. It's arrogant for us to say we have the solutions for all those people. That doesn't mean giving up on doing our part to reduce our impact on the planet. But Canadians are not the only ones who are in this hot water that's getting hotter every day. It's everybody. Globalism is railed against by some, but it is our salvation if we do it right. If we don't do it right, a lot of this book isn't going to be worth much, because it means no one's looking out for the world.

The kind of role British Columbians can play in that world of ours is something that has really consumed me over the past number of years. It's a bit much to think that five million people in British Columbia are going to affect the lives of eight billion, so you do it in very small steps, and you do it locally. Act locally and you will make a difference globally. At the same time, let's not be ridiculous about this. We have to find a way to be relevant, not only in our own lives but in the lives of our neighbours and in the lives, oftentimes, of our competitors and our adversaries. Those are conversations that don't lend themselves to political speeches.

I also want to relate something I could only have done as premier, and that was go to Juno Beach in 2019 to commemorate the seventy-fifth anniversary of D-Day. That meant so much to me. My riding had three cenotaphs: one in Shawnigan, one in Langford and one in Sooke. When I was elected as an MLA, going to all three on Remembrance Day was difficult, but I did my best. I've talked about what a pinch-me moment it was when I became premier. During almost all my time in opposition, I'd been anxious to be energy minister—if only I could be energy minister! Sadly, I had to settle for premier. And once I was premier, the challenge of my desire to be in all places at all times became more difficult. Now I had to make choices, even on Remembrance Day. The Legion in Sooke had the best clam chowder, it was just spectacular, but the largest crowd was in Langford, so that's generally where I went to honour the vets and the community. I remember when it used to be in the parking lot at the site of the future rec centre, and there was only an obelisk. Boy Scouts, Girl Guides and a handful of paramedics might show up, maybe forty people. There would be a moment of silence, and that would be that. This last Remembrance Day in Langford, we had two thousand people surrounding a replica of the Vimy Ridge monument built by the local community. We are so much farther away from those times when more than a million Canadians made sacrifices fighting fascism to make our world free. Seeing the transformation of Remembrance Day in my local community moved me deeply.

I'd already been to Normandy as a private citizen with my kids. I remember weeping at Dieppe. Every year, Frenchmen would open up the little town hall in Dieppe as an area of Canada. The British had wanted to launch a raid on Dieppe three years into the war, and they said, "Well, we'll send in the Canadians. If it works, good, and if it doesn't, what's the loss?" Forgive me, historians, for simplifying the suicidal invasion of Dieppe, but I have been to Dieppe. I've been to Normandy so that my kids would understand these things. My wife is of Dutch ancestry, and Holland was liberated by Canadians. All of that was important to me, and when I got the opportunity to represent British Columbia for the seventy-fifth anniversary of the landing at Juno Beach on D-Day, I jumped at it.

We built a trade mission around the trip, but before we left we met with veterans who were going to be there. One of them was George Chow. As a Chinese Canadian, his rights had been less than other Canadians. He didn't have the right to vote. He couldn't be a citizen. Yet he walked into the Bay Street Armoury and signed up at the age of seventeen. He fought in Europe, and I had the honour of meeting him in Victoria and then again on the sand at Juno Beach. Another veteran from North Vancouver was highlighted in a video presentation they made. It was immensely powerful to be there.

All the Allied countries were represented. Nancy Pelosi was there for the United States. The prime minister was there. Jagmeet Singh was there. I was the only premier. One of the veterans said, "Where the hell are the rest of them? I've been waiting seventy-five years for this. I made it. Why didn't they?" I couldn't answer that. But to see these men... seventy-five years had passed and there they were. Many were in tears. They were reliving a horrifying period in their personal lives, yet they had come back, proudly representing Canada one more time in a place where they had fought fascism and they had prevailed. And because of that, we can gather as free people to talk about different points of view, disagree on this and disagree on that. At the end of the day, our institutions and the people who supported them were stronger than the vile, hateful ideologies that put us into war in 1939.

When I watch Ravi Parmar, my replacement as an MLA, criss-crossing all over the constituency, and I see David Eby meeting all the people I would have been talking to, I realize I have zero ability to do that anymore. My time in that sphere is over. Do I still love people? Absolutely. Do I like grappling with challenging and sometimes unsolvable problems? You bet. But the energy to go around and do all the other work that has to be done—along with the travel, the prospect of having Kevin Falcon, who replaced Andrew Wilkinson as Liberal leader, call me all sorts of names—I'm just not interested in that. Sorry.

The weight of all that pushed me to where I wasn't prepared to do it anymore. It's a shame, because I absolutely loved the job, and I met some people who are going to remain in my life. Geoff Meggs is one of them. Without being too hyperbolic and comparing it to a war footing, we formed a comparable bond. We were in a situation where we had more information than anyone else, and we had to figure how to get through it all, and we did our best. I realize that's a disservice to those who have had to go through a real war, but it felt similar. I also think of Carole James. I have always been very close with her. Now my respect for her is right through the roof because she just continued to plough away. She could have walked away from this a long time ago, but she didn't. She stuck with it until she, too, couldn't do it anymore.

Okay, now having said all that, and I meant every word, I'll let you in on a little secret. I have no regrets today, in this hospital in Berlin, but there have been times prior to this most recent setback when I thought I probably should have stayed. I remember phoning Bob Dewar—I think I was still an MLA at that point, so it might have been in 2023—and complaining about something that David Eby had done. And Bob said something like, "Oh, fuck off. If you don't like it, you could have stayed. It's your own damn fault, so no more whining from you." He said, "Let the kids play. They're going to break stuff. They're going to make their mistakes, but they'll find their way." That was good advice.

So much goes back to values. People who are jerks don't get rewarded for being jerks. But if you are open to someone offering you a hand up, you're more inclined to get more of those people, if you also offer a hand up to someone else around you. That is the essence of my politics. I don't know why people who were never comfortable with the NDP were comfortable with me, but they were. It wasn't that I wasn't a lefty in terms of my values and seeing government as an institution of good, not something to be torn down because it was inefficient and wasn't run like a business. It was a whole bunch of people with expertise coming together with a mission to improve people's lives. That's ultimately what government is all about. And if you can explain that to people, if you're seeking to represent them, then they're more inclined to listen. What's the point of just rolling through saying, vote for me because such and such is bad, or vote for me because the Socreds suck? That's why we're getting such low voter turnouts. There's no connection. And I don't mean a connection to an ideology or worldview, but a connection to representatives. I look at the shit show in the US, and wonder why anyone would go out and campaign for anybody. I simply don't understand. It's so broken down there.

For those stepping into political leadership today, relationships are critically important, and you can't dispatch someone else to build those relationships. You have to do it yourself. You then have to have a team of people who are in it for the right reasons. That's not an easy thing to do. I was blessed with having not just one former leader of the NDP in Carole James, but two, with Adrian Dix as well. I can't think of a political party that went into an election with three leaders like that. Carole brought her constituency, Adrian brought his, and I brought mine. We had a downtown Vancouver guy (Adrian), we had a suburban guy (me), and we had a Victoria school trustee (Carole). We had a history of doing things together. If you are going to lead a political movement, you need to have allies who are genuinely allies.

I had stood with Carole to the bitter end. I stood with Adrian pretty well every step of the way. And both of them stayed with me. During my darkest days as leader, I knew that Adrian and Carole were going to be there, and I was able to learn from the challenges they faced. My issues seemed insignificant compared to what they had gone through. Carole went through a horrific time, as did Adrian. The guy who couldn't lose lost. I have been critical of the way he campaigned in that election, but he was devastated by the outcome, as anyone would be. That did not deter him from standing up with me and saying, "Let's carry on. Let's make the world a better place."

So, for new leaders, for people who want to take over organizations, make sure you're doing it with a lot of friends and don't take yourself too seriously. Also know, as I have learned, that you're replaceable. If you lose sight of that, you will find yourself replaced even faster. Accept the fact you're just passing through, do good deeds while you can, and then get out of the way for someone with more energy and more vitality. That's what I was able to do.

It's a shame that cancer got in the way. I would love to have stayed. But right now I don't miss a minute of it.

Looking back on all of the challenges we faced—the fires, the floods, the heat dome, the pandemic, the personal issues around my health—in my mind, they were just part of my time. I did what I could. We came through them successfully in some cases and unsuccessfully in others. But what a great time.

What a great life.

AFTERWORD

ROD MICKLEBURGH

JOHN HORGAN TOOK UP RESIDENCY IN BERLIN IN DECEMBER OF 2023. Seven months later, after being diagnosed with cancer for a third time, he announced that he was taking a medical leave. In what turned out to be the final interview we did, from his hospital bed, he talked about his time in Germany.

> Stéphane Dion had been Canada's previous ambassador to Germany, until he went to Paris, where he should have gone in the first place. The post had been vacant for a year, and there were people trying to ferry another political appointment into the job. I was so unlike anybody who had ever been there, and it seemed to work well. The staff was a bit taken aback at first, but as they got used to me, I think I was a breath of fresh air for the place. They soon knew about my love of science fiction, mostly *Star Trek* but *Star Wars* too. One night at the Canadian Embassy, I had a Baby Yoda, a green drink with limes on the glass and two blueberries for eyes. And of course, we had our *Star Wars* Day on May 4.
>
> Germany also had a Social Democratic government with a Green coalition partner. That was a pretty familiar situation for me. I spoke their language. I knew politics,

and I was able to feel their pain. Of course, I was also there representing Canada, and for the those first five months, it was great. Then the diagnosis came, and that was that.

Until then, we were having the time of our lives. It was fantastic. Ellie has lots of family in the Netherlands. We took a weekend trip to Amsterdam. We went to Hamburg, Prague, Munich, Düsseldorf. We were doing trips inside Germany and had plans for Portugal, Greece and Croatia. It was different from going on holiday for a few weeks, getting exhausted and saying, "I'm never doing that again." In Germany, we could take small trips and have a place to come home to. Nothing was a nine-hour plane trip. That's what's wonderful about Europe: Everything is so close.

We were living in the official residence with a chef and a housekeeper. It was unlike anything we'd ever done before. The driver would come in the Audi and pick me up every morning, take me to the embassy, and everyone would say, "Mr. Ambassador" or "Your Excellency." I'd go to receptions, although I wasn't really a fan of them, because everybody spoke German. However, I managed to pick out a few people, particularly the Finnish ambassador. We became friends. He lived in the same town as Jyrki Lumme, who played many years for the Vancouver Canucks. During the World Hockey Championships, we travelled to Prague together to watch Canada play Finland. I'm glad to say that Canada won, so I got bragging rights.

I also got to know the ambassador from Latvia fairly well. This was during the NHL playoffs, and we had Arturs Silovs in common. Silovs was playing for the Canucks after Thatcher Demko got hurt. I mentioned Silovs to the ambassador, and she said, "Oh, yes, the great goaltender from Latvia. He is a national hero, and he's a Vancouver Canuck." That all worked out.

> To be honest, I think I was doing pretty well at the job, and it's a shame that I don't see it coming back. At the slow rate of my recovery, I can't imagine returning to what I was doing.

John Horgan's battle against thyroid cancer was unsuccessful. He passed away in Victoria on November 12, 2024. At his memorial, held appropriately in a sports arena, Chargée d'Affaires Evelyne Coulombe made a special trip from Berlin to speak about the impact he had made on people and the workings of the embassy:

> John had a way about him that left a positive and lasting impression on everyone he met. He got to know all our staff and established individual connections with them. He knew where all the Canadians were from, which came in handy when the Canucks beat the Edmonton Oilers or the Calgary Flames and especially the Toronto Maple Leafs. Lots of teasing. When John died, the embassy was flooded with visitors to sign a condolences book. So many ambassadors and other contacts he had made along the way showed up, and they had a lot of stories.
>
> When he had functions at night, we kept his schedule light in the late afternoon so he could return home, change and relax. When he was leaving, he would stick his head in my office and say, "Work harder," even if I was working flat out. He had a lot of humour. Although he was ambassador for a relatively short time, he created a buzz in Germany. We obtained all the meetings we requested, and we were able to advance our priorities, whether it was energy, trade, network building, diversity or inclusion.
>
> Diplomacy is all about relationships and building bridges, and John was a people person. He was a great

> ambassador, a great public speaker, and a great representative of Canada. He displayed a perfect balance of strengths and vulnerability that made him a true and authentic leader. John never denied he was a homer. He missed BC very much. He missed the smell of the ocean, and he missed the mountains.
>
> I could speak about John for a long time, but I want to conclude by saying I miss him very much. I miss his bigger-than-life personality and his authenticity. I will continue to be inspired by him, and he will continue by my side as I pursue the path we started together to advance Canada's interests in Germany. I can still hear him say, with that big deep voice: "Get back to work!"

The memorial took place at the Q Centre Arena in Colwood, a few kilometres from his beloved Langford. The arena was packed, just as it had been for so many sporting events. John had asked Carole James to give the eulogy for his time in politics. She began by noting where the memorial was held:

> Some of you may have been expecting a more traditional or formal setting today, but of course John had something to say about that. Around the time he announced that he was stepping down as premier, he was busy packing up his office. Someone from protocol dropped by, telling him they had a routine question that they had to ask: "If something happens to you, John, after you leave office, would you want a formal state funeral?" John, without missing a beat, said, "Do I have to be there?" The protocol person hesitated for a moment, and said, "It is usually expected, Premier." "Well then, no thanks," John said. "Nothing stuffy for me." And so here we are, at the Q Centre Arena, one of John's favourite places. Just as we should be.

In late October, John had told a few of us a PET scan had revealed that the cancer had spread to other parts of his body, and no one was holding out much hope. At the end of the email, he wrote:

> Despite my current situation, I consider myself a very lucky guy.

His younger son, Evan, was the last person to speak with John before he died. At his father's memorial, Evan recounted their final hours together:

> He and I just sat there chatting for hours, as we had done a thousand times before. We talked into the night about all manner of things. We talked about how the Canucks were doing, and "if Petey [Elias Pettersson] could just find his scoring touch again, they'd be unstoppable. Quinn Hughes is the future." We talked about how he was still upset with the ending of *Game of Thrones*. We talked about some heavier things. We talked about advice he might have for me as an expecting father, and what his greatest triumphs and regrets were in life.
>
> Before I left, I asked him what he would want me to say about him if today ever came. He said, "Just tell everyone I did my level best."

ACKNOWLEDGEMENTS

ROD MICKLEBURGH

WHILE THIS IS JOHN HORGAN'S MEMOIR, IT IS LEFT TO ME TO ACKNOWLEDGE the individuals who contributed to its finished form. Geoff Meggs, John's chief of staff for the five years he was premier, drove the project forward every step of the way. His meticulously kept diary was essential in correcting the record on the rare occasions when the author's memory failed him. John Pearce of Westwood Creative Artists first approached John Horgan with the idea of doing a book and obtained the support of Harbour Publishing, which saw the project through to completion. Thanks as well to Carole James, Don Bain, Shirley Ackland, Amber Nash, Sheena McConnell, Sage Aaron, Richard Blais and Karolinka Zuzalek. Philip Steenkamp and his team at Royal Roads University, particularly Ann Reeves, played a key role by hosting the first three interview sessions. Noel Hudson edited the book, and Pam Robertson was the copy editor. A tip of the hat to Air Quotes Media's *Hotel Pacifico* podcast for permission to draw on its interview with John Horgan to emphasize a few points. Huge personal thanks to my life partner, Lucie McNeill, who was not only a source of encouragement throughout the project, but also set up the Zoom meetings with John, a technology both of us Luddites preferred to leave to someone who knew what they were doing. We called Lucie "our roadie." And finally, my heartfelt appreciation to Ellie Horgan. Without her reassurance and support, during such a difficult, emotional time for her, this book would not have happened.